La vida de
Lazarillo ð Tormes;
y ðe sus fortunas
y aduersida-
des.
M. D. liiij.

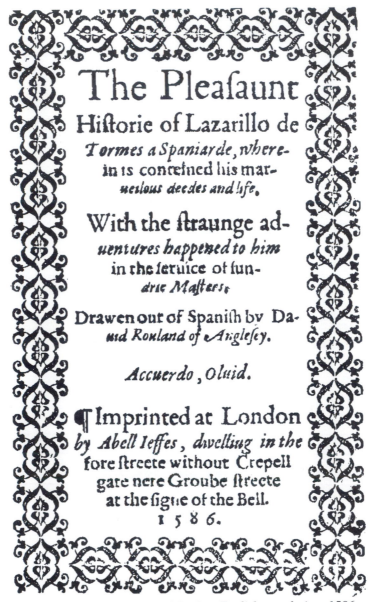

The Pleasaunt

Hiſtorie of Lazarillo de

Tormes a Spaniarde, where-
in is conteined his mar-
uellous deedes and life.

With the ſtraunge ad-

uentures happened to him
in the ſeruice of ſun-
drie Maſters,

Drawen out of Spaniſh by Da-
uid Rouland of Anglesey.

Accuerdo, Oluid.

¶ Imprinted at London
by Abell Ieffes, dwelling in the
fore ſtreete without Crepell
gate nere Groube ſtrecte
at the ſigne of the Bell.
1 5 8 6.

Above (Fig. 2): title page of the first English translation, 1586.

On the previous page (Fig. 1) is the title page of the edition of Lazarillo de Tormes
found hidden from the Inquisition in a house in Barcarrota

The Life of
LAZARILLO DE TORMES
(La Vida de Lazarillo de Tormes
y
de Sus Fortunas y Adversidades)

English Translation
by
David Rowland

with Introduction and Notes
by
Keith Whitlock

Aris & Phillips Ltd – Warminster – England

iv

ISBN 0 85668 728 6 Paper

British Library Cataloguing-in-Publication Data
A catalogue record for this book is available from the British Library.

For David, Lizzie and Isabel
and in memory of
Edwin Nodder

Published in England by Aris & Phillips Ltd, Teddington House, Warminster, Wiltshire BA12 8PQ in association with The Open University, Walton Hall, Milton Keynes, MK7 6AA

Printed at The Open University, Walton Hall, Milton Keynes, MK7 6AA

CONTENTS

Acknowledgements

I wish to express my sincere thanks to Victor Dixon for his help and encouragement and to the copyright holders for allowing the reproduction of the illustrations in this book.

Illustrations
Cover: Matthias Gerung *Lazarus and the Rich Man's Table*, section of a wing panel from the Mompelgarter Altarpiece, sixteenth century, oil on panel 41 x 28 cm, Kunsthistorisches Museum, Vienna. Photo: Bridgeman Art Library.

Preface

Lazarillo de Tormes is one of those very rare books that never cease to intrigue, amaze and delight.

Though many early readers, like Rowland, assumed it to be a factual autobiography, it is plainly a cunning and complex piece of imaginative fiction. But the date of its composition, the story of its publication, and above all its author's identity, all remain mysterious. Since every word was supposedly penned by its invented first-person narrator, we shall never know (though countless critics have been confident they could tell us) not only who really wrote it but how he may have expected us to interpret his creation – to what extent, for example, we are meant to suppose its anti-hero to be knowing or naïve. The uncertainty this engenders makes it seem engagingly modern; we might easily forget, were its depiction of its society not so vivid and convincing, that its puzzles have been with us for almost four centuries and a half.

It gave birth to a literary genre —the episodic, "worm's-eye view" style of narrative later known as the Picaresque— that was to spread via seventeenth-century Spain throughout Europe and beyond, and indeed to "Hurry on Down" to the present day. But even more broadly prophetic was its portrayal of a character moulded as he developed by his environment, his experience and his interaction with others.

Such historical significance aside, there is an enormous amount to enjoy and admire in this jewel of a work: its unforgettable characters, its verbal wit, its coruscating satire on shallow piety and false pretence, the cross-references and recurrent motifs that despite its frequent shifts of focus lend it overall coherence, and especially its author's mastery of the story-teller's art. As with *Don Quixote* (fifty years later), after decades of sharing its pleasures with new generations of readers, I can open it at random still and be sure of laughing aloud.

Victor Dixon   February 2000
Fellow Emeritus, Trinity College Dublin

Introduction

Editions and translations

Lazarillo de Tormes is shrouded in unresolved mysteries and first appeared in public in 1554, published as far as we know in Burgos, Alcalá de Henares, a town near Madrid with a recently founded humanist university, Medina del Campo and Antwerp, then the main city of the Spanish Netherlands. All four editions are dated 1554, but there must have been an archetype, not necessarily printed, to which 'Burgos' is probably nearest. 'Alcalá' bears the date 26th February, but since it calls itself a second impression, that date may have been copied from an earlier one, and the additions (generally not regarded as by the author) may have been added later in the year. 'Medina' bears the date 1st March. 'Antwerp', it has been argued, was printed later in the year. Rowland's translation is based upon the Antwerp text and the second edition of the French translation published by the printer Jean Saugrain in Paris in 1561. The first French edition had come out in 1560 in Lyons which was then a centre of French Protestant activity. Rowland may also have used the first edition. There is unresolved scholarly debate over when the book was first written: internal evidence could support arguments for a date of composition as early as the 1520's or 1530's, but the weight of critical opinion now seems to favour a date closer to 1554.

The book is an early example of a Europe-wide best-seller because of the speed with which it was published and translated into all the major Western European languages. There are many possible reasons for its enormous and immediate popularity, apart from the merit of being written in a vigorous and entertaining style. Certainly there was interest in the ways of rogues and beggars throughout Europe and the book spawned many imitations. Similarly there was the long-standing popularity from medieval times of jest (or joke) books, a tradition that the work obviously taps. Lazarillo's revenge upon his first master, the blind beggar, occurs in books of merry tales. Shakespeare possibly referred to the same incident in *Much Ado About Nothing* (Act II scene I, 206–7) and for this reason has been suspected of reading jest books. In all likelihood he did, but there was another probable reason for the book's huge popularity: its contents were a propaganda gift to powers hostile to Spain, like France and England. The surviving edition of Rowland's translation dates from 1586, when relations between England and Spain had broken down, both countries drifted into war and the Spanish Armada notably failed in 1588. Rowland's translation was regularly reprinted especially at moments of Anglo-Spanish crises during the following ninety years. Indeed a version of the book was even issued in the United States at the time of the Spanish-American war of 1898!

Lazarillo de Tormes is also notably anti-clerical and a propaganda gift to Protestants attacking the Roman Church. The censorship of the book in sixteenth-century Spain mirrors the loss of religious freedom in that country: the Inquisitor, Valdés, placed it on the Index of forbidden books in 1559 and a version expurgated of the fourth and fifth Treatises and some other anticlerical material was published in 1573. The recent discovery of a previously unknown 'Medina' edition is illuminating. It was found walled up with several other books in an old house in Barcarrota, Extremadura. With it were a Hebrew text, an Erasmian humanist book, a book on chiromancy (palmistry) and a manuscript of obscene material. All the listed works were on the Inquisition's Index and the owner had presumably feared or not wanted to recover them. Erasmus' works were widely read and studied in Spain at the beginning of the sixteenth century but even the mention of his name was dangerous at the end. Elizabeth Eisenstein writes:

> … In the course of the sixteenth century, vernacular Bibles that had been turned out on a somewhat haphazard basis in diverse regions were withheld from Catholics and made compulsory for Protestants. An incentive to learn to read was thus eliminated among lay Catholics and officially enjoined upon Protestants. Book markets were likely to expand at different rates thereafter. Bible printing, once authorized, often became a special privilege, so that its decline in Catholic centres had a direct impact on a relatively small group of printers. The entire industry, however, suffered a glancing blow from the suppression of the large potential market represented by a Catholic lay Bible-reading public. Furthermore, vernacular Bibles were by no means the only best sellers that were barred to Catholic readers after the Council of Trent. Erasmus had made a fortune for his printers before Luther outstripped him. Both, along with many other popular authors, were placed on the Index. Being listed as forbidden served as a form of publicity and may have spurred sales. It was, however, more hazardous for Catholic printers than for Protestant ones to profit thereby.
>
> Given the existence of profit-seeking printers outside the reach of Rome, Catholic censorship boomeranged in ways that could not be foreseen. The Index provided free publicity for titles listed thereon. Lists of passages to be expurgated directed readers to "book, chapter, and line" where anti-Roman passages could be found, thus relieving Protestant propagandists of the need to make their own search for anti-Catholic citations drawn from eminent authors and respected works. Early copies of all the original Indexes found their way as soon as they were produced to Leiden, Amsterdam and Utrecht and were promptly utilized by the enterprising Dutch publisher as guides. Indeed, there was much to be gained and little to be lost for the Protestant printer who developed his list of forthcoming books with an eye on the latest

issue of the Index. Decisions made by Catholic censors thus inadvertently deflected Protestant publication policies in the direction of foreign heterodox, libertine, and innovative trends. This deflecting action is worth pausing over. It suggests why printers have to be treated as independent agents when trying to correlate Catholic-Protestant divisions with other developments. It was the profit-seeking printer and not the Protestant divine who published Aretino, Bruno, Sarpi, Machiavelli, Rabelais, and all the other authors who were on Catholic lists. When the intervening agent is left out of account, it becomes difficult to explain why such a secular, freethinking, and hedonist literary culture should have flourished in regions where pious Protestants were in control. (*The Printing Revolution in Early Modern Europe*. Cambridge University Press, 1993, pp.173–177)

Eisenstein's observations suggest that *Lazarillo de Tormes* enjoyed publicity, perhaps notoriety, because it had been placed on the Index in 1559. This may have been a spur to sales in societies where a lay Bible reading public was growing.

Abell Jeffes' 'Logo' on the front page of the English translation carries the words:

'Praise the Lorde with Harp and Songe',

and the bell, presumably a play upon Jeffes' first name Abell, is further suggestive of the ringing out of Protestant Christian news.

Authorship

The authorship of *Lazarillo de Tormes* has remained one of the best kept secrets of European literary history. The initial act of publishing in four locations may simply be a sign of the book's immediate popularity rather than to evade authorial identification. Anonymity has not precluded much guesswork. The two front contenders for authorship amongst scholars who have investigated the matter, are Diego Hurtado de Mendoza named in this connection in 1607–8 and in Rome during the Papal elections of 1550, whose literary style and anticlericalism are judged to match the text's; and Juan de Ortega, named as author in 1605, a Hieronymite friar, elected General of his Order in 1552. Both men suffered reverses in fortune which could have prevented their admitting authorship. My preference is for Juan de Ortega. He studied in Salamanca and entered the Hieronymite monastery in the nearby town of Alba de Tormes. The church of the village, Tejares, where Lazarillo was born, belonged to that monastery. The novel's first location is Salamanca. The Roman bridge of course remains to this day, with its bull (I suggest it is a pre-Roman boar) against which the blind man dashed Lazarillo's head, recently raised upon a plinth. Salamanca as a university enjoyed scholarly and intellectual pre-eminence with Paris, Bologna, Oxford and Cambridge.

The possibility that Juan de Ortega wrote the book has received scholarly support partly because a member of his Order reported so and partly for circumstantial reasons: the surname Ortega (meaning 'stinging nettle') suggests a 'New Christian', born of recent converts to Christianity, presumably of Jewish or Muslim ancestry, like the famous humanist Juan Luis Vives, friend of Erasmus, whose parents were Jewish. We know that Juan de Ortega was a cultured man, noted for a reformist spirit. His election as General of the Hieronymite Order proved too much for conservatives who engineered his fall from grace and banishment as a common friar to Valencia. He had begun to arrange for Charles V's retirement to Yuste and so he was recalled to complete this task. He died in Alba de Tormes in 1557. A supposed authorship cannot be the focus of analysis of a literary work; but there is textual support for the view that the book's social critique is strongly influenced by an authorship reaching across an ethnic divide.

Is the book anti-Catholic?

The manner in which *Lazarillo de Tormes* was subsequently censored and expurgated in Spain suggests that it was judged irreligious; however whether this charge was truly or falsely brought is a matter requiring much further reflection; perhaps a marvellously 'spoof' autobiography smuggles in a plea for a meaningful spiritual life of the sort that an Erasmian and humanist favoured. Rowland seems to have taken the tale as a genuine autobiography, which it is not, and as a 'documentary' on Spain rather than as an imaginative literary work involving selection, exaggeration, allusiveness, parody, burlesque and so on. Rowland, for example, fully grasps the sacramental ironies of bread and wine in the Second Treatise but his translation, as several footnotes point out is sensitive and mutes the full ironic force of the Spanish original perhaps out of sensitivity to some Anglican readers. Tuberville's doggerel at the end suggests that Rowland's translation sold as a 'documentary':

> Then Lázaro deserves
> no blame, but praise to gain,
> That plainly pens the Spaniards' pranks
> and how they live in Spain.

Is the book humanist?

A rapid reading identifies features of humanism, the classical and Biblical quotations and references, the parody of learned terms and structure – the sections are 'treatises' not chapters as in the Penguin translation by Michael Alpert – the anti-clerical satire on members of the Church, the studied dissonance of scholarly and vernacular forms of speech, and the confessional and autobiographical structure that holds the work's narrative together. The standard humanist vehicle of moral philosophy was the treatise; and there was a broad humanist campaign to rescue moral philosophy from scholasticism.

Vernacular Writing
Our anonymous Spanish author used the vernacular; *Lazarillo de Tormes* is written in Castilian. By the sixteenth century Castilian had become a standard national speech against several competitors; it became the dominant tongue through the military and political pre-eminence of Castile which drove a wedge down through the Iberian peninsula and ultimately after unification with Aragon destroyed the last Moorish stronghold in Granada. Humanists played a key role in standardising major modern tongues like Italian, German, French, English and Spanish, their grammar and vocabulary against the counter charge which survived into the eighteenth century that vernaculars, as opposed to Latin, were inherently unstable and prone to obsolescence; hence Swift's satire on the struldbruggs or immortals of Laputa (*Gulliver's Travels*, Book 3, Chapter X). All languages, including Latin, change. A vernacular obviously had a greater potential audience and could reach all levels of society when read aloud. *Lazarillo de Tormes* and numerous other Spanish Golden Age texts, through their popularity and canonisation, helped to stabilise and standardise a 'nation language', achieving dominance of one variant of the numerous dialects of Latin romance to be found in the Iberian peninsula to the present day. Renaissance humanists saw literature as having a civilizing role, or in the opening words of *Lazarillo de Tormes*:

> I am of opinion that things so worthy of memory, peradventure never heard of before nor seen, ought by all reason to come abroad to the sight of many, and not be buried in the endless pit of oblivion.
>
> (Prologue, p.2)

Form, Structure and Content
The book is of course written in the first person, indeed the very first word is 'I'; it is then a sort of fictional autobiography or letter addressed to someone called 'Your Reverence' or 'Your Worship', whom we may infer to be a member of the church hierarchy in Toledo. The relationship appears to be one of naïve layman and ecclesiastical superior. The organisation of the book into Prologue and Treatises could have been a late imposition but suggests a formal academic text perhaps intended to carry the presentation of a profound, abstract and searching moral or philosophical topic.

The Prologue
In the Prologue there are appeals to classical authority perhaps rather commonplace and pretentious – Pliny says, Tully (i.e. Cicero) says – typical of humanist display, quoting authorities in order to reinforce arguments. This practice clashes with the book's contents, a sequence of adventures, ostensibly raw life experience itself. The narrator rejects Horace's famous dictum about epic poetry, that it starts in the middle ('in medias res'), serving notice that he will record presumably the 'epic' of his life, from its chronological beginning. There is then a comical but straight faced

demolition of learned and literary conventions. We are in the presence of a subversive text, but subversive in a peculiarly modern sense: since the work's authorship is completely unresolved, the reader must rely upon a first person narrator to take him or her through a sequence of sordid adventures. The narrator is the only witness; but is that witness reliable? Does Lazarillo retain the reader's sympathy throughout? Is the narrator a consistent piece of fiction or broken between child and adult? Is the narrator gullible or a worldly wise entertainer? Is the reader not led into a literary game, a fiction itself drawing upon a tradition of confessional literature or even a deposition for an inquisitor, but taking the form of comic parody, which has the effect of destabilising the reader's certainties; are events to be treated as comical or serious? Speaking personally I find the book morally disturbing because there is no judgmental or guiding narrative voice to shape my reactions. I further suggest that the sophisticated author intended his writing to have this effect, on the grounds that he chose to suppress the sort of narrative framework which could have supplied the reader with certainty. The reader is thus forced to arrive at his or her own moral position vís a vís what he or she reads.

Lazarillo justifies the writing of the book on the classical grounds that it may prove instructive, may bring fame and may give pleasure. There is a clerical vocabulary – preach, confess, holy – and classical allusions are conveyed in a Spanish so colloquial that the narrator calls it 'coarse'. Indeed there is an apology – doubtless tongue-in-cheek – for the inadequacy of the written expression.

Lazarillo ends his Prologue contrasting those who inherit fine estates with those, like himself, who even when fortune has been hostile, with effort and resourcefulness, nonetheless reach safe anchorage. This metaphor is picked up in the final sentence of the Seventh Treatise:

> Since at the present moment I was enjoying prosperity and at the
> height of all good fortune.

Prosperity originally could also mean good weather and fair sailing, though only a trained Latinist is likely to have known this. The Prologue and Seventh Treatise are also linked by reference to the wheel of fortune, according to which, as it revolves, we are either at the top or bottom. The political term 'revolution' obviously derives from this metaphor. Fortune and God seem synonymous. Lazarillo seems to be insinuating that merit depends not on birth and inherited wealth, but personal excellence. As we set the last Treatise against the Prologue, we meet the most astonishing bathos: the height of good fortune is to be a complaisant cuckold to an immoral and corrupt arch priest, 'Your Reverence's' subordinate. The simulated ignorance (if that is what it is) of the narrator is so perfectly held that we must infer that 'Your Reverence' will agree: Lazarillo has indeed reached safe harbour and good fortune, a success story to which the Church is complicit. Lazarillo is like the brazen complaisant husband Allwit in Middleton's *A Chaste Maid in Cheapside* (first performance 1613) who actually connives at his wife's adultery because he thereby guarantees himself a comfortable life. This 'mènage à trois' is 'the matter' which apparently the first person narrator has been charged to report on, and links the Prologue to the Seventh Treatise. Honour, a pervasive theme of Spanish Golden Age drama (roughly 1560–1680), is claimed by Lazarillo for himself and his wife.

The book has more coherence than its episodic nature may suggest. It is a story of human survival and an exposé of a corrupt society whose moral policemen are party to the corruption and, if we are to believe the narrator, a senior Churchman required him to write 'the matter' down.

Should we take the opening of the Prologue at face value? It seems likely the real author expects us to be amused by the narrator's self-importance (e.g. the 'yo' [I] is redundant, and 'cosas tan señaladas' [things so worthy of memory] etc. is patently absurd). In the first part of the Prologue Lázaro hopes for a wide audience for his work, but in the remainder reveals that he was required only to explain 'el caso' [the matter] but has taken it upon himself to tell his whole life-story, and sees it as 'proof' that the lowliest can rise. This 'modernity' was largely missed by those (like Rowland?) who took it literally, and by many later writers who imitated its (auto)biographical, episodic form and delineation of character.

Incidentally the emperor Charles V held his 'Cortes' or parliament in Toledo in 1525 and 1538. Charles Habsburg was born Flemish and his followers in Spain included many who were influenced by Erasmus and northern European pietism. Is the cutting in of such historical detail an attempt ultimately to eradicate any residual disbelief in the story being told: or possibly a glance outward at a larger society beyond Lazarillo's experience, but not beyond the moral scope of the book? Certainly it is a chance remark suggestive that the author's religious perspective may have found support in Charles V's entourage.

The First Treatise

The first paragraph of the First Treatise has become a precursor of numerous others in the history of Western prose fiction: like Pip in Charles Dickens' *Great Expectations*, Lazarillo tells us his name and how he came by it. Lázaro (the diminutive form is Lazarillo) was born, not in an oxstall like Jesus, but in a watermill. His parents' surnames were of the very commonest, the Spanish equivalent of Smith and Jones. The form of Lazarillo's surname, with a 'de' has chivalresque resonances, like the champions of romances that Don Quixote was later to try to emulate, Launcelot du Lac, Amadís de Gaula, Palmerín de Inglaterrra, and so on. Lázaro gives first his high sounding surname, claiming that he was born 'dentro del río' [within the river], and afterwards, a much more banal explanation. The Spanish word used to describe Lazarillo's mother giving birth is more commonly reserved for animals; there was no lying in; Lazarillo's mother 'dropped' him amongst the sacks, doubtless in the manner of the rats and mice that commonly infest such places.

The name Lázaro, or as we say Lazarus, did occur as the name of a proverbial simpleton in Spain at that time; but it is also the name of the Biblical beggar who lay suffering at the rich man's gates, his sores licked by dogs:

> There was a certain rich man, which was clothed in purple and fine linen, and fared sumptuously every day:
>
> And there was a certain beggar named Lazarus, which was laid at his gate, full of sores,
>
> And desiring to be fed with the crumbs which fell from the rich man's table: moreover the dogs came and licked his sores.
>
> And it came to pass, that the beggar died, and was carried by the angels into Abraham's bosom: the rich man also died, and was buried;
>
> And in hell he lifted up his eyes, being in torments, and seeth Abraham afar off, and Lazarus in his bosom.
>
> And he cried and said, Father Abraham, have mercy on me, and send Lazarus, that he may dip the tip of his finger in water. and cool my tongue; for I am tormented in this flame.
>
> But Abraham said, Son, remember that thou in thy life time receivest thy good things, and likewise Lazarus evil things: but now he is comforted, and thou art tormented.
>
> (Luke 16, 19–25)

I have deliberately quoted from the King James Bible, the Authorised version of 1611 because this, itself an English Renaissance and Christian humanist text, is based on earlier English translations like those of William Tyndale and Miles Coverdale, that are contemporaneous with *Lazarillo de Tormes* and because its grammar and syntax are the same as Rowland's. At that time, lepers, social outcasts, were treated in hospitals dedicated to Saint Lazarus. It was this figure, rather than Lazarus of Bethany, whom Jesus brought back to life from dead (*John* II, 1–4), who became an archetype for human destitution and degradation, and with Pauper (poor man) was polarised against Dives (rich man) in morality plays and homiletic stories that in turn had their roots in the preaching of the Medieval Church. Some critics, however, argue that the other Lazarus may also fall within the book's meaning: whereas Lazarus dies physically but is reborn into a spiritual life, Lazarillo dies spiritually but enters into a life of material well-being. Such a heavy structural irony, like the numerous sacramental ironies and Biblical allusions, assumes considerable Bible knowledge on the part of the reader.

Lazarillo's father, a miller, stole flour; a recurrent motif of the book is bread and starvation, terms which can be metaphors for spiritual as well as material deprivation. The Spanish text refers to the miller not stealing from, but bleeding the sacks. This could be thieves' slang or comic writing; but equally could refer to the bread and wine of Holy Communion and theological disputes over whether the bread and wine are the body and blood of Christ, the issue of transubstantiation. On being charged, Lazarillo's father acted according to *John*, 1. 20:

And he confessed, and denied not; but confessed, I am not the Christ.

Lazarillo describes his father's fate quoting Christ's Sermon on the Mount, which includes the Beatitudes, which in full are as follows:

Blessed are the poor in spirit: for theirs is the kingdom of heaven.

Blessed are they that mourn: for they shall be comforted.

Blessed are the meek: for they shall inherit the earth.

Blessed are they which do hunger and thirst after righteousness: for they shall be filled.

Blessed are the merciful: for they shall obtain mercy.

Blessed are the pure in heart: for they shall see God.

Blessed are the peacemakers: for they shall be called the children of God.

Blessed are they which are persecuted for righteousness' sake: for theirs is the kingdom of heaven.

(Matthew 5, 3–10)

Although our text quotes the final verse of this famous Sermon, it is difficult not to believe that the author did not have in mind the whole, surely one of the greatest Christian appeals on behalf of the marginalised and down trodden; and nowadays, secularised, a moral cornerstone of Western civilization. The grammar of both the Spanish and the English indicates not hope but certainty that Lazarillo's father is in heaven.

The first paragraph ends by recording that the erstwhile miller, as punishment, was forced to take part in a war against the Moors, Muslims, as a muleteer. In fact the Spanish text uses not the romance word but the Arabic word for a watermill; and the word for muleteer is also Arabic. Millers and muleteers were often of Moorish origin, muleteering particularly was one of their favourite professions. We should bear in mind that at the time *Lazarillo de Tormes* was written, Granada, the last Moorish stronghold in the peninsula had fallen, in 1492, and war was continuing on the other side of the Mediterranean in North Africa. Perhaps Lazarillo's father had died in the unsuccessful action at Los Gelves (Jerba) in 1510 or 1520. The fortunes of Moors who remained in the peninsula declined; promises of religious toleration were broken, many were forcibly re-distributed, armed rebellion in the Alpujarras was suppressed in the 1560's and by the second decade of the seventeenth-century, mass expulsions were completed.

The opening paragraph is on a knife edge between knock-about comedy and a moral challenge that, in pointedly quoting key Christian teaching, comes close to blasphemy. Surely this is a humanist attempt to Christianise society. If we may make such a distinction the author appears to mean us to understand a perversion of Christian values, but the narrator seems to misunderstand through ignorance or to make a blasphemous joke.

Lazarillo's mother now a destitute widow, still tries to hold the family together. In keeping with the pervasive irony, she decided in the words of a Spanish saying 'to lean against good folks in order to become one of them', or as Rowland translates:

> determined to inhabit among such as were virtuous and honest, to be
> of that number,

reminiscent of another Spanish saying 'tell me who you go round with and I will tell you who you are.' The same Spanish refrain with its suggestion of immoral earnings is repeated in the Seventh Treatise. She cooked for university students in Salamanca, washed clothes for stable hands of a military–religious order that drew income from a parish in Salamanca, dedicated to Saint Mary Magdalen, a fallen woman rehabilitated by Jesus (see *Luke* chapters 7 and 8 and *John* chapter 8), and used the stables to practise as a prostitute. A blackamoor slave, doubtless originally Muslim, and ironically named Zaide, the Arabic *sayyid* means 'lord ' [as we find in 'El Cid'], becomes the breadwinner and completes the family. Then comes the moment of recognition for the baby of the liaison, that his father is black, the colour of the bogeyman of childish terror, his mother white! Zaide's laughing rejoinder that the half caste is the son of a whore, produces the aside given to Lázaro as adult narrator but like several similar remarks, is possibly an authorial intervention to warn the over-judgmental reader;

> There are many such in the world, which do abhor and flee from
> others because they cannot see what shape they have themselves.

Zaide also stole to provide his adopted family with basic necessities, and was punished with whipping and basting. The narrator or author again intervenes observing that we should not be surprised that a priest or friar steals from the poor or from his convent when love moved a poor slave to steal too, implying that thieving is more to be expected in clerics than in a destitute slave. This was one of the passages expurgated in the Spanish edition of 1573. Rowland following the French translations mutes the directness of the Spanish. This latter is bitter sarcasm: Zaide, denied all rights including a family, acted out of basic human instincts and love; the Church, we are to understand, betrayed those who in Christian charity should have been relieved. Morally, life must take precedence over property.

Both Lazarillo's father and stepfather might have perished in the same military campaign, in 1510 or 1520.

Throughout these paragraphs we may identify the Sermon on the Mount and an attack upon society's perversion of Christian and humane values. The most marginalised of family units collapses and Lazarillo is handed over to a blind beggar, the first of a succession of masters. The blind man, in reciting prayers for money, is parasitic upon the Catholic church. He clearly abuses Christian belief by his hypocrisy and acceptance of money, and indoctrinates and corrupts Lazarillo.

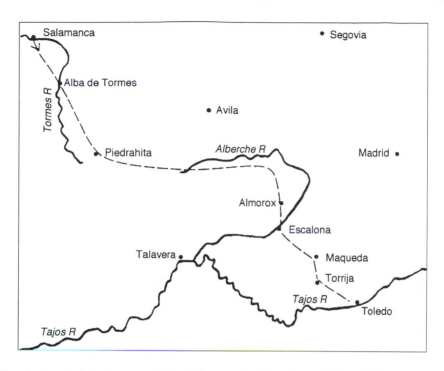

Fig. 3. Lazarillo's journey (Allen Bjornson), taken from Richard Bjornson, *The Picaresque Hero in European Fiction*, University of Wisconsin Press, 1979, fig 5

The Second Treatise
In the Second Treatise Lazarillo goes from the frying pan into the fire, voluntarily entering the service of a priest of Maqueda, a man in holy orders, who is a cruel and pathological miser. There are classical references, to Alexander the Great and Penelope for example, but the entire episode is dominated by sacramental ironies and Biblical allusions. The liturgy is surely mocked when a priest gives bones to a starving boy with the words:

> Take down this to thee, and rejoice, seeing that thou hast the world at
> will. I am sure the Pope himself hath now no better life than thou hast.

This last remark could be interpreted both as hypocrisy by the priest and as an Erasmian swipe at Papal pomp.

The role of bread in the Christian liturgy and as a metaphor for religious communion and spiritual renewal must be understood. The priest denies the key to this paradise; and the climax of the story, the snake that never was, surely alludes to the Garden of Eden myth in *Genesis* 2 and 3. The entire episode reads like a satirical extension of the Dives – Lazarus, rich man – poor man motif. The priest, who should relieve the poor and suffering, behaves like Dives, begrudging Lazarillo even the crumbs from his bread coffer. The Spanish, by the way, uses the word 'arca' for chest, thereby reminding the original readers of the Ark of the Covenant [the wooden coffer containing the tables of the law, kept in the Holiest Place of the Tabernacle] as well as a common piece of church furniture, the Tabernacle which is used to store the Blessed Sacrament.

The entire episode, and especially the scope of its allusions, read like a parodic commentary upon *Matthew* Chapter 12.

> [David] entered into the house of God, and did eat the shew bread, which was not lawful for him to eat.....[the shew bread was the twelve loaves that were placed every Sabbath 'before the Lord' on a table beside the altar of incense, and at the end of the week were eaten by the priests alone.]   (verse 4);

> He that is not with me is against me;   (verse 30);

> All manner of sin and blasphemy shall be forgiven unto men; but the blasphemy against the Holy Ghost shall not be forgiven unto men.
>   (verse 31);

> O generation of vipers, how can ye being evil, speak good things?
>   (verse 34).

It was not the consecrated priest but a lay figure who saved Lazarillo's life, an old woman who recited popular charms, thereby confirming verse 50:

> For whoever shall do the will of my father which is in heaven,
> the same is my brother, and sister, and mother.

The priest rejects Lazarillo, crossing himself as if Lazarillo were possessed of the devil, recalling verse 26:

> And if Satan cast out Satan, he is divided against himself: how shall
> then his kingdom stand?

The priest directly contradicts the work of Jesus:

> Then was brought unto him [Jesus] one possessed with a devil, blind,
> and dumb: and he healed him...   (verse 22).

Rowland himself picks up the religious parody by repeating the original's reference to Jonah (see footnote 61), upon which *Matthew*, Chapter 12, could scarcely be more explicit:

> For as Jonas was three days and three nights in the whale's belly: so
> shall the son of man be three days and three nights in the heart of the
> earth.   (verse 40).

Re-working jest book material does not necessarily make the book a jest book. Its anonymity and first person narrator suppress the sort of background information or narrative framework which could have offered guidance on matters of tone and interpretation. The Second Treatise, ostensibly knock about-comedy of the broadest kind, assumes a darker tone when its allusions to *Matthew* chapter 12 are allowed full force. We do not have to restrict the book's message to the bodily misfortunes of its protagonist and narrator, Lazarillo. The book's structure is so unstable that a remarkably complex range of moral and religious possibilities are in play. The book was placed on Valdés' 1559 Index as we have noted, along with the works of Erasmus; and Rowland's translation, influenced in part by the French translation published by Saugrain (1561), offers further evidence that the book was sensitive to the religious disputes of that time. His marginal gloss on the chance arrival of the tinker:

Lázaro was a good Christian, believing all goodness came from God

has Lutheran resonances of which Gresham, the dedicatee of Rowland's translation, may well have approved. As the footnotes make clear, Rowland was also uncomfortable with the anti-clerical venom in several passages, again following the Saugrain, adopting a euphemistic practice that surely suggests that both English and French translators saw the text as embedded in religious controversy and perhaps did not wish gratuitously to offend a book purchasing public, Catholic or Protestant.

The Third Treatise

Lazarillo meets the master of the Third Treatise in 'this noble city of Toledo' or 'esta insigne ciudad de Toledo', a very Latinate Spanish way of saying 'in this distinguished ancient and illustrious city of Toledo.' Toledo had been the Visi-Gothic capital of Spain before the Moorish invasion and its first recapture from the Moors in 1085 was of great significance. To this day five churches there preserve the pre-invasion liturgical rite, called the Mozarabic. Toledo's archbishop, usually a cardinal too, is Spain's primate, first churchman, and his revenues were once judged second only to the Pope's. Toledo enjoyed renown for its swords, the best quality in Europe. For long the capital city was where the court resided, and Madrid did not become the established capital of Spain until the early seventeenth-century. An analysis of the Spanish aristocracy is then well located in Toledo, since many Castilian aristocratic families claimed pre-Moorish ancestry, to be 'Old Christians', to be blue-blooded, that is white-skinned and therefore able to show blue veins.

The material poverty of a squire, the lowest echelon of the aristocracy, was proverbial in Spain at that time. Our squire is in virtually unfurnished accommodation. He has a way of walking suggestive of pride, traditionally a nobleman's gait, not a merchant's or a Jew's. He is learned in the arts of courtship in the manner of the fourteenth-century Galician troubadour Macías, a proverbial model for faithful lovers, and more skilled than Ovid, who wrote of the art of loving; but he cannot afford even the most immediate sexual relief by the river side. Our anonymous author must have been aware that according to a popular Spanish ballad, the last Visi-Gothic King of Spain, Rodrigo, seduced La Cava, daughter of his governor of Ceuta, by the river Tagus at Toledo, an event which folk tradition blamed for the Moorish invasion in 711. The linking idea would seem to be that of a collapsed aristocracy or social élite. The squire is scrupulous about etiquette, the forms of address appropriate to his rank; back home he had corrected a journeyman for addressing him with the words 'May God preserve your worship' instead of the appropriate 'I kiss your worship's hands'. He had abandoned his dilapidated property rather than doff his cap to a better off neighbour. He exhibits a fastidiousness in eating and commends Lazarillo for daintiness:

> It is a virtue to live soberly, therefore I commend thee much. Hogs fill themselves, and wise men eat discreetly what is only sufficient for them.

Fig. 4 *View of Toledo and the Alcantara Bridge, engraving by M. A. Rouargue, L'Illustration, 1858.*

The theme of bread and destitution continues. Religion is ever present; Lazarillo attributes his finding this master to God's intervention; the squire hears Mass and the Canonical hours sung every day, in Protestant eyes religious practices or good works that were unlikely to secure salvation. The Third Treatise is dominated by the adjectives 'dark' and 'gloomy', such that Lazarillo, to the amusement of his master, misunderstanding the laments of the followers of a funeral cortège, believes the destination of the coffin is his master's lodging, not the usual burial ground, a joke, if that is what it is, traced to an Arabic source. Biblical allusions appear to be more to the Old Testament than the New, notably to *Job* and *Deuteronomy*, the author through Lazarillo quoting *Job* chapter 5:

> [God] Which doeth great things and unsearchable; marvellous things
> without number...:
>
> Behold, happy is the man whom God correcteth: therefore despise
> not thou the chastening of the Almighty:
>
> For he maketh sore, and bindeth up: he woundeth, and his hands
> make whole.   (Verses 9, 17, and 18)

The squire takes on a servant whom he cannot feed. His caste forbids him profitable employment; he represents the economic collapse of a military caste and rentier mentality. He even depends upon his servant to feed him by his begging. He is so disabled socially that, far from holding together a family, like Lazarillo's father and step-father, he cannot procure a harlot's services in the open air. The house of this master may indeed be construed as a grave. He embodies social entropy. His religious devotion is an activity of empty forms. His only accoutrements of value are his cloak and sword.

Propaganda, Literary Imitation and Satire

Protestants, ignoring the fact that this caricature arose originally as a humanist critique in Spain itself, fastened upon it with glee. *Lazarillo de Tormes* became a propaganda gift and in his dedication to the English translation (1586), David Rowland of Anglesey, the translator, elaborating upon the French version, wrote:

> besides much mirth, here is also a true description of the nature and
> disposition of sundry Spaniards. So that by reading hereof, such as
> have not travelled Spain, may as well discern much of the manners
> and customs of that country, as those that have there long time
> continued.

Rowland's running heading and marginal glosses (he borrowed and adapted fourteen from the French and added twenty of his own) insistently rub in the propaganda purpose:

> *The Spaniard's Life.*
>
> *There is not such provision of meat in Spain as in England.*
>
> *Poor Lázaro did bear his master's dinner and his own in his
> bosom for fear of losing it.*
>
> *In Spain many drink nothing but water, and some that may, have
> wine, but the squire drank it for want of better.*

The recurrent motif of bread and hunger is exploited. Of all Lazarillo's masters, it was the third, the destitute country gentleman who best lent himself to searching ethnic satire:

> he taketh his sword and kisseth the pommel, and as he was putting it
> in his girdle, said unto me:

'My boy, if thou knewest what a blade this is, thou wouldest marvel, there is no gold that can buy it off me, for as many as Antonio made, he could never give such temper to any as he gave to this.'

Then drawing it out of the scabbard he tasted the edge with his fingers, saying,

'Seest thou it? I dare undertake to cut asunder with it a whole fleece of wool.'

I answered him softly to my self, saying,'And I with my teeth though they be not of such hard metal, a loaf of bread weighing four pound.'

This dialogue identifies honour and material destitution.

Of course figures like Lazarillo's master the squire gravitated naturally to Spain's wars and armies, especially in the Low Countries and Italy. Doubtless many in the Spanish forces, in reality rogues, thieves and vagabonds, swore and postured as if gentlemen born back home. The following example of Europe wide pamphleteering, printed in London in 1599 and thought to be a translation from Dutch or German, pursues the satire:

But *Signor* is a Cavalliero, he must be reverenced, *Guarda su Signoria*, [i.e. the Lord preserve your worship] he must be soothed and flattered.... Moreover, you ought to know he is a *Hidalgo*, [i.e. a son of something] although he have no patents thereof, even whose name and race, doth terrify the Moors ....

This is a *Signior's* diet at another's cost, but alas if you find him at his owne Table, you may see it stately furnished with a *Sardinia*, [i.e. Sardine] or a crust of bread, a pot of *Aqua*, [i.e. water] and perhaps a bone, yet abroad, if there be a Wolf at the Table, *Signor* is one...

Signor being in the street, or any other public place, his first gestures are to bend the head, turn the eye, and Peacock-like to behold himself; if nothing be amiss, his gait is like one who treads the measures....[i.e. dances]. His Trade in *Spain* perhaps was to sew hand-baskets, or to blow glasses in the furnaces, scarce trusted to guard a flock of *Cabritos* [i.e. young goats]. And here he will bear the name of a *Hidalgo* or don....he frieth in Love's searching flames like a fiery furnace.[1]

---

1   Jones, R.O., (ed) *La vida de Lazarillo de Tormes*, Manchester University Press, 1966, Introduction, pages xxiii-xxiv. Jones' excellent introduction quotes a Spanish proverb:
    La comida de hidalgo poca vianda y mantel largo [i.e. the Spanish gentleman's meal, little meat and a lot of table cloth].
Jones' quotation from *Viaje de Turquia* (1557) illustrates the extent to which the satire was home produced.

[Note: this passage confirms a widespread practice of that time, of using Spanish and Italian forms of address almost interchangeably. There are abundant examples in English drama during the reigns of James I and Charles I, perhaps because Spaniards dominated so much of the Italian peninsula, or possibly because of a popular assimilation of Mediterranean Latin peoples in northern European eyes.]

Spaniards are portrayed as displaced military adventurers, projecting destitution, parasitism, pride, violence and lust. These themes, sometimes comic, at others serious and tragic, became staples of late Elizabethan and Jacobean plays.

Shakespeare's comedy *Love's Labour's Lost*, published in quarto in 1598, was first performed when Spain and England were at war. The play is set in Navarre and has as one of its characters 'a fantastical Spaniard' Don Adriano de Armado. The Roman Emperor Hadrian was born a Spaniard; the 'de' indicates aristocracy or knighthood, 'Armado' means an armed man. He is pilloried throughout the play: his lust seduces the country wench Jaquenetta, he claims familiarity with the king

it will please his grace (by the world) sometime to lean upon my poor
shoulder, and with his royal finger, thus dally with my excrement,
with my mustachio ...   (Act V, scene i, lines 91–94)

he impersonates Hector in a masque, and under challenge confesses that he has no shirt (Act V, scene ii, line 699). Like Don Quixote not yet born, he models his life upon literature:

I have vowed to Jaquenetta to hold the plough for her sweet love three
years...   (Act V, scene ii, lines 865–866)

Shakespeare had surely either read Rowland's translation or heard a close account of it, the comic resemblance to Lazarillo's third master being so obvious.

Othello (probably written 1602–1604 and performed at court November 1604) opens with two Spanish adventurers in Italy, Roderigo and Iago, the one bearing the name of the last Visi-Gothic king whose failure let the Moors into Spain, the other named after Spain's patron saint, whose nickname was 'Kill Moors', plotting to destroy another culturally displaced person, a Moorish general. Shakespeare captures the racial mixture of the Italian peninsula bestowing Spanish names where Cinthio's original story has none. It is dramatically consistent that Othello, entrapped by Iago's machinations, kills himself with

a sword of Spain the ice-brook's temper.   (Act V, scene ii, line 254)

Other English Renaissance dramatists like Marston, Dekker, Ford and Middleton created both comic and violent characters for the London Stage to foment popular hispanophobia. Middleton's *A Game at Chesse* attacking the projected Spanish marriage of Charles with a Spanish princess was the first long run stage hit of the London theatre. The Spanish ambassador protested to King James who closed the play in August 1623. London rejoiced when the marriage project proved a fiasco. A character called Lazarillo, knight or servant, occurs in plays like *Blurt Master Constable* (?Middleton, ?1602), *Love's Cure* (Beaumont and Fletcher? 1602–1606),

Match Me in London (Dekker) an old play relicensed without fee at the height of anti-Spanish hysteria, 21 August 1623, and *All's Lost by Lust* (Rowley ?1622). Scholars are not always certain to whom to attribute authorship.

Beaumont's *The Woman Hater* (?1606, registered 1607) subtitled *The Hungry Courtier*, is set in Milan and the hungry courtier is variously called Lazarello and Lazarillo. His hunger presents a peculiarly Epicurean twist; he rejects plain fare and pursues around town the cooked head of a fish called 'umbrana':

> Duke. Lazarello? what is he?
>
> Arrigo. A courtier my Lord, and one that I wonder your grace knowes
> not: for he hath followed your Court, and your last predecessors, from
> place to place any time this seven year, as faithfully as your Spits and
> your Dripping-pans have done, almost as greasely. (Act I, Scene i,
> lines 43–58)

The material destitution of an enemy is an obvious propaganda tool to foment xenophobia.

Jonson's satire was perhaps the most biting:

> A noble Count, Don of Spain, my dear...
> A doughty Don is taken with my Dol... Sweet Dol,
> You must go tune your virginal, no losing O' the least time
> His great Verdugo-ship has not a jot of language;
> So much the easier to be cozened, my Dolly.

> *The Alchemist* (1610) Act III, Scene iii, lines 10, 39, 66–67, 70–72.

'Verdugo' is Spanish for hangman or executioner. Jonson caricatures the Spaniard [he is, of course, the Englishman Surly in disguise] as a noble killing machine, who goes after whores but is too proud to learn English.

His eventual entry milks precisely the same comic famishment as we find in Lazarillo's third master:

> Slud he does look too fat to be a Spaniard....
> You shall be emptied Don: pumped and drawn
> Dry, as they say.   (Act IV, Scene iii, lines 28, 44–45.)

Jonson repeats the stock joke that Spanish aristocrats eat little, are skinny and lascivious but his vocabulary suggests that Dol will prove more than a sexual match and will transmit venereal disease.

In Jonson's late play, *The New Inn*, effete chivalry is embodied in an hispanophile character, Sir Glorious Tipto, who ends up drunk below stairs.

The Fourth and Fifth Treatises

The representations of friars and pardoners of the Fourth and Fifth Treatises were held throughout late medieval Western Christendom and the English poet Geoffrey Chaucer (?1340–1400) had anticipated them over one and a half centuries before. In the General Prologue to *The Canterbury Tales,* Chaucer gives vignettes of both a

Friar and a Pardoner. Chaucer's Friar like Lazarillo's was a womanising convivial
rogue, a drunk who knew barmen and landlords

> Bet than a lazar or a beggestere;
> For unto swich a worthy man as he
> Accorded nat, as by his facultee,
> To have with sike lazars aqueyntaunce. (Lines 241–245)
> [Trans.: Better than a diseased man or beggar,
> for to such a distinguished man as he,
> it was not appropriate, if his profession be borne in mind
> to have anything to do with the sick and destitute.]

The 'lazar' of the passage means of course a poor, diseased man, possibly a leper
and etymologically, the word is the same as a Lazarus or Lázaro. Chaucer repeats a
conventional sarcasm. Perhaps then the narrator of *Lazarillo de Tormes* saw no
reason to repeat what was widely known to his readers. There might however have
been other reasons.

We do not, of course, know amongst whom this narrative may have circulated
before it found its way into print, and as we have seen, its author could himself have
been a friar. Perhaps our anonymous author exercised caution or alternatively
assumed that his readers knew so much of such cases that to write further would be
redundant. However short though the Treatise is, there are thematic links to the rest
of the book: Lazarillo's fourth master was of the Order of Mercy, an order chiefly
engaged in the redemption of Christian captives from the Muslims in North Africa.
Otherwise the anti-clerical satire is conventional: another priest without vocation
who hated church services and monastic life. Some critics have however also
inferred that this Friar was bisexual, and a pederast, and hence the final sentence of
the paragraph: Lazarillo was his catamite, the full story being suppressed.

Pardoners of course were not members of the priesthood, not in holy orders.
Chaucers's Pardoner too had all the resource and skills of his Spanish counterpart:

> His wallet lay before hym in his lappe,
> Bretful of pardon, comen from Rome al hoot.   (lines 686–687).
> [Trans.: His wallet lay before him on his lap, brimful of pardons, just
> come all hot from Rome.]

In the prologue to his tale, Chaucer's Pardoner boasts of his skills in the pulpit,
his capacity to deceive ordinary church goers and rob them. Indeed, his criminality
and immorality (the text also suggests sexual perversion) is presented so openly to
the other pilgrims that the revelations which the pardoner makes in the prologue and
conclusion of his tale, seem more Chaucer's than the ostensible narrator's. Again
there is a Spanish detail of thematic importance: our Spanish Pardoner is of the
'Santa Cruzada', or 'Holy Crusade' and sold indulgences granting full remission of
their sins to those who contributed in this manner toward the campaigns against the
infidels [i.e. Muslims] in North Africa and elsewhere. Their activities brought profits
to the state but serious abuses were condemned repeatedly in the Castilian 'Cortes'

[i.e. Parliament] and in 1524, Charles V issued a decree to prevent pardoners from forcing their indulgences upon the people. The portrait of a Pardoner in so short a book cannot be adventitious. Such satire was a late medieval Europe wide convention, this particular incident being very close to a story of Masuccio of Salerno, but its presence here links the book more to Lutheran reform than Erasmian satire.

The Sixth Treatise

Brief though the Sixth Treatise is, its very spareness is telling. Lazarillo apparently makes a foray into the real economy assisting a painter of tambourines. The nature of Lazarillo's work is explicit in the Spanish, though muted in Rowland's translation: it was to grind the Tambourine Painter's colours. This apparently innocent narrative detail may well be playful disguise. Lazarillo was apprentice to a master tambourine-painter who practised skilled craftwork which at that time was still in the hands of Moors. Lazarillo's father might have been Moorish, his step father certainly was one. Perhaps then he briefly took refuge in his caste. Moors were often associated with money-making and music. They were also well known for hard work! This, then, in sum, could be the implications of this narrative incident.

Spanish however is very rich in proverbs and refrains, and these include many, about tambourines and grinding. A tambourine has fun-loving associations, of music, rhythm and dance, and not surprisingly we find refrains like:

> There's no marriage without a tambourine.

Even at the present day, there still survive amongst the Moors of Morocco, communal satirical poetry competitions, impromptu, to the rhythms of tambourines. The topics satirised may range widely across family rivalries, business greed, sexual philanderings and so on.

The tambourine then has resonances of the pleasures of song and dance, festivity and sex. Grinding, of course, takes us into sexual semantic territory, especially when we recall that the sort of grinding that Lazarillo did was with pestle and mortar. Again, there is sound contemporary evidence in refrains for an association of milling and love-making:

> when my dark girl turns her eyes, it's a sign that the mill is not grinding sand;

> grain in the hopper of the mill, who comes first, grinds first.

Perhaps in the Seventh Treatise the adult Lazarillo is but a 'miller' for an Archdeacon who 'grinds' his wife![2] A very popular Mexican song of a few years ago was called quite simply, 'Moliendo Café', 'grinding coffee'. The Spanish

---

2   Shipley George, 'A Case of Functional Obscurity' in *Modern Language* Nolci, 1982, Volume 97, pages 225–253.

speaking world is far less inhibited about sexual matters than the Anglo Saxon. Rarely does a Spanish speaking politician lose his job over sexual peccadillos.

Perhaps the Tambourine-Painter was a skilled womaniser, who drew Lazarillo into his activities. Rowland's reticence may support this interpretation. The original perhaps embarrassed him.

The inclusion of such an incident may remind us of the bawd, Pompey, in *Measure for Measure* Act II Scene i (performed, 1604), who seeks to deflect a magistrate's interrogation by comical reference to a dish of prunes, a deliberate attempt to change the agenda.

One can understand one critical view that *Lazarillo de Tormes* is more the notes for a novel than a novel itself[3].

Lazarillo reverts to a master who is a chaplain of the Church who, in a manner of speaking, sub-contracts him as a water seller. The concession that allowed Lazarillo to keep Saturday takings has led some critics to infer that the chaplain was a converted Jew, and to point out that Toledo Cathedral in 1547 laid down severe 'estatutos de impieza', that is statutes of clean blood, to exclude New Christians. Ethnic cleansing is nothing new. The expression 'received me for his own' can bear several interpretations, Christian, racial and sexual. Surely the reader is challenged to ponder the vocation of the chaplain and the importance of the metaphor of water: the carrying of water marks genuine employment, whereas, as we shall see, the crying of wines in the Seventh Treatise coincided with hypocrisy and corruption. There is a cross reference to the Prologue, where Tully's [Cicero's] remark 'Honour nourishes the arts' was followed by the image of a soldier mounting a ladder. We learn in the Sixth Treatise that the chaplain enabled Lazarillo to mount the first social rung and he thereby achieved 'buena vida', as opposed to 'triste vida', that is good life, both in quality and honour, against a sad life. Lazarillo then dresses himself in second hand clothes, what he calls 'hábito de hombre de bien', that is, the dress of a respectable man and a man of means – and gives up work! Lazarillo follows his third master, the squire, and retains a second hand sword from the same place of manufacture. There is irony in his imitating the dress of a squire whose whole false appearance he had exposed.

The Seventh Treatise
Immediately after the chaplain, Lazarillo briefly serves a constable the lowest officer in the organisation of Justice and the only untarnished master. The physical insecurity proves too much and he abandons him; he then becomes a civil servant – town crier – held at that time to be the lowest of employments, vile and contemptible. There are linguistic reasonances about Lazarillo's description of this

---

3   Castro, C. *La Vida de Lazarillo de Tormes*, Taurus Ediciones, Madrid, 1985, Fifteenth Reprint, page 29.

choice of career that are especially noteworthy: Lazarillo says in Rowland's translation that

God by his grace lightened my mind

in Spanish 'alumbrarme'. The same verb was used in the First Treatise after the Blind man had bashed Lazarillo's head against the stone bull and taught him underworld slang, when he blasphemously remarks

Neither gold nor silver can I give thee, howbeit, I do mean to teach
thee the way to live.

The narrator/Lazarillo, after using the verb 'alumbrar' comments in Rowland's translation:

It was he that gave me sight and taught me how to know the world.

And in the Second Treatise at the point when Lazarillo had a second key made, Lazarillo says he was 'alumbrado por el Espíritu Santo', that is, in Rowland's words.

By inspiration of the Holy Ghost.

In the early sixteenth-century in Spain, there was a movement within Spanish Catholicism whose members were called 'alumbrados', guided by the light of God, also sometimes called by historians, illuminists. It was suppressed as heretical. God and pious allusions are pervasive to the book, and it may be unwise to latch on to this metaphor. There is however startling irony in using the language of a movement associated with fostering an inner spiritual life to characterize acquiring the worldly wisdom of a blind beggar, getting a key made in order to steal bread, and joining the Civil Service. Lazarillo says that nobody prospers without a government job, and that through it, he lives at the service of God and 'Your Reverence'.

The Unity of the Text

A common reaction to a reading of *Lazarillo de Tormes* is that the book is a masterpiece, but a flawed masterpiece on the grounds that the brilliance of the first three treatises is not sustained. Some such reaction must have troubled the original French and Tudor English translators because they included, presumably as a balancing makeweight, the first chapter of the spurious sequel. In other words, they found the final four treatises too lightweight against the first three. This edition has expunged the spurious material as extraneous.

Most scholarly criticism of the text of the last seventy years has followed F. Courtney Tarr in treating *Lazarrilo de Tormes* as a literary and artistic unity. In effect he argues that the fragmentary appearance of the last four treatises arises from their division and the accompanying rubrics or captions; for Courtney Tarr, these are not authorial, and treatises four and six are transitional paragraphs; the conclusion, the seventh treatise, is deliberately ironical and anticlimactic; the book ends as it begins with co-habitation. Courtney Tarr concludes:

The foregoing analysis of *Lazarillo de Tormes* has revealed, I trust, a
coherent development and a literary unity greater than that of a series
of episodes grouped around a single figure. Each stage is the natural

outcome of the preceding ones and together they form an organic whole. The translations are everywhere clear and logical. The last four *tractados* [treatises], short as they are in comparison with the first three, are neither fragmentary nor cut down. If we discard the misleading division into *tractados* and keep in mind that in the prologue it was clearly implied that stress would be laid on Lázaro's *adversidades* [adversities] (the first three *tractados*), the space devoted to his rise does not seem unduly small, especially in view of its modest nature and ironical treatment. After the climax of his misfortunes is reached, it is only natural to usher in the conclusion already announced in the prologue, which is given an unexpected ironical turn quite in keeping with the spirit of the first few paragraphs of the book. There are other connections between the beginning and the end: the similarity of the situation of Lázaro's wife with that of his mother, and the *spíritu de prophecía* [gift of prophecy] of the blind man, whose influence runs through the book like a fine connecting thread. The many ways in which the various stages – or chapters – are linked together have already been pointed out. The consistent use of transitional figures or occupations is worthy of note, as is also the persistence of certain characteristics in Lázaro's masters. They exemplify two vices, avarice and hypocrisy. The blind man was a rogue and a miser, the priest a miser and a hypocrite, the *escudero* [squire], despite his insistence on honor, allows himself to be fed by his servant and to leave his creditors in the lurch, the *buldero* [pardoner] was both a hypocrite and a rogue, and the archpriest likewise a hypocrtie. The prevalence of hypocrisy coincides with the anticlerical satire which is present throughout the book, but which is especially emphasized after the hunger theme has been used up. Although the rôle of the protagonist undergoes changes, these changes fit naturally into each other and do not belie the underlying conception of his character. From all these standpoints the work possesses an undeniable coherence and a definite literary unity.

But the unity of the whole is surpassed by that of the first part. The climactic treatment of the hunger theme gives to the first three *tractados* an artistic unity and elaboration superior to that of the work as a whole. The artistic climax is reached before the literary goal is in sight. The resulting let-down is inevitable. The latter portion of the book becomes, then, an anticlimax, an effect which is heightened by the ironic and anticlimactic character of the ending itself. Moreover, the technique and motivation used in the first three *tractados* were carried to their logical conclusion there and could not be utilized for the remainder of the work. Is it any wonder, then, that this portion of the work should be artistically inferior to the first three *tractados*? Thus, the very technique which is largely responsible for the excellence of the first part of the book is, in a certain sense, also responsible for the comparative inferiority of the latter portion. This disparity in both merit and length between the two parts of the book is heightened – and even an air of incompleteness given – by the inadequate and arbitrary division into chapters, a division which occurred subsequent to the writing of the text.

If each of Lázaro's masters and protectors had been treated at relatively equal length, the book would undoubtedly have had better mechanical proportions, but would its literary worth have been increased? I doubt it, and the fact that Tractado V, good as it is, does not measure up to the preceding ones, seems to corroborate this belief. And I shall venture to suggest that the very shortness of the last four *tractados* may even enhance the literary merit of the work by bringing out in contrast the first three, the real artistic unit. The unknown author found for the latter portion of his story no technique comparable to that evolved in the first part, but he did the next best thing: he did not obscure its effect by developing all his later figures at equal length.[4]

Courtney Tarr's argument is persuasive. Its weakness is that nothing is known of the form of *Lazarillo de Tormes* before its publication in 1554. We do not know therefore whether author or publisher is responsible for the division into treatises and the accompanying captions. Courtney Tarr is hazarding a guess about authorial motive.

More recently Bruce Wardropper, after praising Courtney Tarr's pioneering essay as

The first truly critical study of the book (revealing at one stroke more
than any single scholar has since achieved)

concludes rather contradictorily

A complete understanding is beyond critical reach, the *Laazarillo* is,
and will remain, a mystery story.[5]

He however is not beyond hazarding his own solution to the mystery. He justifies the apparently fragmentary last four treatises on the grounds that the text is a burlesque of the Dives-Lazarus, Rich Man-Poor Man motif, and the final treatises, a cynical account of Abraham's bosom, a form of bliss after the temporal hell of the first three masters.

---

4   Courtney Tarr, F. 'Literary and Artistic Unity in the *Lazarillo de Tormes*' in
     Proceedings of the Modern Language Association of America, 42, 1927, pages 404–
     421. The section quoted is from pages 418–421.

5   Wardropper, Bruce, W., 'The Strange Case of Lázaro Gonzales Pérez', in *Modern
     Language Notes* 92, Hispanic Issue, March 1977, page 212.

Certainly scholarly speculation upon the literary and artistic unity of the text is in order; but without knowledge of the author's intentions, no conclusive verdict is possible.

Economic Realities

In commenting upon the economic decay and collapse that set in in Spain during the second half of the sixteenth century, an eye witness wrote in 1626:

> Those who travel through the fertile fields of Spain, see them covered with nettles and thorns, because there is no one to till them. Most Spaniards have been reduced to idleness... and it is something worth seeing that all the streets of Madrid are full of lay-abouts and tramps, playing all day at cards, waiting for the time to go to the convents to eat[6].

There are contrasting views on interpreting a multivalent text like *Lazarillo de Tormes*. Some scholars regard it as essentially reworking medieval materials, as a sort of comic and irreligious entertainment and deny any critique of social and economic collapse; other scholars locate the text firmly in the religious ferment of that time and as a biting critique of a society shortly to experience such economic collapse. Of course, poverty was a Europe wide phenomenon, but Alan Deyermond's view that

> Spain's economic and political decline was half a century away in the future when *Lazarillo* was published[7]

will not stand against the evidence:

> Between 1511 and 1549 the price of wheat rose from 89 to 187 maravedises, that of wine from 20 to 151, and that of oil from 80 to 238...
>
> From 1550 to 1562 there was a marked recession, and, in 1557, a severe financial crisis, the first of many to come. The finances of the Crown were in confusion, a state of affairs that was to prevail under the rule of the remaining Habsburg kings. The reluctance or inability of Charles V to cut his coat according to his cloth must surely be seen as in itself a sufficient cause for the economic ruin of Spain.

The Emperor's Finances

Charles the First of Spain and Fifth of the Holy Roman Empire was essentially a warrior. His imperial destiny claimed all his thoughts and energies, and he shared the traits that one day were to be embodied in

---

6   *Modern Language Notes*, (93), 1976 page 316: 'The Wine Against the Water' by James Herrero, My translation

7   Deyermond, A *Lazarillo de Tormes* A Critical Guide, Grant and Cutler Ltd London 1993, page 16.

another pathetic knight [i.e. Don Quixote], the sublime image of Spanish idealism.

Frugal, even parsimonious in his personal expenditure, the emperor spent recklessly on his military enterprises. The struggle against France, against the Turk, and against Protestantism and revolt in Germany left him permanently short of funds. At first it was the Netherlands and Italy that bore the heaviest burdens. Later the emperor fell back more and more on Spain. Since the contribution of the Crown of Aragon remained relatively small throughout his reign, this meant in practice Castile.

Perhaps I should point out that by 'Castile' is meant ... not only the modern territory that we know under that name but the whole Crown of Castile, which at this period covered about two-thirds of the total area of the Iberian Peninsula and included Galicia, Asturias, León, Extremadura, Old and New Castile, Murcia and Andalusia. These regions formed a single state with common frontiers, Cortes [i.e. Parliament] and legislation, currency and fiscal system. The Crown of Aragon comprised Navarre, the modern Aragon, Catalonia and Valencia, which were autonomous in these respects.

The Castilian resources were considerable for that day. The revenues payable by the Spanish Church to the Crown were an important item. The secular taxes included a bewildering array of customs duties, taxes on the transit of cattle and a tax on the Granada silk industry. The *alcabala,* a tax paid on nearly everything that was bought and sold, had been collected throughout the fifteenth century and was a rich source of revenue to the Crown. Now, however, it was converted into a fixed quota that was paid by each town or village, and as prices rose it declined in value.

These and other revenues were insufficient to meet the cost of empire. Charles was often obliged to ask the Cortes for a *servicio,* traditionally a temporary subsidy but which after 1523 became a regular tax amounting to some 400,000 ducats a year. The royal share of the American treasure that arrived from the Indies came to about the same sum.

The clergy and the *hidalgos* [noblemen and gentlemen who enjoyed the ancient privileges of their rank as a reward for the services rendered by their ancestors to the Crown] were exempt from payment of the *servicio*, which fell as an additional burden on the shoulders of the *pechero,* or person liable to pay this and other direct taxes. The proportion of *hidalgos* to *pecheros* is difficult to determine and varied greatly from place to place. In León, for instance, there were as many *hidalgos* as *pecheros,* while in the south there were relatively few *hidalgos.* Grants of *hidalguía* [i.e. titles of nobility] were readily sold by the Crown, and were bought by everyone who could afford to do so.

Even with the aid of the *servicios,* sales of patents of *hidalguía,* and other expedients, the emperor was unable to meet his commitments. In 1534, for instance, the Crown's net income amounted to some 110,000 ducats, whereas its anticipated outgoings came to 420,000. In order to close the gap between income and expenditure Charles resorted to methods that were bound to prove ruinous. On nine occasions he seized the remittances of American treasure destined to private persons, compensating the latter by issuing them with *juros* or government bonds that yielded a high rate of interest and were assigned in turn to the various sources of revenue. The *juros* multiplied like weeds and ended by devouring more than half the royal revenues, which went to meet the interest payments. Any suggestions by the Crown that it might attempt gradually to redeem *juros* evoked an outcry from the holders, who formed a rapidly growing class of rentiers.

Another and even more pernicious method of deficit financing was to borrow from German, Genoese, Flemish and Spanish bankers against payment from the next treasure-fleet or against future tax revenues. In short, the emperor's lack of prudent financial policy ensured that the resources of Castile were mortgaged for years ahead. As J. H. Elliott points out, the reign of Charles V saw three dangerous developments that were to be of incalculable importance for sixteenth- and seventeenth-century Spain. In the first place, it established the dominance of foreign bankers over the country's sources of wealth. Second, it determined that Castile would bear the main weight of the fiscal burden within Spain. In the third place, it ensured that within Castile the brunt of the burden was borne by those classes which were least capable of bearing it.

The economic plight of Castile was clearly perceived by the first of the Spanish political economists and one of the earliest mercantilists to appear in any country: Luis Ortiz, controller of the royal finances, in a memorial which he addressed to Philip II in 1558, two years after the latter's accession to the throne....

Agriculture

The decay, or perhaps I should rather say the stagnation, of Castilian agriculture in the sixteenth century has received less attention from historians than other branches of the economy. Yet the sorrows of the *campo* – the word means more, perhaps, to the Spanish farmer than our own word 'land' to his English counterpart – played a decisive part in the larger tragedy of the economic decadence of Spain.

At the beginning of the sixteenth century agriculture was far from flourishing. The Catholic kings had made some attempt to improve matters, but with only moderate success. They tended, also, to favour sheep-farming, on which the profitable wool trade depended, at the expense of tillage.

At some point not as yet fully defined the inflation outpaced the rise in the prices of farm-products, and the market price no longer covered costs. Nor was the farmer, in theory at least, allowed to receive even this market price. He was hampered by the *tasa* or fixed price imposed on grain and other products, and by a multitude of regulations that were intended to ensure a cheap and plentiful supply of foodstuffs [for the cities], but which in fact achieved little except to encourage fraud and the growth of a black market....

we may add the recurrent series of epidemics, droughts and famines that were the scourge of town and countryside alike...

The Poor Law Controversy
Sixteenth-century Spain was an unsettled place to live in. The texts of the period leave us with the impression of people always on the move, fleeing from disaster or allured by the promise of riches. Soldiers on their way to the wars, emigrants to the Indies, Castilians and Galicians to the more prosperous south, hangers-on drifting after the court, French immigrants attracted by the promise of high wages, all were to be found on the Spanish roads. The problem of destitution or, as we should say, unemployment, grew more and more acute. Five times between 1523 and 1534 the Cortes complained of the host of beggars and vagrants who were over-running Castile. Several books and pamphlets offered solutions[8]...

As J. E. V. Crofts observed in 1924, the first French version of *Lazarillo de Tormes* of 1560 sold as a picture of Spanish life and manners and its second edition in 1561 explicitly states this in its revised title:

The pleasant and witty history of *Lazarillo de Tormes a Spaniard*, in which can be recognised a good part of the customs, life and conditions of the Spanish people.[9]

---

8   Grice Hutchinson, M. *Early Economic Thought in Spain.* George Allen and Unwin, London 1978, pages 124-131.
9   Crofts, J. E. V. (ed) *The Pleasant Historic of Lazarillo de Tormes,* The Percy Reprints, VII, Oxford, Basil Blackwell, 1924, Introduction, page VIII, my translation.

David Rowland amplifies this revised title. Some fifty years later, Spain's financial reality did not escape those who had attempted unsuccessfully to negotiate Charles' Spanish marriage in 1623:

> The King is expected in London, when Buckingham intends to feast the Spanish Ambassador at York House, but rather 'pro forma' than 'ex animo' [i.e. for appearances, not because he wished to]. The courtiers who were in Spain complain of coarse entertainment, and of finding 'nothing but penurie and prowde beggarie'[10]

In *The Staple of News (1625),* Ben Jonson satirically summarises the condition of the Spanish Exchequer. The central female personage is Pecunia (money), Infanta (Spanish princess) of the Mines, a comic Spanish stage female explicitly identified as princess of

> The rich mines of Potosí,
>
> The Spanish mines i' the West Indies. (Act IV, Scene IV, lines 20-21.)

Her nurse is Mortgage.

Rowland's Dedication

It cannot then have been an accident that David Rowland dedicated his translation to Sir Thomas Gresham, (?1519-1579), Royal Agent or King's Merchant in Antwerp on behalf of the English government under Henry VIII, Edward VI, Mary and Elizabeth, founder of the Royal Exchange, and judged to have had

> an understanding of the behaviour of money unprecedented in a native of these islands and unsurpassed by any of his foreign contemporaries.[11]

Whether true or false, Gresham was a smart operator at playing with exchange rates. At Antwerp, Gresham had first resided in the house of Gasper Schetz his 'very friend', who was none other than factor to Charles V, temporarily he was ambassador to the Duchess of Parma, regent of the Netherlands, he undertook a financial mission to Seville in Spain and as an intimate of Cecil, Lord Burghley, vigorously acted for English interests, spying upon Spain and frustrating Spanish machinations. He was in fact present at Charles V's abdication in Brussels in 1556.

The words of Rowland's dedication were then well chosen:

> I was so bold as to dedicate the fruit of my simple labour unto your worship, who both for travel, daily conference with divers nations and knowledge in all foreign matters is known to be such a one, as is well able to judge, whether these reports of little Lázaro be true or not.

---

10   *Calendar of State Papers, Domestic Series,* London, 1858, vol. CLIII, p.103, October 23rd, 1623.

11   Bindoff, S. T., *The Fame of Sir Thomas Gresham,* The Fourth Neale Lecture in English History December 6 1973 at University College, London. Jonathan Cape, London, 1973, page 13.

Further Gresham was undoubtedly a Protestant. He sheltered Foxe the martyrologist who stayed in his house in Antwerp as a refugee during Mary's reign on his way to Strasbourg; and acted as intermediary with the Prince of Orange and a leading member of the local Protestant Church, the wealthy banker of Spanish Jewish ancestry, Marcus Pérez [12]. Pérez was well known to the Spanish government for a project to send Protestant literature to Seville and for trying to purchase the religious freedom of the Netherlands.

The Translator

Little is known of David Rowland (active 1569-1586), yet what little there is, has recently become controversial. The tradition summarised in the *Dictionary of National Biography* is that he was a native of Anglesey, studied logic and grammar in St. Mary's Hall Oxford, left without taking a degree, subsequently became tutor to the son of the Earl of Lennox and accompanied him on travels through France and Spain where he obtained some knowledge of modern languages. Controversy has arisen from the published research of Gareth Alban Davies, Emeritus Professor at the University of Leeds. In two articles in *Transactions of the Honourable Society of Cymmrodorion,* 1991 and 1992, and a third in *The National Library of Wales Journal XXVIII,* 1995, Professor Davies attempts to argue that David Rowland should be identified with the Antwerp Catholic recusant and scholar Richard Verstegen Rowlands (active 1565-1620) whose entry in the *Dictionary of National Biography* is much longer and need not detain us. Professor Davies produces much curious evidence upon David Rowland's possible career, for instance that he might have been of an Anglesey family with a London base and been admitted as a Queen's Scholar to Westminster School in 1553-4 and that Welsh gentry and settlement in Yorkshire could have secured Rowland's position as tutor to Charles Stuart, son of the Earl of Lennox. Professor Davies'examination of the English translation yields many valuable fresh insights; but his identification of David Rowland with Richard Verstegen Rowlands must be judged implausible and unproven, indeed Professor Davies' cited evidence and critical acumen surely undermine his own case. It is difficult to believe that Rowland could have become tutor to a possible claimant to the English throne as a direct descendant of Henry VII without the closest scrutiny of his religious – Protestant – credentials. Elizabeth was on the throne, the Earl of Lennox was cousin of the future James VI and I. Professor Davies writes

> Can we deduce from what point of view, so to speak, Rowland translated? I have noted already how he toned down his anticlerical references, and what he presumably regarded as unseemly irreverences. In contrast, in his treatment of the more specifically

---

12   *Dictionary of National Biography* London 1908. Volume VIII, Pages 585-596. See also Rekers, B., *Benito Arias Montano*, Warburg, London, 1972, pages 71, 72, 75 and 122.

Catholic aspects of Spanish life and devotion, he pushed the knife in more deeply. When commenting, for instance, on the blind man's great repertoire of prayers, the English text adds ' and the life of all the holy saints'. The specifically Catholic nature of the occasion is also underlined when Lázaro refers to 'otras tantas bendiciones' [so many other blessings], which is translated as 'have of me many blessings and prayers for his soule'. Interestingly too, when the hungry Lazarillo looks at the 'cara de Dios' [the face of God] in the loaves of bread inside the priest's forbidden chest, Rowland, representing a context that was often playfully Eucharistic, makes a half allusion to transubstantiation in the words 'beholding always that bread as a God'. Rowland, quite consistently, suppressed the reference to Extreme Unction [the Christian sacrament at death]. These examples and others suggest that the translator was more interested in portraying Catholic practices in a critical light than in exalting them. His point of view may, therefore, be described as Protestant, but at the same time very critical of the Anglican Church in the seventies [i.e. 1570's].

The *tratado* [i.e. treatise] of the seller of indulgences raises rather different issues. He was, of course, a favourite target of both traditional and Erasmist criticism; that, in turn, is consistent with the translator's desire to present a text that was critical of the Catholic past. However, Rowland seems to have had something else too in his sights. For example, where the exact meaning of the Spanish had escaped him he uttered what could as readily have been a gibe from Marprelate; 'I meane such as are made priestes, more for money than for learning and good behaviour'. [The anonymous Marprelate pamphlets, 1588–1589, attacked the bishops' style of living and defended the Presbyterian system of discipline.] But the key scene in the *tratado* is the account of the false miracle played in order to boost the sale of indulgences.

The episode turns, of course, on people's simple-mindedness, and on the cruel deceptions used by unscrupulous persons. At that level, this is a criticism fairly levelled at Catholic practice, and the main target is the bullmonger himself. Nevertheless, in a simulated English context there is more to it, for the interrupter of the sermon uses language that betrays its Puritan origin: 'ye honest and godly people, give eare'. Those that then attempt to eject him are in one sense sectaries of a different persuasion, and are certainly accorded greater sympathy.

All in all, the scene depicts satirically – for anyone wanting to see it that way – the kind of public disagreements between pulpit and

congregation that erupted sometimes in the overheated atmosphere of
religious controversy. [13]

With due respect to Professor Davies, I suggest that he may have been misled by
a passage in Burgon's *Life and Times of Sir Thomas Gresham* suggesting friendship
between Richard Verstegan Rowlands and Gresham[14]. Certainly Gresham gave
hospitality to Catholics at his home in Antwerp, notably Cardinal Pole in June 1555
when Mary was on the throne; but previously, Burgon had commented upon
Gresham as 'notorious for his strong Protestant bias'[15]. Burgon does not record
David Rowland's dedication of *Lazarillo de Tormes* to Gresham and appears to have
known nothing of it.

Rowland's Translation as Literature

Contrary to the opinion of Professor Crofts in his introduction to the 1924 edition,
that Rowland was a beginner in Spanish and depended upon the French, Professor
Davies rejoins:

> More recent work has demonstrated that Rowland, in fact, not only
> knew Spanish well, but that where there were divergences between the
> Spanish and the French versions he often preferred the original text...
>
> The [marginal glosses] often supplemented the local colour,
> thereby revealing quite incidentally, the translator's own direct
> knowledge of Spain. More idiosyncratically, five glosses gave English
> currency values to coins mentioned in the text ... thus suggesting the
> translator's own commercial interest and experience. He also assumed
> that such information would be welcomed by his readers.
>
> But Rowland also had a Spanish text to hand... An examination of
> the early editions (characterized as they were by numerous variants
> and textual omissions) demonstrated that the text followed by
> Rowland, and distinct from the edition used by the French translator,
> was that which first appeared in an Antwerp edition of *La vida de
> Lazarillo de Tormes,* published by Martin Nucio in 1554; but that the
> text which he actually handled was the edition of the following year
> (1555), in which the [spurious] Second Part made its first appearance.
> It was the first chapter of this which was incorporated by the translator
> (emulating the French example) [and which this edition excludes]...

---

13   Davies, G. A., David Rowland's *Lazarillo de Tormes (1576);* The History of a
     Translation in *The National Library of Wales Journal* XXVIII, October 1995, pages
     370-372.
14   Burgon, J. W., *The Life and Times of Sir Thomas Gresham* Two Volumes, 1839,
     reissued Burt Franklin, New York 1968, Volume I, page 203.
15   Burgon, Volume I, page 127.

If we bear in mind the remark made about the *Lazarillo* in Rowland's dedication to Gresham, 'perceiving that in France many delighted therein, being turned into their tongue', he seems to refer to his own direct experience; furthermore, the fact that he had been in a position to handle copies of both the 1560 and 1561 editions of the French translation lends strength to the argument that he had purchased his own copy (or copies) while on a visit to France. As for the Spanish text, he possibly acquired a copy of the Nucio edition in the Low Countries, maybe in Antwerp itself when he was there in Gresham's service...

How did Rowland set about his translation? ... Rowland picked his own way through a labyrinth of different readings and renderings, not only choosing those renderings of the original text which he considered most accurate, but also taking at times from the French text a turn of phrase more suited to his own interpretation of the meaning, whilst at others striking out on his own.

What, in fact, are the most important features of this English translation? In the first place, it is remarkably accurate...

In general, the changes and modifications which Rowland introduced clearly indicate that he regarded the *Lazarillo* as a serious piece of criticism of society and religion, particularly at the point of interaction between both. The tendency to play down the references to certain practices that were no longer part of Anglican worship and to highlight abuses suggests that for Rowland it was the message that counted.

The extraordinary liveliness of Rowland's prose is obvious to any reader. His occasional use of periphrasis shows how attentive he was to getting the meaning across, although he did now and again over-indulge. He noticeably wanted to give the reader a sense of the vigorous 'low-style' – occasionally heightened where required – that marked the original narrative. The Spanish is colourful and down-to-earth, qualities that Rowland sought to reproduce. For instance, 'shee kept an ordinarie table for divers Students'. 'throwe the helve after the hatchet', 'went about to marry me with his mayd'. '[hunger] commonly maketh man have ready wittes': these examples also indicate Rowland's command of English everyday speech. In contrast, where greater elegance or solemnity were required, then the *Book of Common Prayer* and the English Bible [Cranmer's] provided adequate support.

At first sight therefore, Rowland's affection for archaisms seems oddly placed. Among the words that were either archaic or unusual by mid-century or thereabouts, one can mention *noughtly* (for wickedly), *milner, Morrien* (for Moor or blackamoor), *keept, suspection, inquirance, blowing* (for bragging), *covent, nee* (for nigh), *moyle* (for mule), *overwhart* (for *overthrawt*), *letany* (possibly affected by Spanish *letanía*). Apart from these archaisms, Rowland showed a preference for a prose-style which was Anglo-Saxon rather than Latinate or Norman, an ambition easier to achieve given the environment of the street rather than the court. In such a context Lázaro's own narrative, that of the brash *'homo novus'* [new man], mirrors linguistically the aspirations of an ambitious and radicalised underclass.

Rowland's preference for archaisms, however deliberate, may here and there have owed something to his 'provincial' origins, where older speech habits and vocabulary had been preserved; or to the fact that his English had been for him a learnt language, often more conservative. Did he show any trace of his Anglesey origins? One or two instances do outcrop: for instance, his *'I never slept a winke* seems closer to' 'chysgais I ddim winc' than to English usage; *did teare more shoes* probably mirrors Welsh 'rhwygo'*; he rose on his feet* points to Welsh usage, 'cododd ar ei draed'. However, the sparsity of such examples suggests that these are vestiges, rather than characteristics, in Rowland's use of English...

George Turberville went on to express the admirable constraints within which the true translator worked:

Nothing mor leese than libertie you knowe
Which no translatour hath I undertake
Unless that he his Authors sense forsake.

[*leese* = untruthful]

That ideal of exactness was one to which Rowland also adhered. It helped create a landmark in the history of English translations; and like certain other translated works of that period, it hastened the process of enrichment that made possible the Renaissance in English letters that followed.

It is essential to emphasise that the evidence presented here does not constitute incontrovertible proof of the circumstances in which David Rowland operated, or of the intellectual environment that was his. What I have done is to suggest a scenario that best fits in with the little that we do know.[16]

These are perceptive remarks by a native Welsh speaker. I would add that they accord more plausibly with Gresham's activities in Antwerp as a spy and agent of a

---

16   Davies G. A., 1995, pages 373-379.

Protestant English crown than the subversive writing of a recusant. The dedication to Gresham must be read for what it states. The five marginal glosses upon exchange rates are similarly appropriate for a dedicatee like Gresham whose unrivalled grasp of the money markets saved the English crown from the financial mishaps of other European powers. Further, the sensitivity to religious interpretation which Professor Davies identifies seems entirely appropriate to a tutor still loyal to a family whose fortunes were bound up with its religious affiliations [see under Stuart Esmé, 1542?–1583, in the *Dictionary of National Biography*] Rowland's translation better reflects Elizabeth's settlement than a recusant's concerns. There is no record that Rowland quarrelled with, or was dismissed by, the family of the Earl of Lennox, and cousins of the future James I. He dedicated his Latin text *A Comfortable Aid for Scholars* published in London in 1578, to the Earl of Lennox.

We do not know whether Gresham obtained the Nucio Antwerp edition of *Lazarillo de Tormes* for Rowland or encouraged him to translate it. The facts of the history of the translation are well established. The Stationer [printer-publisher] Thomas Colwell sought a licence to publish the *marvelus Dedes and the Lyf of Lázaro de Tormes* in 1568–69. As Rowland states in his dedication, he dropped the translation for some time. It is highly plausible that Rowland had worked in his patron's Antwerp office, especially as Gresham had financial interest in Yorkshire where the household of the Earl of Lennox was confined for some time by the English crown. Colwell sold his licence to print the book to Henry Bynneman on 19th June 1573 and it was Bynneman who published the complete translation in 1576. Bynneman was a high class scholar stationer who also published Turberville, Gascoigne and Spenser, Byrd and Tallis. No copies of the 1576 edition have survived, though Hazlitt is thought to have seen a copy. Sir Thomas Gresham died in 1579 but the dedication to him remained in the 1586 edition. Bynneman died in 1583 leaving his widow in straitened circumstances. A writ was issued for his assets which included

'twohundred bookes of the Spanyardes lyfe.'

The 1586 edition of *Lazarillo de Tormes* was printed and published by Abell Jeffes at the Sign of the Bell, with the additional verses by Turberville. It is, of course, perfectly possible that the form of the author's name David Rowland of Anglesey was a comical calque upon the Spanish 'little Lazarus of Tormes'. The translation went through several editions down to 1677.

Lazarillo de Tormes and Western Literary Tradition

If *Lazarillo* reflects particular historical relationships as perceived by its anonymous author, it also established a precedent which would be followed under quite different circumstance in later picaresque novels. Besides delineating the major outlines of this myth [i.e. the rise of the low-born individual], the anonymous author contributed to the evolution of the modern European novel. Earlier works – anatomies of roguery like *Liber vagatorum* (1510) or jest books like *Till Eulenspiegel* (1515) – had depicted low-life scenes and drawn upon popular anecdotes, but by sustaining a consistent pseudo-autobiographical perspective while allowing readers to glimpse the flaws and inadequacies of the narrator's personality, the author of *Lazarillo* achieved a much higher degree of artistic organisation and moral seriousness than did his predecessors. Furthermore, his extended portrayal of a lower-class character's life placed a new emphasis upon the primacy of individual experience and reflected a heightened interest in creating the illusion of verisimilitude, suggesting that the anonymous author of *Lazarillo* was among the first Europeans to seize upon the novel's potential as a serious form of literary expression.[17]

Nearly fifty years after *Lazarillo* first appeared, Mateo Alemán's *Guzman de Alfarache* was published in Madrid in two parts, 1599 and 1604 and achieved an extraordinary popular success. Although Alemán called the second part of his novel *Watch Tower of Man's Life*, the work became popularly known as *Pícaro, Rogue*, because the lighter, racy and entertaining aspects appealed much more to the public: Guzmán was born in Seville, the illegitimate son of low and disreputable parents; his father was an usurer, his mother a prostitute; when his father died, Guzman decided to venture forth .... Perhaps not surprisingly 1605 saw the publication of *La Pícara Justina* by Francis Lòpez de Úbeda, *The Female Rogue Justine*, which quotes Alemán's novel and makes jokes of Lazarillo's witticisms. The vogue for such fiction was well launched and translations rapidly followed. James Mabbe, who spent the years 1611–1613 in Madrid, and delighted to call himself Diego Puede-Ser [James May-be] was translator of *The Rogue or the Life of Guzmán de Alfarache*, published in London in 1622/1623 and reprinted in Oxford in 1630 and London in 1634. Ben Jonson wrote dedicatory verses. A chain of direct and verifiable influences leads from the Spanish picaresque through *Gil Blas* (Lesage, 1715) and *Roderick Random* (Smollett, 1748) but

> despite a continuity suggested by the recurrence of the picaresque myth, the first person narrative and the panoramic perspective, differences in social and literary conventions bring about a change in the picaresque hero and reflect points of view which are diametrically opposed to those more commonly associated with the earlier Spanish novels.[18]

Lazarillo de Tormes was not the first (or last) book to entertain with stories of low life and practical jokes. Its significance is that it reworked such material in the

---

17   Bjornson, R., *The Picaresque Hero in European Fiction*, Wisconsin, 1977, page 42.
18   Bjornson, Richard, *The Picaresque Hero In European Fiction*, Wisconsin, 1979, pages 12–13.

form of a fictional autobiography or memoire-letter, that this form allowed the reader to access the narrator's mind and personality, that the form highlighted characterisation as an enduring feature of the novel, and that this illusion of autobiography and individual experience, contributed to what we later call the realist novel. Just reflect for a moment on the almost endless list of English novels called after the key protagonist, and in autobiographical form: *Robinson Crusoe*, *Moll Flanders*, *Evelina*, *Jane Eyre*, and so on, and thousands more, dominated by the destiny of a single protagonist, not in fictional autobiographical form, like *Tom Jones*, *Emma* and *Pickwick Papers*. Within Spain and beyond, the fictional form grew to incorporate female personages, and as it evolved, jumped class to include young noblemen. We find novels with clear picaresque features adapted to philosophical, educational, even psycho-analytical studies, *Candide*, *David Copperfield*, *Ulysses*....

Literary Experiment and Innovation
Lazarillo de Tormes is the sort of literary work that resists closure.

Notwithstanding its concluding two paragraphs, the experience of reading the book denies us the sense of 'they all lived happily ever after'. Lots of questions keep coming to mind such as:

> Is the eponymous hero of the book a moral agent or a product of relations of power in a particular society?

> Or is the narrator/hero a 'fictive' person who should not be considered to own his words and actions?

> Is the book a witty parody, a burlesque ridiculing those who seek glory and renown?

> Is the book evidence of a prudential self and a prudential ethic, a rhetorical posture that subordinates honesty to decorum?

> Who is the mysterious 'Your Worship'?

> What is the nature of his relationship with Lázaro?

> What sort of authority does he have?

> Is the whole situation a bluff?

In fact, the questions come pouring out and appear to be almost unlimited. The book deconstructs all authority, even its own authority as a book.

In 'The Case of the Purloined Letter', a humorous title that effectively removes authorship and problematizes authorial intent, Peter Dunn ponders aloud (the article was originally a lecture) upon what grounds the book may be judged innovatory, modern and subversive.[19]

Dunn sets out to surprise, tease and entertain. Notwithstanding, his pleasure in the sheer paradoxes of *Lazarillo de Tormes* leads him to make the following points:

> the book's structure does not allow resolution of a host of questions raised;

> there is parody of several modes of discourse, such as medieval writing on the three estates, chivalresque romance with the intervention of providence, confessional literature, depositional testimony before a court and epistolary conventions;

> the interior life of the narrator is unresolved and inexplicit;

> there are many gaps and omissions, matters of fact and causality are not clear or not known and questions proliferate out of control;

> the text appears not to have been written for the public because its context is one of a private communication; but the Prologue, with its mention of writing to achieve fame, is predicated upon an aesthetics of reader reception; the text is then, in a sense, written yet requires its readers to re-write it;

> the matter ('el caso') giving rise to the communication is not precisely known, just inferred;

> the author is not known;

> the recipient is not known;

> Lázaro appears to want to substitute his own agenda for that of his enquirer;

> the book is an act of masking rather than communicating.

There is then a self-consciousness and range of narrative practices that anticipate those of a modern writer like Joyce or Borges. It could be said of *Lazarillo de Tormes* as of *Don Quixote* that it anticipated a very large number of the later experiments and developments in prose fiction.

This Bilingual Edition
This bilingual edition has been prepared as follows:

My Spanish text is the 1554 Burgos text, edited by the late Professor R. O. Jones and collated with the 1554 Antwerp edition, from which it differs very little. Rowland used the 1555 Antwerp edition which included the spurious sequel and accordingly his translation ends with the first chapter of that sequel, as do the French editions published by P. Sangrain in Lyon in 1560 and in Paris in 1561. This spurious material has been cut from this edition on the grounds that the 1554

---

19   Dunn, Peter, N. 'The Case of the Purloined Letter', *Revista de Estudios Hispánicos* (U.S.A.), 22, (1988), 1–14.

Spanish text should have primacy. My overall purpose has been to provide a Spanish text against which Rowland's translation might be read with confidence.

Rowland's facing English translation is a fully modernised text that preserves the running title and the original glosses; and retains the italicization of special names of J. E. V. Crofts' Percy Reprint VII of 1924. As Professor Crofts explains, this italicization represented roman in the 1586 edition. Punctuation and paragraphing have been brought into line with modern practice. Upon punctuation, it should be noted that English Renaissance use of colons, as in the passages from the Authorised Version of the Bible already cited in this introduction, reflects oral rather than silent reading practices and then commonly indicated pauses in oral delivery for the taking of breath. The printing of punctuation has changed significantly especially since the beginning of the nineteenth century; colons, semi-colons and even to a lesser extent commas and full-stops, have acquired semantic force which would not have applied in Rowland's time.

40

Bibliography

All scholars owe an overwhelming debt to their teachers and those who have gone before. A text like *Lazarillo de Tormes*, of seminal importance in modern western prose fiction, has attracted to itself such a vast corpus of critical writings that any bibliographical guidance in support of this first facing text of a Spanish original and Rowland's translation, must be highly selective if it is to avoid confusion and be helpful. The following references are then chosen because of the general respect in which they are held by scholars, and their usefulness to me.

A bilingual text of sixteenth century Spanish prose and its Tudor English translation must face a particular bibliographical problem. There has been a long historical convention amongst many scholars of English literature to deny or regard as insignificant, Spanish cultural influence. This is regrettable. Dramatists like John Fletcher and James Shirley cannot be fully understood without their Spanish source material; and consequently the cultural politics of the pre-Civil War Stuart Court, where the taste of writers like Fletcher and Shirley was dominant, may not be fully understood either. Sir Philip Sydney's circle translated Spanish literature, Shakespeare certainly moved in hispanophile company, Jonson read Spanish and admired writers like Góngora, Donne had a profound grasp of Spanish. Yet Professor Crofts in his 1924 edition of *Lazarillo de Tormes* bluntly denied that David Rowland was competent in Spanish, emphasizing the French translation. In fact, one suspects that Crofts like so many Professors of English Literature, had a competence in French and little Spanish. Hence, however, the unfortunate truth that Spanish speaking American scholars have shown far more curiosity in the sources of so much English literature of the Renaissance than their English speaking counterparts. In the United States, where Spanish is the second language, and bilingual scholarship is commonplace, there is far more openness and a less defensive attitude. Claudio Guillén in the brilliant Laurel Language Library edition of *Lazarillo de Tormes* and *El Abencerraje* (the latter incidentally translated into English by Bartholomew Young in 1598) used Rowland's translation to explain the Spanish. Guillén is an outstanding representative of the new bilingual scholarship which has emerged in the last forty years. I cannot, therefore, apologise for including such scholarship in the bibliography. Indeed, conference after conference of the Spanish Society for English Renaissance Studies has examined Spanish material in English translation. One can only wonder when the English speaking world of Britain will drop its defensiveness and join in.

Finally the following bibliography has been drafted to reflect a bilingual not a monolingual text.

BIBLIOGRAPHY 41

Editions

Castro, C. (ed.), *Lazarillo de Tormes*, Taurus, Madrid, 1985 (fifteenth printing).

Crofts, C. E. V. (ed.), *Lazarillo de Tormes*, drawn out of the Spanish by David Rowland of Anglesey, Percy Reprint VII, Blackwell, Oxford, 1924.

Davies, G. A. (ed.), *The Pleasant History of Lazarillo de Tormes Drawn out of Spanish by David Rowland of Anglesey*, Newton: Gwasg Gregynog, 1991. (A modern spelling edition with woodblock illustrations and notes.)

Guillén, C. (ed.), *Lazarillo de Tormes*, Laurel Language Library, Dell, New York, 1966.

Jones, R. O. (ed.), *La Vida de Lazarillo de Tormes y de sus Fortunas y Adversidades*, Manchester University Press, 1966.

Ricapito, J. V., *Tri-Linear Editions of Lazarillo de Tormes of 1554: Burgos, Alcalá de Henares, Amberes*, Hispanic Seminary of Medieval Studies, Madison, 1987.

Trend, J. B. (ed.), *Spanish Short Stories of the Sixteenth Century*, World Classics, Oxford University Press, 1928.

Criticism

Archer, R., 'The Fictional Context of *Lazarillo de Tormes*' in *Modern Language Review*, 80, part 2, April 1985, pages 340–350.

Carey, Douglas, M., 'Lazarillo de Tormes and the Quest for Authority', *Proceedings of the Modern Language Association of America*, 94, 1979, pages 36–46.

Davey, E.R., 'The Concept of Man in Lazarillo de Tormes', *Modern Language Review*, Volume 72, 1977, pages 596–604.

Deyermond, Alan, *Lazarillo de Tormes A Critical Guide*, Grant and Cutler, London, 1993.

Dunn, P. N., 'Lazarillo de Tormes: The Case of the Purloined Letter', *Revista de Estudios Hispánicos* (U.S.A.), 22, 1988, pages 1–14.

Ferrer Chivite, M., 'Sustratos Conversos en la creación de Lázaro de Tormes', *Nueva Revista de Filología Hispánica*, 33, 1984, pages 352–379.

Fiore, Robert L., *Lazarillo de Tormes*, Boston, Twayne, 1974.

Hanrahan, T., '*Lazarillo de Tormes*: Erasmian Satire or Protestant Reform?' *Hispania*, U.S.A., 66, 1983, pages 333–339.

Herrero, J., 'The Ending of Lazarillo: The Wine against the Water', *Modern Language Notes*, 93, 1978, pages 313–319.

Herrero, J., 'Renaissance Poverty and Lazarillo's family: The Birth of the Picaresque Genre' *Publications of the Modern Language Association*, 94, 1979, pages 876–886.

O'Reilly, T., 'The Erasmianism of *Lazarillo de Tormes*; in *Essays in Honour of Robert Brian Tate*, Nottingham University, 1984, pages 91–100.

Shipley, G. A., 'A Case of Functional Obscurity: The Master Tambourine-Painter of *Lazarillo*, Tratado VI, *Modern Language Notes*, 97, 1982, pages 225–253.

Shipley, G. A., 'The Critic as Witness for the Prosecution: Making the Case against Lázaro de Tormes', *Publications of the Modern Language Association*, 97, 1982, pages 179–194.

Truman, R. W., 'Parody and Irony in the Self-Portrayal of Lázaro de Tormes' in *Modern Language Review* 63 (1968) pages 600–605; and 'Lázaro de Tormes and the "Novus Homo" Tradition', in *Modern Language Review*, 64 (1969) pages 62–67.

Waley, Pamela, '*Lazarillo's* Cast of Thousands, or the Élites of Poverty', *Modern Language Review*, Volume 83, part 3, July 1988, pages 591–601.

Wardropper, B. W., 'The Strange Case of Lázaro Gonzales Pérez', *Modern Language Notes*, 92, 1977, pages 202–212.

Woods, M. J., 'Pitfalls for the Moralizer in *Lazarillo de Tormes*',*Modern Language Review*, 74, 1979, pages 580–598.

Zappala, M., 'The Lazarillo Source – Apuleius or Lucian? – and Recreation', *Hispanófila*, 97, 1989, pages 1–16.

The Picaresque

Adams, Percy G., *Travel Literature and the Evolution of the Novel*, Kentucky, 1983, Chapter 1, 'The Evolving Novel', Chapter 2, 'Travel Literature'.

Alter, Robert, *Rogue's Progress*, Harvard, 1964.

Bjornson, R., *The Picaresque Hero in European Fiction*, Wisconsin, 1979, Chapter 2: 'The Birth of the Picaresque: *Lazarillo de Tormes* and the Socialising Process'.

Booth, W. C., *The Rhetoric of Fiction*, Penguin, 1991, Chapter 13: 'The Morality of Impersonal Narration'.

Dunn, Peter N., *The Spanish Picaresque Novel*, Boston, Twayne 1979; and *Spanish Picaresque Fiction*, Ithaca, Cornell, 1993.

Guillén, C., *Literature as System*, Princeton, 1971, Chapters 3, 4 and 5, 'Toward a Definition of the Picaresque', 'On the uses of Literary Genre' and' Genre and Countergenre: The Discovery of the Picaresque'.

Guillén, C., *The Anatomies of Roguery*, New York, Garland, 1987.

Ife, Barry W., *Reading and Fiction in Golden-Age Spain: A Platonist Critique and Some Picaresque Replies*, Cambridge, 1985.

Parker, A. A., *Literature and the Delinquent*, Edinburgh, 1967, Chapter 1: 'The Genesis of the Picaresque'.

Pellon, G. and Rodriguez-Luis, J. (eds.) *Upstarts, Wanderers or Swindlers: Anatomy of the Pícaro*, Rodopi, Amsterdam, 1986.

Reed, Helen H., *The Reader in the Picaresque Novel*, London, Támesis, 1984.

Rico, F., *The Spanish Picaresque Novel and the Point of View*, Davies, C. and Sieber, H. trans., Cambridge, 1984.

Sieber, H., *The Picaresque*, The Critical Idiom, 33, Methuen, 1977.

Whitbourn, Christine J., *Knaves and Swindlers*, Oxford, 1974.

Background

Elliott, J. H., *Imperial Spain 1469–1716*, Penguin History Reissue 1999, Chapters 5–6, 'The Government and the Economy in the Reign of Charles V' and 'Race and Religion'.

Eisenstein, E. L., *The Printing Revolution in Early Modern Europe*, Cambridge University Press, 1993.

Grice-Hutchinson, M., *Early Economic Thought in Spain, 1177–1740*, George Allen, London, 1978, Chapter 4: 'The Political Economists'.

Kamen, H., *The Spanish Inquisition, An Historical Revision*, Weidenfeld and Nicolson, London, 1997, Chapter 5: 'Excluding the Reformation', Chapter 6: 'The Impact on Literature and Science'.

Kraye, J. A., (ed.) *The Cambridge Companion to Renaissance Humanism*, Cambridge University Press, 1997, and especially Chapter 6: 'Humanists and The Bible', and Chapter 10: 'Vernacular Humanism in the Sixteenth Century'.

Russell, P. E., *Spain: A Companion to Spanish Studies*, Methuen, London, 1971, Chapters 4 and 8, 'Monarchy and Empire (1474–1700)' and 'Spanish Literature (1474–1681)'.

Sir Thomas Gresham

Bindoff, S. T., *The Fame of Sir Thomas Gresham*, Neale Lecture in English History, 1973, Jonathan Cape, London, 1973.

Burgon, J. W., *The Life and Times of Sir Thomas Gresham*, 1839, Two Volumes, reissued, Burt Franklin, New York, 1968.

Rekers, B., *Benito Arias Montano* (1527–1598), Warburg, London, 1972, Chapter IV 'The Family of Love', surely one of the most illuminating accounts of religious life in Antwerp during Gresham's time there.

Salter, F. R., *Sir Thomas Gresham 1518–1579*, Parsons, London, 1925.

See also the long entry in the *Dictionary of National Biography*.

David Rowland

The entry in the *Dictionary of National Biography* repeats the agreed facts of Rowland's known career but is not correct in respect of his translation of *Lazarillo de Tormes*. He did not work with the expurgated 1573 Spanish text.

The fascinating but controversial recent studies are:

Davies, G. A., (i), 'The English *Lazarillo de Tormes* (1586) and its Translator: David Rowland of Anglesey or Richard Rowland Verstegan?' in *Transactions of the Honourable Society of Cymmrodorion*, 1991, pages 99–128 and 1992, pages 45–78.

(ii) 'David Rowland's *Lazarillo de Tormes* (1576): The History of a Translation' in *National Library of Wales Journal*, 1995, pages 349–387.

Tudor Translations from Spanish

López Fernandez, A., 'The Renaissance environment of the first Spanish Grammar published in sixteenth-century England' in *Sociedad Española de Estudios Renacentistas Ingleses*, Volume VII La Coruña, 1996, pages 99–105.

Randall, D. B. J., *The Golden Tapestry. A Critical Survey of Non-Chivalric Spanish Fiction in English Translation (1543–1657)*, Duke University Press, Durham, 1963.

Sánchez Escribano, F. J., (ed.) *Picaresca Española en Traducción Inglesa*, University of Zaragoza, 1998.

Santoyo, J. C., *Ediciones y traducciones inglesas del Lazarillo de Tormes (1568–1977)*, University College of Álava, Victoria, 1977.

Ungerer, G., (i) *Anglo-Spanish Relations in Tudor Literature*, Swiss Studies in English, 38, Francke, Berne, 1956 and AMS Press, New York, 1972.

(ii) 'The Printing of Spanish Books in Elizabethan England' in *The Library*, Fifth Series, 20, 1965, pages 177–229.

Wilson, E. M., 'Spanish and English Literature of the Sixteenth and Seventeenth Centuries' in Cruickshank, D., (ed.) *Studies in Discretion, Illusion and Mutability*, Cambridge University Press, 1980.

Fig 5. Title verso of the first English translation, showing publisher's emblem.

Fig. 6 Engraved portrait of Sir Thomas Gresham.

To the right worshipful
Sir Thomas Gresham[1]
Knight

When I had read over this little treatise[2] (right worshipful), finding it for the number of strange and merry reports very recreative and pleasant, I thought it no labour evil bestowed to occupy myself in the translation thereof. And being moved thereto the rather, perceiving that in France many delighted therein, being turned into their tongue[3], I fully determined to bring my former pretence to end[4], considering that besides much mirth, here is also a true description of the nature and disposition of

---

1   Sir Thomas Gresham (1518?–1579) was an eminent financier who served Henry VIII, Edward VI, Mary and Elizabeth and amassed colossal wealth. For many years he represented the financial interests of the English crown in Antwerp. Since Spain then ruled the Netherlands, he had ample dealings with that country. For years he had lodged with a Spaniard in Antwerp, he undertook a financial mission to Seville for several months in 1554–5 and had served as ambassador to Charles V.

   Gresham is perhaps best remembered today for building the Royal Exchange and founding the famous lectures. For the purposes of this present study it is important to note that he had strong Protestant sympathies, defended Protestant and English national interests against Spanish machinations, was an intimate friend of Cecil, Elizabeth's Secretary of State, and gave hospitality to John Foxe, author of *The Acts and Monuments*, a massive and enduring piece of Protestant propaganda.

   For a full summary of his life see *Dictionary of National Biography*, Oxford University Press, 1968, Volume VIII pages 585–596.

   The date of Gresham's death, 1579, is further confirmation that there was an earlier edition of Rowland's translation, entered in the Stationers' Register of 1568–9 and known to have been published in 1576. No known copy survives.

2   This word could mean 'tale' or 'narrative' as well as academic topic in English, though not in Spanish. Rowland uses the term for the entire novel, the Spanish original, for its parts. This suggests that Rowland, in keeping with present day scholarship, regarded the work as a whole.

3   This is a reference to Saugrain's translation of 1561. Rowland used the French as well as the Spanish, following Saugrain's modifications of anti–clerical material and some excisions, as well as the practice of marginal glosses.

4   This 'pretence' is not known. Perhaps Rowland means 'plea' or 'excuse', but the word could mean 'aim, purpose or design', in which case Rowland could be referring to the Stationers' entry of 1568–9 which had secured the licence to publish.

sundry Spaniards[5]. So that by reading hereof, such as have not travelled Spain may as well discern much of the manners and customs of that country as those that have there long time continued. And being now finished, I was so bold as to dedicate the fruit of my simple labour unto your worship, who both for travel, daily conference with divers nations, and knowledge in all foreign matters, is known to be such a one as is well able to judge whether these reports of little Lazaro be true or not. Wherefore I most humbly beseech your worship favourably to accept this poor present, as offered of one who wisheth unto you and yours all health, wealth, long life, with increase of all virtue and worship[6]. Trusting that after your weighty and important affairs, to ease your tedious exercises[7], you will recreate yourself with reading of some pleasant part hereof.

Your worship's most humbly to command,
David Rowland.

---

[5] Hence the running heading 'A Spaniard's Life'. An element of hispanophobia is explicit.

[6] i.e. respect, esteem.

[7] i.e. wearisome or irksome demands of working and public life.

La Vida De
Lazarillo De Tormes
Y
De Sus Fortunas
Y
Adversidades

Of the four separate editions of *Lazarillo de Tormes* that are known to have appeared in 1554, I have accepted the arguments of R.O. Jones that the Burgos is the oldest and least polished, that those of Antwerp and Alcalá had been polished with a consequent loss in vigour and vitality.[2] Since the Burgos is the most vigorous and archaic, it is reproduced here. The recently discovered copy of Medina del Campo has yet to receive scholarly assessment. However, since Rowland used the Antwerp for his translation, the Spanish text carries footnotes which indicate the Antwerp variant readings with some small glosses intended to assist the reader attempting the Spanish.

PRÓLOGO

Yo por bien tengo que cosas tan señaladas, y por ventura nunca oídas ni vistas, vengan a noticia de muchos y no se entierren en la sepultura del olvido, pues podría ser que alguno que las lea halle algo que le agrade, y a los que no ahondaren tanto los deleite; y a este propósito dice Plinio que no hay libro, por malo que sea, que no tenga alguna cosa buena; mayormente que los gustos no son todos unos, mas lo que uno no come, otro se pierde por ello. Y así vemos cosas tenidas en poco de algunos, que de otros no lo son. Y esto, para que ninguna cosa se debría romper ni echar a mal, si muy detestable no fuese, sino que a todos se comunicase, mayormente siendo sin perjuicio y pudiendo sacar della algún fruto; porque si así no fuese, muy pocos escribirían para uno solo, pues no se hace sin trabajo, y quieren, ya que lo pasan, ser recompensados, no con dineros, mas con que vean y lean sus obras, y si hay de qué, se las alaben; y a este propósito dice Tulio: La honra cría las artes. ¿Quién piensa

PROLOGUE

The Prologue of Lazaro de Tormes, unto a Gentleman of Spain,
which was desirous to understand the discourse of his life[1].

I am of opinion that things so worthy of memory, peradventure never heard of before nor seen, ought by all reason to come abroad to the sight of many, and not be buried in the endless pit of oblivion[2], there perpetually to be forgotten; for it is possible that those which shall read this treatise of my life may find some pleasure therein. Wherefore true it is that Pliny[3] recordeth *there is no book so evil but hath some goodness in it contained*, considering all men taste not alike[4], that which one man will not eat, another longeth sore for; we see many despise things which others do greatly esteem. Therefore nothing ought to be broken and cast away unless it were detestable, but that first divers men should see the same, and especially being not hurtful, but rather able, instead of damage[5], to yield profit and utility. If the world were otherwise, very few would take pen in hand to pleasure one man only, seeing that they can not bring their works to end without great travail[6]. And when they have ended their labour, they rightfully desire to be recompensed, and not with money, but only that all men with courteous mind will read and allow[7] their works, yea, and if there be cause why, give them praise. For to this end Tully saith, *Honour*

---

1   The italicized captions of each treatise and the italicized marginal notes follow the practice of the French translation of Saugrain, of 1561. These glosses are not in the Spanish text.

     This caption reminds us that the novel takes the form of a deposition or confession, not unlike some made to the Inquisition. Whether the person addressed is a gentleman of Spain may be wondered; the Seventh Treatise offers the possibility that he is a senior Church dignitary in Toledo.

2   The original frontispiece of Rowland's translation reproduced on page 45, carries the words 'accuerdo olvid.'; these Spanish words are mispelt and unclear, but could stand for 'acuerdo lo olvidado' i.e. I remember what has been forgotten. Rowland's image alludes to classical notions of the underworld where we go on death and the river Lethe which, after being crossed, causes us to forget.

3   Pliny the younger in his *Letters* III. 5. This quotation was a commonplace. The rhetorical flourishes and classical allusions at once establish a humanist text or the parody of one.

4   i.e. do not have the same taste in reading.

5   i.e. harm.

6   i.e. hardship, toil.

7   i.e. tolerate.

que el soldado que es primero del escala, tiene más aborrecido el vivir? No, por cierto; mas el deseo de alabanza le hace ponerse al peligro; y así, en las artes y letras es lo mesmo[1]. Predica muy bien el presentado, y es hombre que desea mucho el provecho de las ánimas; mas pregunten a su merced si le pesa cuando le dicen: '¡Oh, qué maravillosamente lo ha hecho vuestra reverencia!' Justó muy ruinmente el señor don Fulano, y dio el sayete de armas al truhán, porque le loaba[2] de haber llevado muy buenas lanzas. ¿Qué hiciera si fuera verdad?

Y todo va desta manera: que confesando yo no ser más santo que mis vecinos, desta nonada, que en este grosero estilo escribo, no me pesará que hayan parte y se huelguen con ello todos los que en ella algún gusto hallaren, y vean que vive un hombre con tantas fortunas, peligros y adversidades.

Suplico a vuestra M. reciba el pobre servicio de mano de quien lo hiciera más rico si su poder y deseo se conformaran. Y pues V.M. escribe se le escriba y relate el caso muy por extenso, parecióme no tomalle por el medio, sino del principio, porque se tenga entera noticia de mi persona, y también porque consideren los que

---

1   mismo.
2   lo loaba.

doth maintain art or cunning[8]. Do you think that the soldier that first mounteth on the wall with his ladder is wary of his life? No surely, the desire of honour enourageth him so to venture into such danger. So likewise in Art[9] and learning, we use to say, master Doctor[10] hath preached well, he is a man that seeketh the health of souls; but I pray you demand of him whether he will be offended that one shall say, 'O how divinely you have preached, master Doctor'. The like happeneth in men of arms, as men commonly report. O how such a knight jousted noughtly[11], and notwithstanding he hath given his coat armour to a jester which commended him for running well[12]; what would he have given if he had said the truth?

Wherefore now that all things pass after such a sort[13] I, confessing myself to be no holier than my neighbours, am content that such as find any taste in this my gross style and novelty[14] may pleasure and delight themselves therewith; and they may perceive how a man liveth after[15] so many fortunes[16], dangers, and adversities.

Therefore now I beseech your Worship[17] receive with willing heart this poor token of my true affection, which should have been much richer if power and ability had been equal with desire. And seeing that you[18] have commanded me to write the matter[19] at length, I have thought good not to begin[20] the midst of my life, but first to tell you of my birth, that all men may have full knowledge of my person, that those which possess great rents[21] and revenues may understand what small praise is

---

8   Marcus Tullius Cicero, in his *Tusculanum* I. 4., and again a common quotation : more literally 'Honour nourishes the Arts and all men are fired to study by glory'.

9   Plural in the Spanish. Read 'the Arts'.

10   i.e. a student friar or monk about to be graduated, or theology student who has finished his studies and is about to take his Master's.

11   i.e. badly.

12   i.e for having borne his lance well on horseback.

13   i.e. since that is the way things are .....

14   'Novelty' seems a misreading of the Spanish word. 'Trifle' is more accurate. The attitude of affected modesty was a familiar device of a prologue.

15   i.e. survives.

16   i.e. blows of fortune. These words echo the full title of the book.

17   'Worship' has upper case in the Spanish. The entire novel is a statement made to someone in authority, and the address to 'you' or 'your worship' is to be found throughout the narrative.

18   The Spanish repeats the more elaborate 'Your Worship'.

19   i.e . relate the facts of the case, legal terminology in the Spanish, which Rowland rightly echoes. Lazarillo returns to this point at the end, see Seventh Treatise (31). 'The case' links prologue and ending and strengthens a reading of Lazarillo's life story as a deposition or parody of such a deposition.

20   i.e. read 'at'. The narrator here echoes Horace in his *Letters* 149, where he praises a writer who brings the reader quickly to the middle of his subject.

21   i.e. incomes.

heredaron nobles estados cuán poco se les debe, pues fortuna fue con ellos parcial, y cuánto más hicieron los que, siéndoles contraria, con fuerza y maña remando, salieron a buen puerto.

due unto them, seeing that Fortune[22] hath dealt partially with them; and how much commendation they deserve, which[23] in despite of cruel fortune, with force and industry, by rowing out of tempestuous seas, have arrived to fortunate and happy havens[24].

---

22 Rowland has given Fortune an uppercase, a reading which the Spanish suggests. Fortune was a sort of power in human affairs, classical rather than Christian; and it was common to represent human affairs in terms of the wheel of fortune, hence the political metaphor 'revolution'.

23 i.e. who. The relative pronoun 'who' was not common in standard English until James I's reign. Rowland prefers 'which' throughout.

24 These words anticipate the ending of the Seventh Treatise. 'Prosperity', we must remember, could also mean fine weather.

LAZARILLO DE TORMES

Tratado Primero
Cuenta Lázaro su vida, y cuyo hijo fue

Pues sepa V.M. ante todas cosas que a mí llaman Lázaro de Tormes, hijo de Tomé Gonzáles y de Antona Pérez, naturales de Tejares, aldea de Salamanca. Mi nacimiento fue dentro del río Tormes, por la cual causa tomé el sobrenombre, y fue desta manera. Mi padre, que Dios perdone, tenía cargo de proveer una molienda de una aceña, que está ribera de aquel río, en la cual fue molinero más de quince años; y estando mi madre una noche en la aceña, preñada de mí, tomóle el parto y parióme allí: de manera que con verdad me puedo decir nacido en el río. Pues siendo yo niño de ocho años, achacaron a mi padre ciertas sangrías mal hechas en los costales de los que allí a moler venían, por lo cual fue preso, y confesó y no negó y padeció persecución por justicia. Espero en Dios que está en la gloria, pues el Evangelio los llama bienaventurados. En este tiempo se hizo cierta armada contra moros, entre los cuales fue mi padre, que a la sazón estaba desterrado por el desastre ya dicho, con cargo de acemilero de un caballero que allá fue, y con su señor, como leal criado, feneció su vida.

Mi viuda madre, como sin marido y sin abrigo se viese, determinó arrimarse a los buenos por ser uno dellos, y vínose a vivir a la ciudad, y alquiló una casilla, y metióse[1] a guisar de comer a ciertos estudiantes, y lavaba la ropa a ciertos mozos de caballos del Comendador de la Magdalena, de manera que fue frecuentando las caballerizas. Ella y un hombre moreno de aquellos que las bestias curaban, vinieron

---

1   metíase.

LAZARILLO DE TORMES

First Treatise
Lazaro declareth his life, and whose son he was.

Your worship shall understand before all things, that my name is *Lazarillo de Tormes*, son of *Thome Gonzales* and *Antona Perez* native of *Tejares*, a village near *Salamanca*. I was born within the river called *Tormes*, whereof I took my surname, as hereafter you shall hear: my father whom God pardon, had the charge of a mill standing upon that river wherein he supplied the room of[1] a miller about fifteen years. It fortuned on a night my mother being great with child, was there brought to bed, and then was I born; therefore now I may truly report the river itself to be the place of my nativity. And after the time I came to the age of eight years, there was laid to my father's charge that he had shamefully cut the seams of men's sacks that came thither to grind, wherefore he was taken and imprisoned, and being tormented he confessed the whole matter, denying nothing wherefore he was persecuted. I trust in God that he is now in paradise, seeing that the Gospel doth say, that blessed are such as confess their faults. About the same time an army was made against the Turks,[2] and my father being then banished for the mishap aforesaid, chanced to be one supplying the room of a muleteer under a knight which went thither, in whose service, like a true and faithful man, he ended his life.

My mother being then a comfortless widow, after the loss of her dear husband, determined to inhabit among such as were virtuous and honest,[3] to be of that number, and therefore came immediately to this noble city,[4] where, after that she had hired a little house, she kept an ordinary table for divers students,[5] and washed shirts for a company of horsekeepers, belonging to the Commander of *Magdalena*,[6] by means whereof she had occasion to make often resort unto the stables. Where in

---

1   i.e. carried out the job of.

2   Possibly the battle for the island of Djerba, off the coast of Tunis in 1510, one of several such hard fought and futile battles.

3   Literally the Spanish original adapts a proverb: 'she decided to lean against the good in order to be one of them'. The same refrain occurs in the last treatise, and suggests living on immoral earnings.

4   The original reads, 'she came to live in the city', that is, Salamanca.

5   i.e. she cooked them a lunch for which they paid.

6   A knight of the military-religious order of Alcántara, which enjoyed the income of various estates, one of which was the parish Church of Santa Maria Magdalena of Salamanca.

en conocimiento. Éste algunas veces se venía a nuestra casa, y se iba a la mañana; otras veces de día llegaba a la puerta, en achaque de comprar huevos, y entrábase en casa. Yo, al principio de su entrada, pesábame con él y habíale miedo, viéndo el color y mal gesto que tenía; mas de que vi que con su venida mejoraba el comer, fuile queriendo bien, porque siempre traía pan, pedazos de carne, y en el invierno leños, a que nos calentábamos. De manera que, continuando la posada y conversación, mi madre vino a darme un negrito muy bonito, el cual yo brincaba y ayudaba a calentar. Y acuérdome que, estando el negro de mi padrastro trebejando con el mozuelo, como el niño vía a mi madre y a mí blancos, y a él no, huía dél con miedo para mi madre, y señalando con el dedo decía: '¡Madre, coco!'

Respondió él riendo: '¡Hideputa!'

Yo, aunque bien mochacho, noté aquella palabra de mi hermanico, y dije entre mí:

'¡Cuántos debe de haber en el mundo que huyen de otros porque no se veen a sí mesmos!'[1].

Quiso nuestra fortuna que la conversación del Zaide, que así se llamaba, llegó a oídos del mayordomo, y hecha pesquisa, hallóse que la mitad por medio de la cebada que para las bestias le daban hurtaba, y salvados, leña, almohazas, mandiles, y las mantas y sábanas de los caballos hacía perdidas, y cuando otra cosa no tenía, las bestias desherraba, y con todo esto acudía a mi madre para criar a mi hermanico. No nos maravillemos de un clérigo ni[2] fraile, porque el uno hurta de los pobres y el otro de casa para sus devotas y para ayuda de otro tanto, cuando a un pobre esclavo el amor le animaba a esto. Y probósele cuanto digo y aún más, porque a mí con

---

1   mismos.
2   ni de un fraile.

continuance of time, a black Moor, one of master Commander's men, became to be familiarly acquainted with her, so that for his part he would oftentimes arrive at midnight to our house, and return again betimes in the morning, otherwhiles at noontide, demanding at the door whether my mother had eggs to sell, and so come in prettily without suspicion. At the beginning I was right sorry to see him make repair thither, being afraid to behold his black uncomely visage; but after that I once perceived how only by his resort our fare was so well amended, I could by no means find in my heart to hate him, but rather bear him good will, rejoicing to see him; for he always brought us home with him good round cantels[7] of bread and pieces of broken meat, and in the winter time wood to warm us withal.

To be short, by his continual repair thither, matters went so forward that my mother found good time to bring forth a young blackamoor, whom I daily played withal, and sometimes helped to warm. And I remember very well, that on a time as my stepfather played merrily with his young son, the little child perceiving that my mother and I were white, and his father black as jet, he ran away for fear to my mother, and stretching forth his finger, cried, '*Mamma*, the bug'![8] Whereat my black stepfather would laugh, and say, 'Whoreson, art thou afraid of thy father?'[9] Although I was then but young, I rightwell marked the child's words, and said to myself, there are many such in the world, which do abhor and flee from others because they cannot see what shape they have themselves.

Within a while after, it pleased fortune that the daily conversation of Zaide (for so was my father's name) came to the ears of him that was steward to master Commander, who made such strait[10] inquiry, that he was advertised how the black Moor did used *All was fish that came to the net* to steal half the provender that was allowed the horses, yea, horse coverings, sheets, and curry combs, otherwhiles wood and bran; which things indeed he always said were lost, and when nothing could be gotten to serve his turn he would never stick to unshoe the horses, to get some gain, presenting daily all such gifts to my mother, as a help to bring up my little black brother. Let us never therefore marvel more at those which steal from the poor, nor yet at them which convey from the houses they serve, to present therewith whom they love in hope to attain thereby their desired pleasure,[11] seeing that love was able to encourage this poor bondman or slave to do thus much as I have said, or rather more, which by evident trial was afterwards

---

7   i.e. slices or pieces.

8   or, as we say today, bogey-man. Perhaps Rowland had in mind the Welsh bwgan.

9   The Spanish literally reads: 'he answered, laughing, "Son of a whore!"'

10   i.e. strict, vigorous.

11   This is one of several instances where Rowland softens anti-clerical material in the original Spanish. A more literal translation would be: 'Let us not be surprised at a priest or friar, because the one steals from the poor, and the other from a monastery for the benefit of his female followers and whatever, seeing that a poor slave gave into love and stole.'

amenazas me preguntaban, y como niño respondía, y descubría cuanto sabía con miedo, hasta ciertas herraduras que por mandado de mi madre a un herrero vendí. Al triste de mi padrastro azotaron y pringaron, y a mi madre pusieron pena por justicia, sobre el acostumbrado centenario, que en casa del sobredicho Comendador no entrase, ni al lastimado Zaide en la suya acogiese.

Por no echar la soga tras el caldero, la triste se esforzó y cumplió la sentencia, y por evitar peligro y quitarse de malas lenguas, se fue a servir a los que al presente vivían en el mesón de la Solana; y allí, padeciendo mil importunidades, se acabó de criar mi hermanico hasta que supo andar, y a mí hasta ser buen mozuelo, que iba a los huéspedes por vino y candelas y por lo demás que me mandaban.

En este tiempo vino a posar al mesón un ciego, el cual, pareciéndole que yo sería para adestralle, me pidió a mi madre, y ella me encomendó a él, diciéndole como era hijo de un buen hombre, el cual por ensalzar la fe había muerto en la de los Gelves, y que ella confiaba en Dios no saldría peor hombre que mi padre, y que le rogaba me tratase bien y mirase por mí, pues era huérfano. Él respondió que así lo haría, y que me recibía no por mozo sino por hijo. Y así le comencé a servir y adestrar a mi nuevo y viejo amo.

Como estuvimos en Salamanca algunos días, pareciéndole a mi amo que no era la ganancia a su contento, determinó irse de allí; y cuando nos hubimos de partir, yo fui a ver a mi madre, y ambos llorando, me dio su bendición, y dijo:

'Hijo, ya sé que no te veré más. Procura de ser bueno, y Dios te guíe. Criado te

proved true. For I being examined of the deed, after much threatening was constrained as a child, for fear, to discover the whole matter, confessing how I had sold certain horseshoes to a smith at my mother's commandment. Wherefore my miserable stepfather was by judgment of the law, as the order is there, whipped and larded, and to my mother express commandment was given upon the usual pain of a hundred stripes, no more to enter into the house of the above named Commander, nor yet entertain into hers the unfortunate *Zaide*[12].

There is an order in that country that when any Moor doth commit any heinous offence, to strip him naked and being bound with his hands and his knees together to baste him with hot drops of burning lard.

My sorrowful mother fearing to throw the helve[13] after the hatchet, determined by all means to keep their commandment, wherefore she entered into service with those which at the time dwelt at the ordinary inn called Solona[14], so to escape danger and to avoid the dangerous reports of evil tongues, where she suffered much sorrow, and there brought up my black brother, until he was able to run abroad, and that I being a good stripling, could go up and down the town to provide the guests with wine, and candles, and other things necessary. In this mean time, there happened a blind man to come thither to lodge, who thinking me to be a fit man to lead him, desired my mother that I might serve him, wherewith she being right well content, most earnestly prayed him to be a good master unto me, because I was an honest man's son,

There is no provision there in inns, for the guests must send abroad into the town for all such victual as they need.

who in maintaining the faith of Jesus Christ against Turks, died in the battle of *Gelves*[15], and how that she trusted in almighty God I would prove as honest a man as he; therefore in any wise that he would be careful over me, being a fatherless child.

'Let me alone then,' answered he, 'I will not use him as a servant, but as a son.'

Then in happy time I began to serve my old and new master. And after we had remained certain days at *Salamanca*, my blind master perceiving his gain there to be but small, determined to depart thence; and a little before our departure, I went to see my mother. When I came where she was, we shed both most bitter tears, and she gave me her blessing, saying,

'Now my dear son I shall see thee no more, therefore be a good child. I pray God be thy help, I do thank the Lord I have brought thee up well hitherto, and I have

---

12 Zaide was a common Arabic name meaning 'Lord' and occurred frequently in Spanish romances with Arabic protagonists, hence, 'El Cid'.

13 Rowland's delightful rendering of a proverb: 'to throw the rope after the bucket'.

14 Solona for the original Solana, an inn formally on the site of the present town hall.

15 The island nowadays known as Djerba. The two most significant military expeditions were in 1510 and 1520. Both Lazarillo's father and step–father might have died in the same battle.

he y con buen amo te he puesto. Válete por ti.'

Y así me fui para mi amo, que esperándome estaba. Salimos de Salamanca, y llegando a la puente, está a la entrada della un animal de piedra, que casi tiene forma de toro, y el ciego mandóme que llegase cerca del animal y allí puesto, me dijo:

'Lázaro, llega el oído a este toro, y oirás gran ruido dentro dél.'

Yo simplemente llegué, creyendo ser ansí[1]; y como sintió que tenía la cabeza par de la piedra, afirmó recio la mano y diome una gran calabazada en el diablo del toro, que más de tres días me duró[2] el dolor de la cornada, y díjome:

'Necio, aprende que el mozo del ciego un punto ha de saber más que el diablo', y rio mucho la burla.

Parecióme que en aquel instante desperté[3] de la simpleza en que como niño dormido estaba. Dije entre mí:

'Verdad dice éste, que me cumple avivar el ojo y avisar, pues solo soy, y pensar cómo me sepa valer.'

Comenzamos nuestro camino, y en muy pocos días me mostró jerigonza, y como me viese de buen ingenio, holgábase mucho, y decía:

'Yo oro ni plata no te lo puedo dar, mas avisos para vivir muchos te mostraré.'

Y fue ansí[4], que después de Dios éste me dio la vida, y siendo ciego me alumbró y adestró en ansí carrera de vivir. Huelgo de contar a V.M. estas niñerías para mostrar cuánta virtud sea saber los hombres subir siendo bajos, y dejarse bajar siendo altos cuánto vicio.

Pues tornando al bueno de mi ciego y contando sus cosas, V.M. sepa que desde que Dios crió el mundo, ninguno formó mas astuto ni sagaz. En su oficio era un águila; ciento y tantas oraciones sabía de coro: un tono bajo, reposado y muy

---

1   así.
2   turó.
3   disperté.
4   así.

now put thee to a good master; from henceforth provide for thyself, seeing that I have done my part.'

I took my leave and returned in haste to my master, which tarried for me ready to take his voyage[16]. So we departed out of *Salamanca*, and came on our way as far as the bridge, at the entrance whereof standeth a beast of stone, fashioned much like a bull[17]. As soon as we came near it, the blind man willed me to approach, saying:

'*Lazaro*, put thine ear to this bull, and thou shalt hear a terrible noise within it.' As soon as he had said the word, I was ready like a fool to bow down my head, to do as he had commanded, thinking that his words had been most true; but the traitorous blind man suspecting how near it my head was, thrusteth forth his arm upon a sudden, with such force, that my sore head took such a blow against the devilish bull, that for the space of three days my head felt the pains of his horns. Wherefore he was right glad, and said:

'Consider now what thou art, thou foolish calf; thou must understand, that the blind man's boy ought to know one trick more than the devil himself.'

It seemed then immediately that I awaked out of simplicity, wherein I had of long time slept (like a child), and I said to myself:

'My blind master hath good reason. It is full time for me to open mine eyes, yea, and to provide and seek mine own advantage, considering that I am alone without any help.'

We continued on our journey, and within few days I came to good knowledge[18], so he perceiving what a ready tongue I had, was right glad, and said:

'Neither gold nor silver can I give thee, howbeit, I do mean to teach thee the way to live.'[19]

And so certainly he did; for next after God he made me a man, and although he was blind, it was he that gave me sight and that taught me how to know the world. I rejoice to declare unto your worship these childish toys, that you may see how commendable it is for a man of low estate to be brought to authority and exalted, and contrariwise what a shame it is for a man of dignity and estimation to be pulled down to wretched misery.

But to return to my blind master, and to show his nature, I assure you that since the beginning of the world God never made man more deceitful and crafty. For in his art and trade of living he far passed all other: he could recite by heart a hundred

---

16   i.e. journey.

17   The stone object now stands on a new plinth by the old Roman bridge over the river Tormes, together with a modern sculpture of Lazarillo and the blind man. Very possibly the 'bull' was a pre–Roman boar.

18   Literally the Spanish means that he taught Lazarillo a sort of peddlars' slang.

19   This is Biblical parody, e.g. 'Silver and gold have I none; but such as I have give I thee' (Acts 3.6); and 'Receive my instruction, and not silver; and knowledge rather than choice gold. For wisdom is better than rubies; and all the things that may be desired are not to be compared to it' (Proverbs 8. 10–11.).

sonable que hacía resonar la iglesia donde rezaba, un rostro humilde y devoto que con muy buen continente ponía cuando rezaba, sin hacer gestos ni visajes con boca ni ojos, como otros suelen hacer. Allende desto, tenía otras mil formas y maneras para sacar el dinero. Decía saber oraciones para muchos y diversos efectos: para mujeres que no parían, para las que estaban de parto, para las que eran malcasadas, que sus maridos las quisiesen bien; echaba pronósticos a las preñadas, si traía[1] hijo o hija. Pues en caso de medicina, decía que[2] Galeno no supo la mitad que él para muela[3], desmayos, males de madre. Finalmente, nadie le decía padecer alguna pasión, que luego no le decía: 'Haced esto, haréis estotro, cosed[4] tal yerba, tomad tal raíz.' Con esto andábase todo el mundo tras él, especialmente mujeres, que cuanto les decía creían. Destas sacaba él grandes provechos con las artes que digo, y ganaba más en un mes que cien ciegos en un año.

Mas también quiero que sepa vuestra merced que, con todo lo que adquiría y tenía, jamás tan avariento ni mezquino hombre no vi, tanto que me mataba a mí de hambre, y así no me demediaba[5] de lo necesario. Digo verdad: si con mi sotileza y buenas mañas no me supiera remediar, muchas veces me finara de hambre; mas con todo su saber y aviso le contaminaba[6] de tal suerte que siempre, o las más veces, me cabía lo mas y mejor. Para esto le hacía burlas endiabladas, de las cuales contaré algunas, aunque no todas a mi salvo.

Él traía el pan y todas las otras cosas en un fardel de lienzo que por la boca se cerraba con una argolla de hierro y su candado y su llave, y al meter de todas[7] las cosas y sacallas[8], era con tan gran vigilancia y tanto por contadero, que no bastara hombre en todo el mundo hacerle[9] menos una migaja; mas yo tomaba aquella laceria que él me daba, la cual en menos de dos bocados era despachada. Después que cerraba el candado y se descuidaba pensando que yo estaba entendiendo en otras cosas, por un poco de costura, que muchas veces del un lado del fardel descosía y tornaba a coser, sangraba el avariento fardel, sacando no por tasa pan, mas buenos

---

1   sí traían.
2   que not in Antwerp.
3   muelas.
4   Possibly a misprint. The Alcalá reads coged.
5   remediaba
6   i.e. Lázaro filched secretly from his master.
7   todas not in Antwerp.
8   sacarlas.
9   que no bastara todo el mundo hacerle.

long prayers and more, yea, and the life of all the holy saints; at his devotion time he used such a loud tunable voice, that it might be heard throughout the church where he prated, and besides all that, he could counterfeit a good devout countenance in praying, without any strange gesture, either with mouth or eye, as other blind men are accustomed to use. I am not able to recite a thousand other manner of ways which he had to get money; he would make many believe that he had prayers for divers good purposes, as for to make women bring forth children, yea, and to make men to love their wives, although they had hated them before never so much. He would prognosticate to women that were with child, whether they should bring forth a son or a daughter; in matters of physic, he would affirm that *Galen*[20] never knew half so much as he; also for any grief, the toothache, or any other disease, there was never one complained, but that immediately he would say, do this, do that, seethe such a herb, take such a root. So that by this his continual practice, he had daily great resort made unto him (especially of women) which did faithfully believe all that ever he said; by them he had great gain, for he won more in a month, than twenty of his occupation did in a whole year.

Yet for all his daily gains, you[21] understand that there was never man so wretched a niggard. For he caused me not only to die for hunger, but also to want whatsoever I needed.[22] And therefore to confess the truth, if I had not found out means to help myself, I had been buried long since. Wherefore oftentimes I would so prevent him of all his craft, that my portion should prove as good as his; and to bring my matter so to pass I used wonderful deceits (whereof I will recite unto you some) although sometimes my practising of them did cost me bitter pains.

This blind man carried always his bread and his victual in a little bag of cloth, which was shut at the mouth with an iron buckle, under a miserable lock and key. At the time of putting his meat in, and taking it out, he would keep such straight account, that all the world was not able to deceive him of one crumb, and therefore there was no help, but that I must needs be content with that small allowance that he gave me, which always I was sure to dispatch at two morsels; and as soon as ever he had shut his little lock, he would think then that all were sure, imagining that I had other matters in hand. Then would I boldly unrip and sow up again the sides of his covetous sack, using daily to lance one of the sides, there to take out not only bread

---

20   A celebrated Greek physician of the second century A.D., born at Pergamos, Asia Minor, now modern Turkey.

21   Throughout these paragraphs as elsewhere in the novel, the 'you' is the 'your worship', the person of superior rank, to whom Lazarillo addresses his history in his Prologue.

22   The Spanish original contains a word play suggesting that Lazarillo could not cure himself of the disease of hunger by achieving even half of what he needed in order to live.

pedazos, torreznos y longaniza; y ansí[1] buscaba conveniente tiempo para rehacer, no la chaza, sino la endiablada falta que el mal ciego me faltaba[2].

Todo lo que podía sisar y hurtar, traía en medias blancas; y cuando le mandaban rezar y le daban blancas, como él carecía de vista, no había el que se la daba amagado con ella, cuando yo la tenía lanzada en la boca y la media aparejada, que por presto que él echaba la mano, ya iba de mi cambio aniquilada en la mitad del justo precio. Quejábaseme el mal ciego, porque al tiento luego conocía y sentía que no era blanca entera, y decía:

'¿Qué diablo es esto, que después que comigo[3] estás no me dan sino medias blancas, y de antes una blanca y un maravedí hartas veces me pagaban? En ti debe estar esta desdicha.'

También él abreviaba el rezar y la mitad de la oración no acababa, porque me tenía mandado que en yéndose el que la mandaba rezar, le tirase por cabo del capuz. Yo así lo hacía. Luego él tornaba a dar voces, diciendo: '¿Mandan rezar tal y tal oración?', como suelen decir.

Usaba poner cabe sí un jarrillo de vino cuando comíamos, y yo muy de presto le asía y[4] daba un par de besos callados y tornábale a su lugar. Mas turóme[5] poco, que en los tragos conocía la falta, y por reservar su vino a salvo nunca después desamparaba el jarro, antes lo tenía por el asa asido; mas no había piedra imán que así trajese a sí como yo con una paja larga de centeno, que para aquel menester tenía

Fig. 7 - Illustration of a boy stealing wine from a blind man through a straw (decretals of Gregory IX)

---

1   así.
2   i.e. not merely to keep the tricks going, but to make good the need the blind man made me suffer.
3   i.e. conmigo.
4   y: not in Antwerp.
5   i.e. duróme.

at my own pleasure, but also slices of flesh, and sweet carbonados; so that by such means I found convenient time to ease the raging hunger that he was cause of[23].

Moreover all the money that I could convey and steal from him, I changed always into half blanks[24] and when any man demanded any prayer, he had always of ordinary a blank given him for his hire, and because he could not see, it should be delivered me; but he could never so soon put forth his hand to receive it, but I was as ready to throw it into my mouth, and by quick exchange to give him the just value of half of it, whereat he would much murmur, knowing by the only feeling of it what it was, and would say:

'How in the devil's name chanceth it that since thy coming to me, I receive but half blanks, and before I had always a whole blank and sometimes two? I think surely that thy unluckiness be cause thereof.'[25]

From that time forward he thought good to shorten his prayers, cutting them off in the midst: wherefore he commanded me, that soon as the almsgiver had turned his back, I should pluck him by the cloak. Then straightways changing tune, he would begin to cry with loud voice (as blind men use to do) —

Blind men stand therein church porches ready to be hired for money to recite any prayer.

'Who will hear such a devout prayer, or else the life of some holy Saint?'

At dinner or supper time he had always before him a little pot full of wine, which sometimes I would lay hand on, and after two or three kisses send it him secretly home again.[26] But that happy time continued but a while, for I was wont to leave so little behind me, that he might soon espy the fault, as indeed immediately he did mistrust the whole matter, wherefore he began a new order, not to leave his wine any more at random, but to avoid danger, had always his little pot fast by the ear,[27] so to be sure of his drink. Yet notwithstanding all of this, the adamant stone[28] had never such virtue to draw iron to it, as I had to suck up his wine with a long reed

---

23   This narrative material recalls both folk–tale and the lancing of Christ's body on the cross. Rowland's use of the Spanish word 'carbonados' is noteworthy. It means pieces of meat, either cooked on charcoal or stewed. It is not in the original text, which reads 'slices of bacon and long pork sausage.' Rowland's practice illustrates a large influx of Spanish words into English, many ending in – ade and –ada, hence Armada, stockade, lemonade, etc.

24   Again Rowland used a Spanish word widely used in English at that time: the Spanish 'blanca' meant 'white money', a silver coin.

25   Strictly the original reads 'This bad luck must be in you'.

26   'I used to grip it quickly, give it a couple of hushed kisses and put it back'. (ed.)

27   'He never let it go'. (ed.)

28   i.e. magnet.

hecha, la cual metiéndola en la boca del jarro, chupando el vino lo dejaba a buenas noches.

Mas como fuese el traidor tan astuto, pienso que me sintió, y dende en adelante mudó propósito, y asentaba su jarro entre las piernas, y atapábale con la mano, y ansí[1] bebía seguro. Yo, como estaba hecho al vino, moría por él, y viendo que aquel remedio de la paja no me aprovechaba ni valía, acordé en el suelo del jarro hacerle una fuentecilla y agujero sotil[2], y delicadamente con una muy delgada tortilla de cera taparlo, y al tiempo de comer, fingiendo[3] haber frío, entrábame entre las piernas del triste ciego a calentarme en la pobrecilla lumbre que teníamos, y al calor della luego derretida la cera, por ser muy poca, comenzaba la fuentecilla a destillarme[4] en la boca, la cual yo de tal manera ponía que maldita la gota se perdía. Cuando el pobreto iba a beber, no hallaba nada: espantábase, maldecíase, daba al diablo el jarro y el vino, no sabiendo qué podía ser.

'No diréis, tío, que os lo bebo yo — decía —, pues no le quitáis de la mano.'

Tantas vueltas y tientos dio al jarro que halló la fuente y cayó en la burla; mas así lo disimuló como si no lo hubiera sentido, y luego otro día, teniendo yo rezumando mi jarro como solía, no pensando el daño que me estaba aparejado ni que el mal ciego me sentía, sentéme como solía, estando recibiendo aquellos dulces tragos, mi cara puesta hacia el cielo, un poco cerrados los ojos por mejor gustar el sabroso licor, sintió el desesperado ciego que agora[5] tenía tiempo de tomar de mí venganza y con toda su fuerza, alzando con dos manos aquel dulce y amargo jarro, le dejó caer sobre mi boca, ayudándose, como digo, con todo su poder, de manera que el pobre Lázaro, que de nada desto se guardaba, antes, como otras veces, estaba descuidado y gozoso, verdaderamente me pareció que el cielo, con todo lo que en él hay, me había caído encima. Fue tal el golpecillo, que me desatinó y sacó de sentido, y el jarrazo tan grande, que los pedazos dél se me metieron por la cara, rompiéndomela por muchas partes, y me quebró los dientes, sin los cuales hasta hoy día me quedé.

Desde aquella hora quise mal al mal ciego, y aunque me quería y regalaba y me curaba, bien vi que se había holgado del cruel castigo. Lavóme con vino las roturas

---

1   así.
2   sutil.
3   fingiendo.
4   destilarme, i.e. to trickle.
5   i.e. ahora.

which I prepared for the purpose; for as soon as the end of my reed had been once in, I might well desire him to fill the pot again[29].

Yet at the last the crafty blind man chanced to feel me, and being angry, determined to take another way, to place his pot between his legs, covering it still with his hand, so to avoid all former dangers. When he had so done, I being accustomed to drink wine, did long to taste of it, and perceiving that my reed could then no more prevail at all, I devised another kind of fetch,[30] how to make a hole in the bottom of his wine pot, and to stop the same with a little soft wax, so that at dinner time making a show as I were ready to die for cold, I would creep between the blind man's legs, to warm myself at his small fire, by the heat whereof, the wax being little in quantity, would so melt away, that the wine would issue down into my mouth freshly and trim, I being sure to gape upward so just, that one drop should never fall beside. So that when my blind master would taste of his wine, he should never find drop to quench his thirst, whereat he would much marvel, cursing and swearing all manner of oaths, yea, wishing the pot and all that was within at the devil, musing still how his wine should be so consumed away. Then straightways to excuse myself, I would say:

'I trust you will not mistrust me, gentle uncle, seeing that the pot came never out of your own hands.'

Whereupon then to be well informed of the truth, he began to feel and grope the pot over so often, that at last he found the spring, and at that time disembled quietly the matter, as if he perceived nothing.

The next day I began again to prepare myself after my accustomed sort to take my pleasure of his wine, being ignorant of the evil that should ensue, thinking that my master would never have mistrusted me about such a matter, wherefore I was merry and careless. But my cruel master, perceiving after what strange sort I received those sweet drops of wine, which came forth as a quick spring at his pot bottom, my face bent towards heaven, my eyes in manner closed, so to receive with more delight and better taste that pleasant liquor which I thought did preserve my life, the malicious blind man having time of revengement at his will, lifted up the sweet and sour pot (as I may say), and with all his force clapped it so rudely upon my face, that I thought verily heaven above, and all therein, had fallen upon me. The cruel blow was such that it took away my senses, it troubled sore my brains, and my face was all cut with pieces of the broken pot, yea, and some of my teeth were then broken, which as yet is seen, wherefore I never loved him after, howbeit he cherished me daily; yet for all the false love and friendship which he showed, I perceived right well how glad he was that he had so punished me. To make me

---

29   A more accurate reading of the original might be 'I left it empty' or 'it was goodbye or goodnight to the wine'.

30   i.e. dodge, trick.

que con los pedazos del jarro me había hecho, y sonriéndose decía:

'¿Qué te parece, Lázaro? Lo que te enfermó te sana y da salud', y otros donaires que a mi gusto no lo eran.

Ya que estuve medio bueno de mi negra trepa y cardenales, considerando que a pocos golpes tales el cruel ciego ahorraría de mí, quise yo ahorrar dél; mas no lo hice tan presto por hacello más a mi salvo y provecho. Y[1] aunque yo quisiera asentar mi corazón y perdonalle el jarrazo, no daba lugar el maltratamiento que el mal ciego dende[2] allí adelante me hacía, que sin causa ni razón me hería, dándome coxcorrones[3] y repelándome. Y si alguno le decía por qué me trataba tan mal, luego contaba el cuento del jarro, diciendo:

'¿Pensaréis[4] que este mi mozo es algún inocente? Pues oíd si el demonio ensayara otra tal hazaña.'

Santiguándose los que lo oían, decían: '¡Mirá, quién pensara de un muchacho[5] tan pequeño tal ruindad!', y reían mucho el artificio, y deciánle: 'Castigaldo[6], castigaldo, que de Dios lo habréis.'

Y él con aquello nunca otra cosa hacía. Y en esto yo siempre le llevaba por los peores caminos, y adrede, por le hacer mal y daño: si había piedras, por ellas, si lodo, por lo más alto; que aunque yo no iba por lo más enjuto, holgábame a mí de quebrar un ojo por quebrar dos al que ninguno tenía. Con esto siempre con el cabo alto del tiento me atentaba el colodrillo, el cual siempre traía lleno de tolondrones y pelado de sus manos; y aunque yo juraba no lo hacer con malicia, sino por no hallar mejor camino, no me aprovechaba ni me creía más: tal era el sentido y el grandísimo entendimiento del traidor.

Y por que vea V.M. a cuánto se extendía el ingenio deste astuto ciego, contaré un caso de muchos que con él me acaecieron, en el cual me parece dio bien a

---

1   y: not in Antwerp.
2   desde.
3   i.e. coscorrones.
4   pensáis.
5   mochacho.
6   i.e. castigadlo.

amends, he washed with wine the wounds which the unhappy pot had made, and after much laughing, said:

'What sayeth thou to this, my boy, the wine that hath done thee hurt shall now heal thee again,'[31] and such other merry jests, which I utterly misliked .

As soon as I began to recover, and that my face was in manner healed, I considered with myself, how that with few more such blows the blind man might quickly bring me to my grave. And therefore determined to shorten his days if I could, which thing I went not about immediately, but tarried a due time for mine own safety and advantage. And whereas afterwards I went about to forget mine anger,[32] and to forgive him the blow, the evil usage and entertainment which he daily showed me, would in no wise consent thereto. For still he tormented me with sore blows without any offence or fault at all. And when any man demanded why he handled me so cruelly, straight ways he would up and declare the discourse[33] of his pot, saying,

'Do you think that this child is some innocent?'

And always at the end of his tale these would be his words:

'Who unless it were the devil himself could have found out such rare pranks?'

The people would much marvel at my invention, and blessing themselves[34], would say unto my master:

'Punish him, punish him, God will reward you therefore.'

Which thing he did continually, and would have done without their bidding; wherefore I daily led him through the worst ways I could possibly find all for very spite, minding if I could to do him harm; where I might espy stones or mire, I would even through the thickest; and although I could never escape dry foot, I was glad. with losing one of mine own eyes, to put out both his that never had any. At such times of his sorrows, to be revenged, he would take hold with his nails on the hinder part of my head, where with his often pulling, he had left *He was born blind* very few hairs behind; it would never prevail me then to say,

that I could find no better way, nor yet to swear how I did not lead him that naughty[35] way maliciously, for he was so subtle, that to my words he would give small credit.

But now because your worship shall understand how far his craft did extend, I will declare one chance amongst many, which happened in the time I served him,

---

31   Possibly more Biblical parody: 'See now that I, even I, am he, and there is no god with me: I kill, and I make alive: I wound, and I heal: neither is there any that can deliver out of my hand'. (Deuteronomy 32.39). This section could be parody of the taking of wine during Christian mass.

32   i.e. 'although I tried to forget my grievance yet ....'.

33   i.e. story.

34   i.e. crossing themselves.

35   i.e. foul and wicked.

entender su gran astucia. Cuando salimos de Salamanca, su motivo fue venir a tierra de Toledo, porque decía ser la gente más rica, aunque no muy limosnera. Arrimábase a este refrán: 'Más da el duro que el desnudo.' Y venimos a este camino por los mejores lugares. Donde hallaba buena acogida y ganancia, deteníamonos; donde no,a tercero día hacíamos Sant Juan[1].

Acaeció que llegando a un lugar que llaman Almorox, al tiempo que cogían las uvas, un vendimiador le dio un racimo dellas en limosna, y como suelen ir los cestos maltratados y también porque la uva en aquel tiempo está muy madura, desgranábasele el racimo en la mano; para echarlo en el fardel tornábase mosto, y lo que a él se llegaba. Acordó de hacer un banquete, ansí[2] por no lo poder llevar como por contentarme, que aquel día me había dado muchos rodillazos y golpes. Sentámonos en un valladar[3] y dijo:

'Agora quiero yo usar contigo de una liberalidad, y es que ambos comamos este racimo de uvas, y que hayas dél tanta parte como yo. Partillo hemos[4] desta manera: tú picarás una vez y yo otra; con tal que me prometas no tomar cada vez más de una uva, yo haré lo mesmo[5] hasta que lo acabemos, y desta suerte no habrá engaño.'

Hecho ansí[6] el concierto, comenzamos; mas luego al segundo lance el traidor mudó propósito y comenzó a tomar de dos en dos, considerando que yo debría hacer lo mismo. Como vi que él quebraba la postura, no me contenté ir a la par con él, mas aun pasaba adelante: dos a dos, y tres a tres, y como podía las comía. Acabado el racimo, estuvo un poco con el escobajo en la mano y meneando la cabeza dijo:

'Lázaro, engañado me has: juraré yo a Dios que has tú comido las uvas tres a tres.'

'No comí— dije yo— mas ¿por qué sospecháis eso?'

---

1   The day of Saint John was the day proverbially for changing house, master or servant.
2   así.
3   i.e. a stone wall, not valley as Rowland translates.
4   i.e. lo partiremos.
5   mismo.
6   así.

wherein he seemeth to give full understanding of his subtlety[36]. When we departed out of *Salamanca*, his intent was to come to the city of *Toledo*, knowing that the people were richer there than in other places, although not so charitable, yet for all that, leaning to his old proverb: *More giveth the niggard than the naked*, we took our voyage through the best villages we could find, where we found great gain and profit, continuing after such sort a certain time; and whereas we liked not our entertainment[37], the third day we would be sure to take our leave and to end our year[38].

It fortuned at the last, that we arrived to a town called Almorox, at such time as they gathered their grapes[39]; where one of the vineyard gave my master a whole bunch, which by reason of the late time were more than ripe, so that some were ready to fall from the bunch, wherefore he could by no means carry it in his bag, by reason it was so moist. Therefore he determined to make a sumptuous banquet with it, partly because he had no means to carry it with him, and partly because he thought therewith to please me, which had received that day many cruel blows. As soon as we found a valley fit for the purpose, we sat us down, and my master said,

'*Lazaro*, my boy, I will now use a great liberality towards thee; it is my pleasure that both of us shall eat friendly together this bunch of grapes, whereof thy part shall be as much as mine, we will part it after this sort: thou shalt take one grape and I another, promising me faithfully that thou will not take above one at a time, and I will do the like to thee, and so we will quietly end our bunch, without any fraud or guile on either part.'

Upon that condition we agreed and began our banquet. But my master belike forgetting his promise, did soon change purpose, for immediately he began to pick the grapes by two and two, thinking peradventure that I would do like, as he might well think. Indeed I was not far behind him, for as soon as I perceived that he had broken the law, I was not content to go by two and two as he did, but went before him, taking up by two and three together, and sometime more as I was best able. When the bunch was ended, he took the stalk in his hand, and wagging his head, said:

'*Lazaro*, thou hast deceived me, by God thou hast eaten by three and three.'
I utterly denied it, and said,

'Indeed, uncle, it is not true; why should you think so?'

---

36   i.e. cunning.

37   i.e. wherever we were badly received...

38   Literally the Spanish reads 'we would make Saint John'. There was a custom for ending a contract, be it with servants or landlord, on this saint's day, hence Rowland's translation.

39   Almorox (or Almoroj) is a village in the province of Toledo, about 38 miles northwest of that city. It is a wine growing region. The places mentioned in the novel after Salamanca – Almoroj, Torrijos, Escalona, Maqueda – are all on the same road from Salamanca to Toledo. See map.

Respondió el sagacísimo ciego:

'¿Sabes en qué veo que las comiste tres a tres? En que comía yo dos a dos y callabas.'

Reíme entre mí, y aunque mochacho noté mucho la discreta consideración del ciego.

Mas por no ser prolijo dejo de contar muchas cosas, así graciosas como de notar, que con este mi primer amo me acaecieron, y quiero decir el despidiente y con él acabar.

Estábamos en Escalona, villa del duque della, en un mesón, y dióme un pedazo de longaniza que le asase. Ya que la longaniza había pringado y comídose[1] las pringadas, sacó un maravedí de la bolsa y mandó que fuese por él de vino a la taberna. Púsome el demonio el aparejo delante los ojos, el cual, como suelen decir, hace al ladrón, y fue que había cabe el fuego un nabo pequeño, larguillo y ruinoso, y tal que, por no ser para la olla, debió ser echado allí. Y como al presente nadie estuviese sino él y yo solos, como me vi con apetito goloso, habiéndome puesto dentro el sabroso olor de la longaniza, del cual solamente sabía que había de gozar, no mirando qué me podría suceder, pospuesto todo el temor por cumplir con el deseo, en tanto que el ciego sacaba de la bolsa el dinero, saqué la longaniza y muy presto metí el sobredicho nabo en el asador, el cual mi amo, dándome el dinero para el vino, tomó y comenzó a dar vueltas al fuego, queriendo asar al que de ser cocido por sus deméritos había escapado.

Yo fui por el vino, con el cual no tardé en despachar la longaniza, y cuando vine hallé al pecador del ciego que tenía entre dos rebanadas apretado el nabo, al cual aún no había conocido por no lo haber tentado con la mano. Como tomase las rebanadas y mordiese en ellas, pensando también llevar parte de la longaniza, hallóse en frío con el frío nabo. Alteróse y dijo:

---

1 i.e se había comido.

Then he like a crafty blind man answered:

'I did perceive straightways how the matter went, for when I began to take up by two and two, thou never didst find fault, but didst keep silence.'

I then laughed to myself; although I was but young, I considered well his discreet consideration.

Now sir, to avoid long talk, I will leave apart many matters as well pleasant as worthy to be noted, which have fortuned to me with this my first master. I will only tell what happened a little before I departed[40]: we came to *Escalona*, a town of the Duke's[41], and when we were at our lodging, he gave me a piece of a sausage to roast, the which being almost enough, and the fat *Here they use few gridirons but all spits, and do roast overthwart the coals* dropped and pressed out upon thin slices of bread, as the fashion is, and those being eaten, he drew his purse, and boldly drew out a *maravedi*, willing me to fetch the value thereof in wine. The devil who (as they say) is the occasion that men become thieves, was *A maravedi is a sixth part of an English penny.* ready at hand to prepare opportunity to deceive him.

It fortuned that near the fire there lay a little root[42], somewhat long and evil favoured, such a one as belike was not serviceable for the pot, and therefore was left there as abject[43]. And as at that time there was no more but he and I alone, I felt myself pinched with a liquorous[44] appetite, my teeth being set on edge with the sweet savour of his roasted sausage, the which was the only witness that I should be the eater thereof, I not regarding what the sequel might be, leaving aside all manner of fear, for to fulfil my rash desire, in the meanwhile that the blind man was drawing his purse, I whipped off quickly the sausage from the spit, and thereon broached the aforesaid worm–eaten root, which my master most willingly took and began to turn, thinking to roast that which for the goodness was not worthy to be boiled.

So I went for wine, and by the way I made a fair end of my sausage, and as soon as I came in again, I found my master wringing between two slices of bread, the naughty root, not knowing what it was, for with his fingers he had not as yet touched it. Immediately after he had begun to eat, taking a large bit of bread, meaning to have tasted a little of his sausage, but his teeth entered into the root, where he found a cold morsel; whereat he being sore abashed, showed it to me, and said,

---

40   i.e. events leading up to Lazarillo's leaving this master.

41   The Duke of Escalona was a relative of Charles V and an important nobleman, the first of the title dying in 1529, and his son in 1556. The older Duke had supported in Escalona a number of artists and intellectuals, including some of unorthodox Christian views that could be described as pietist or alumbrist. The villages mentioned in the novel cluster in an area associated with this religious unorthodoxy in the 1520's.

42   In the Spanish, a turnip.

43   In its old literal meaning, 'thrown away', 'cast off.'

44   Less common than 'lickerish', or 'liquorish', meaning 'longing', 'greedy'.

'¿Qué es esto, Lazarillo?'

'¡Lacerado de mí![1]— dije yo—. ¿Si queréis a mí echar algo? ¿Yo no vengo de traer el vino? Alguno estaba ahí, y por burlar haría esto.'

'No, no— dijo él— que yo no he dejado el asador de la mano; no es posible.'

Yo torné a jurar y perjurar que estaba libre de aquel trueco y cambio; mas poco me aprovechó, pues a las astucias del maldito ciego nada se le escondía[2].

Levantóse y asióme por la cabeza, y llegóse a olerme; y como debió sentir el huelgo, a uso de buen podenco, por mejor satisfacerse de la verdad, y con la gran agonía que llevaba, asiéndome con las manos, abríame[3] la boca más de su derecho y desatentadamente metía la nariz, la cual él tenía luenga y afilada, y a[4] aquella sazón con el enojo se habían aumentado un palmo, con el pico de la cual me llegó a la gulilla[5]. Y[6] con esto y con el gran miedo que tenía, y con la brevedad del tiempo, la negra longaniza aún no había hecho asiento en el estómago, y lo más principal, con el destiento de la cumplidísima nariz medio cuasi ahogándome, todas estas cosas se juntaron y fueron causa que el hecho y golosina se manifestase y lo suyo fuese devuelto a su dueño: de manera que antes que el mal ciego sacase de mi boca su trompa, tal alteración sintió mi estomago que le dio con el hurto en ella, de suerte que su nariz y la negra malmaxcada[7] longaniza a un tiempo salieron de mi boca.

¡Oh gran Dios, quién estuviera aquella hora sepultado, que muerto ya lo estaba! Fue tal el coraje del perverso ciego que, si al ruido no acudieran, pienso no me dejara con la vida. Sacáronme de entre sus manos, dejándoselas llenas de aquellos pocos cabellos que tenía, arañada la cara y rascuñado el pescuezo y la garganta; y esto bien lo merecía[8], pues por su maldad me venían tantas persecuciones.

---

1   Lázaro puns on his name. Popular etymology incorrectly linked the name to 'lacerar' meaning 'suffer'.

2   ascondía.

3   abrióme.

4   a: not in Antwerp.

5   i.e. golilla, throat.

6   y: not in Antwerp.

7   i.e. mal mascada, poorly chewed.

8   i.e. Lázaro's throat deserved its punishment for leading him into trouble.

'*Lazaro*, what meaneth this?'

I then answered:

'Now Jesus what is this?[45] Alas wretch that I am, do you mean to blame me, you know well that I came but now from the tavern with wine, surely some naughty man hath been here, that hath done this in despite or mockage.'

'No no,' then said he, 'that cannot be possible, for I never let the spit go out of mine own hands.'

Then to clear myself, I began to swear all oaths, that I was innocent of that vile exchange[46]; but all was in vain, for from the subtlety of that ungracious blind man nothing could be kept hid .

He rose up and took fast hold of my head, to smell whether he could feel the savour[47] of his sausage: and as soon as ever he felt occasion to suspect that I had eaten it, he was as glad as a good bloodhound that had his chase in the wind. Wherefore to be better informed of the truth, being sore endued with anger[48], he rashly opened my mouth with the strength of his hands, so that perforce I was fain to gape even to the uttermost; and then he thrusteth with all haste, into my mouth, his worm–eaten nose, which was both long and sharp, yea, which at that time by reason of great anger, was lengthened a long handful, so that the pike[49] thereof did gall my throat. Wherefore, partly by reason of the fear that I was in, and partly because the sausage in such short time was not settled in my stomach, but most of all, by reason of the great trouble[50], which his monstrous nose put me to, wherewith I was in a manner choked, I was forced to discover[51] my gluttony, so that the sausage of necessity returned to his old master again; for my poor stomach was so much altered, that before the blind man had drawn out his hoggish nose, I was even ready to render up the theft. For look as soon as ever he had pulled out his snout, the evil eaten sausage came gushing out after, in honest company.

O mighty God! Who had been then buried, might well have looked for my company, for I was altogether dead; his rage was then so great, that if men had not come in, I think certainly he would have taken away my life. With much ado I got me out of his hands, leaving him with his claws full of that small quantity of hair which I had left (all which torment he most justly deserved, seeing that through his naughtiness[52] I suffered such persecution).

---

45   Not in the original Spanish. Rowland's translation reinforces Biblical parody.

46   i.e. swapping a turnip for a sausage.

47   i.e. catch the breath or smell.

48   The Spanish original conveys that he was suffering agony or anxiety.

49   i.e. tip.

50   The Spanish could also mean 'sounding', 'probing' and 'tickling'!

51   i.e. reveal.

52   i.e. evil conduct. The references to Jesus, God and persecution in this section confirms the parodic echoes of the Bible. Hunger is both physical and metaphorical.

Contaba el mal ciego a todos cuantos allí se allegaban mis desastres, y dábales cuenta una y otra vez, así de la del jarro como de la del racimo, y agora de lo presente. Era la risa de todos tan grande que toda la gente que por la calle pasaba entraba a ver la fiesta; mas con tanta gracia y donaire recontaba[1] el ciego mis hazañas que, aunque yo estaba tan maltratado y llorando, me parecía que hacía sinjusticia en no se las reír.

Y en cuanto esto pasaba, a la memoria me vino una cobardía y flojedad que hice, por que me maldecía, y fue no dejalle sin narices, pues tan buen tiempo tuve para ello que la meitad[2] del camino estaba andado; que con sólo apretar los dientes se me quedaran en casa, y con ser de aquel malvado, por ventura lo retuviera mejor mi estómago que retuvo la longaniza, y no pareciendo ellas pudiera negar la demanda. Pluguiera a Dios que lo hubiera hecho, que eso fuera así que así[3].

Hiciéronnos amigos la mesonera y los que allí estaban, y con el vino que para beber le había traído, laváronme la cara y la garganta, sobre lo cual discantaba el mal ciego donaires, diciendo:

'Por verdad, más vino me gasta este mozo en lavatorios al cabo del año que yo bebo en dos. A lo menos, Lázaro, eres en más cargo al vino que a tu padre, porque él una vez te engendró, mas el vino mil te ha dado la vida.'

Y luego contaba cuántas veces me había descalabrado y harpado la cara, y con vino luego sanaba.

'Yo te digo — dijo — que si un hombre[4] en el mundo ha de ser bienaventurado con vino, que serás tú.'

Y reían mucho los que me lavaban con esto, aunque yo renegaba. Mas el pronóstico del ciego no salió mentiroso, y después acá muchas veces me acuerdo de aquel hombre, que sin duda debia tener spíritu[5] de profecía, y me pesa de los sinsabores que le hice, aunque bien se lo pagué, considerando lo que aquel día me dijo salirme tan verdadero como adelante V.M. oirá.

Visto esto y las malas burlas que el ciego burlaba de mí, determiné de todo en todo dejalle, y como lo traía pensado y lo tenía en voluntad, con este postrer juego que me hizo afirmélo más. Y fue ansí[6], que luego otro día salimos por la villa a pedir limosna, y había llovido mucho la noche antes; y porque el día también llovía, y

---

1   contaba.
2   mitad.
3   i.e. it would have been a good idea to have bitten off his nose.
4   si hombre.
5   espíritu.
6   así.

The ungodly blind man would then declare to as many as came in, my unfortunate disgraces, rehearsing often over, as well the tale of his pot, and of the bunch of grapes, as also this last trick of his sausage. The laughter that men made was so great, that all such as were in the street came in to see the feast[53], where he recited with such grace all my misadventures, that me thought verily I did them great wrong in not laughing for company.

When all this was past, there came to my mind a certain faint and a slothful cowardice, which I had committed in not leaving him noseless, seeing that I had time fit for the purpose. Yea, and that I had gone half the way to do it. For if I had but closed my teeth together, his nose had never gone more abroad; and truly I believe because it was the nose of that naughty man, it would have better agreed with my stomach, than the sausage did, for had it once been invisible, I might well have denied it him again. Now I would to God my teeth had done their part, for it had been better so than otherwise .

The hostess, and other that were there, made us friends, and with the wine that I had brought for his supper, they washed my face, and my throat, which his nails had all torn. Whereat he made much grudging, saying,

'Certainly this boy doth consume me more wine in a year, with washing his wounds, than I do drink in two. Without doubt, *Lazaro*, thou art more bound to wine, than to thy father, for he only begot thee once, and it hath saved thy life a thousand times,' and so declared how many time he had wounded me and healed me again with wine, and then said again:

'I promise thee truly, *Lazaro*, if any man in the world shall have happy chance with wine, it is thou.'

Which words caused those that were there, to laugh heartily, I being still in most sorrowful despair. But look what the blind man prognosticated then, it was not all in vain, for his sayings at that time proved afterwards most true. Wherefore I have oftentimes since called to mind his words, whereby it appeared that he had a great gift in prophesying, and therefore it hath often repented me of my cruel dealing towards him, although his deserts were evil, seeing that his words of prophecy proved so true, as hereafter your worship shall plainly understand.[54]

To conclude, his evil nature and my usage considered, I determined to forsake him for ever, and as I imagined[55] daily thereupon, desirous to depart, this his last deed persuaded me fully thereunto, and the matter chanced to fall out thus. Within two days after, we went through the city to demand men's charities[56], where it had rained much the night before, and because likewise it rained sore that day, my

---

53   i.e. fun, jollity.
54   See the Seventh Treatise (13), where in his prosperity, Lazarillo has the job of crying the wines sold in Toledo. The blind man has a gift of comical prophecy.
55   i.e. thought it through, planned.
56   i.e. begging.

andaba rezando debajo de unos portales que en aquel pueblo había, donde no nos mojamos; mas como la noche se venía y el llover no cesaba, díjome el ciego:

'Lázaro, esta agua es muy porfiada, y cuanto la noche más cierra, más recia. Acojámonos a la posada con tiempo.'

Para ir allá, habíamos de pasar un arroyo que con la mucha agua iba grande. Yo le dije:

'Tío, el arroyo va muy ancho; mas si queréis, yo veo por donde travesemos más aína sin nos mojar, porque se estrecha allí mucho y saltando pasaremos a pie enjuto.'

Parecióle buen consejo y dijo:

'Discreto eres; por esto te quiero bien. Llévame a ese lugar donde el arroyo se ensangosta, que agora es invierno y sabe mal el agua, y más llevar los pies mojados.'

Yo, que vi el aparejo a mi deseo, saquéle debajo de[1] los portales, y llevélo derecho de un pilar o poste de piedra que en la plaza estaba, sobre el cual y sobre otros cargaban saledizos de aquellas casas, y dígole[2]:

'Tío, éste es el paso más angosto que en el arroyo hay.'

Como llovía recio, y el triste se mojaba, y con la priesa que llevábamos de salir del agua que encima de[3] nos caía, y lo más principal, porque Dios le cegó aquella hora el entendimiento (fue por darme dél venganza), creyóse de mí y dijo:

'Ponme bien derecho, y salta tú el arroyo.'

Yo le puse bien derecho enfrente del pilar, y doy un salto y póngome detrás del poste como quien espera tope de toro, y díjele:

'¡Sus! Saltá todo lo que podáis, porque deis deste cabo del agua.'

---

1   debajo (no 'de').
2   díjele.
3   encima (no 'de').

master went praying under certain portals that are there[57], where it was dry. When night did approach, the rain continuing still, he said unto me,

'*Lazaro*, this rain is without end, for the more that night draweth on, the more earnest[58] it is; let us draw homeward to our lodging.'

But as it chanced, we had between us and home, a great wide gutter which the rain had made, wherefore I said,

'Uncle, this gutter is very broad and swift, so that we shall have much ado to pass; notwithstanding, I have now espied one narrow place, where we may well leap over dryfoot.'

He thought verily then, that I had given him good and friendly counsel, and therefore said,

'My good boy, now I perceive thou art wise, I must needs love thee; therefore I pray thee lead me to the narrowest place, where I may best escape, for now in winter it is not good to take water[59], especially to go wet–shod.'

O how glad I was then to see the time which long before I had wished for! Wherefore without delay, I brought him from underneath the portals, and led him right against a great pillar of stone which stood in the market–place, and then said,

'Uncle, this is the very narrowest place of all the gutter. '

Then straightway, by reason of the great rain that fell upon him, and also because of his great haste to be under cover, and chiefly, for that God himself had at that time so blinded his understanding, to give me good time of revengement, he gave full credit to my words and said,

'*Lazaro*, let me see now how thou canst set me where I must take my jump, and then leap thou over on God's name.'[60]

I did so, for when I had taught him his place;[61] I leaped as far as I could and took standing behind the post, as one that had watched the re–encounter of a Bull, and then I said,[62]

'Now, uncle, leap boldly as far as you possibly can, for else you may chance wet yourself.'

---

57   i.e. arcades. Covered walkways may be found still in many Spanish cities, including Alcalà de Henares. The best examples survive in northern cities like Santiago de Compostela and Avilés where there may be monotonous rain for weeks on end.

58   i.e. persistent.

59   Literally, 'water tastes bad'.

60   'On God's name' is an addition of Rowland, again suggesting that he identified the Biblical parody in the text and sought to emphasise it.

61   The Spanish reads 'put him square in front of the pillar'.

62   Literally, the Spanish says that Lazarillo awaits the butt or charge of a bull. The Spanish switches to the present tense for graphic purposes. The Spanish does not give a capital to bull: Rowland possibly identified a framing element in the original Spanish narrative and sought to emphasise it, or to give the practical joke and Lazarillo's experience of this master, a climax.

Aun apenas lo había acabado de decir cuando se abalanza el pobre ciego como cabrón, y de toda su fuerza arremete, tomando un paso atrás de la corrida para hacer mayor salto, y da con la cabeza en el poste, que sonó tan recio como si diera con una gran calabaza, y cayó luego para atrás, medio muerto y hendida la cabeza.

'¿Cómo, y olistes la longaniza y no el poste? ¡Olé! ¡Olé!'[1], le dije yo.

Y dejéle[2] en poder de mucha gente que lo había ido a socorrer, y tomé[3] la puerta de la villa en los pies de un trote, y antes que la noche viniese di conmigo en Torrijos. No supe más lo que Dios dél hizo, ni curé de lo saber.

Tratado Segundo

Cómo Lázaro se asentó con un clérigo, y de las cosas que con él pasó

Otro día, no pareciéndome estar allí seguro, fuime a un lugar que llaman Maqueda, adonde me toparon mis pecados con un clérigo que, llegando a pedir limosna, me preguntó si sabía ayudar a misa. Yo dije que sí, como era verdad; que, aunque maltratado, mil cosas buenas me mostró el pecador del ciego, y una dellas fue ésta. Finalmente, el clérigo me recibió por suyo. Escapé del trueno y di en el relámpago, porque era el ciego para con éste un Alejandro Magno, con ser la mesma[4] avaricia, como he contado.

No digo más sino que toda la laceria del mundo estaba encerrada en éste. No sé si de su cosecha era, o lo había anexado con el hábito de clerecía. Él tenía un arcaz

---

1   Olé is ambiguous, it could be a shout of triumph or a command to smell!
2   déjole.
3   tomo.
4   misma.

I had not so soon said the word, but that incontinently[63] the poor blind man was ready to take his race[64], returning a pace or two back from the standing, and so with great force took his leap, throwing forward his body like a buck[65], that at the last his head took such a monstrous blow against the cruel stony pillar, that his head sounded withal as it had been a leather bottle[66], whereupon he fell back with his cloven pate, half dead. Then gave I a leap and said,

'How now, uncle, could you smell the sausage so well, and why not the pillar, I pray you? Prove now a little what you can do.'[67]

So I left him there between the hands of many men that came in all haste to help him, and took my ready way straight towards the town gate with no slow pace, and then trotted so fast forward, that before night I arrived at *Torrijos*.[68] After that time I never understood nor yet sought to know what God almighty did with him.

Second Treatise

How Lazaro placed himself with a Priest, and what thing happened to him in his service.

The next day, after doubting of mine own safety there, I departed thence and went to a village which is called *Maqueda*[1], where I met for my sins with a priest, who as soon as he espied how that I demanded alms, did inquire whether I could help to[2] mass. I answered saying, 'Yea sir, that I can', as truth it was, for although the blind man had used me scarce well, he taught me to do a thousand feats, whereof this was one. The priest received me for his own; so I escaped then from the thunder and came into the tempest, yea and God knoweth, how from evil, to ten times worse, for the blind man was in comparison of this master, a great *Alexander*[3], howbeit, he was so covetous a niggard, as heretofore I have rehearsed.

All the misery in the world was enclosed within this wretched priest. I know not whether it was his own harvest, or whether he acquired it with his clerical habit.

---

63   i.e. forthwith.

64   i.e make his run or charge.

65   The Spanish in fact says 'like a male goat' or 'billy–goat' a strong term of sexual abuse, too.

66   Literally, a pumpkin or gourd.

67   Thus Rowland renders the Spanish; Olé!, a cry of triumph 'bravo' and ambiguously also meaning 'smell'!

68   Torrijos is about 23 miles northwest of Toledo.

1   Maqueda is half–way between Escalona and Torrijos, on the same road, north west of Toledo.

2   i.e. with

3   Alexander the Great was a classical model of generosity.

viejo y cerrado con su llave, la cual traía atada con un agujeta del paletoque[1], y en viniendo el bodigo[2] de la iglesia, por su mano era luego allí lanzado, y tornada a cerrar el arca. Y en toda la casa no había ninguna cosa de comer, como suele estar en otras: algún tocino colgado al humero, algún queso puesto en alguna tabla o en el armario, algún canastillo con algunos pedazos de pan que de la mesa sobran; que me parece a mí que aunque dello no me aprovechara, con la vista dello me consolara. Solamente había una horca de cebollas, y tras la llave en una cámara en lo alto de la casa. Destas tenía yo de ración una para cada cuatro días; y cuando le pedía la llave para ir por ella, si alguno estaba presente, echaba mano al falsopecto y con gran continencia la desataba y me la daba diciendo:

'Toma, y vuélvela luego, y no hagáis sino golosinar', como si debajo della estuvieran todas las conservas de Valencia, con no haber en la dicha cámara, como dije, maldita la otra cosa que las cebollas colgadas de un clavo, las cuales él tenía tan bien por cuenta, que si por malos de mis pecados me desmandara a más de mi tasa[3], me costara caro.

Finalmente, yo me finaba de hambre. Pues, ya que conmigo tenía poca caridad, consigo usaba más. Cinco blancas de carne era su ordinario[4] para comer y cenar. Verdad es que partía comigo del caldo, que de la carne, ¡tan blanco el ojo![5], sino un poco de pan, y ¡pluguiera a Dios que me demediara![6] Los sábados cómense en esta tierra cabezas de carnero, y enviábame por una que costaba tres maravedís. Aquélla le cocía y comía los ojos y la lengua y el cogote y sesos y la carne que en las quijadas tenía, y dábame todos los huesos roídos, y dábamelos en el plato, diciendo:

'Toma, come, triunfa, que para ti es el mundo. Mejor vida tienes que el Papa'.

'¡Tal te la dé Dios!', decía yo paso entre mí.

---

1   i.e. a kind of cape.
2   i.e. bread commonly offered by women, but not holy.
3   i.e. exceeded my allowance.
4   i.e. daily budget.
5   i.e. Lázaro's plate was white like his eye!
6   i.e. would to God it had met half my needs.

For he had always a great old coffer, wherein he continually locked with a key which did hang at the point of his coat, all the bread[4] that came from the church at offerings, forgetting at no time to leave the same locked, being his only storehouse and buttery.[5] For about all the house a man might discern nothing that could be eaten, neither bacon hung in the chimney, nor cheeses laid upon shelves, nor yet broken bread in some odd corner, as commonly in other houses one should find, which things, so that I might have seen and not tasted, the sight would have comforted me much. All the provision he had was a rose of onions in a high garret, kept also under sure lock and key; my allowance was only an onion every four days. And when I should come for the key to take my due, if there were any stranger by, he would thrust his hand into his bosom, and with much modesty[6] would say,

'Take the key, see it be immediately delivered me again, thou dost nothing but cram up meat.' So that he that had heard him, would have judged there had been under the custody of that key, all the confectures of *Valencia*.[7] But for anything that was there, beside the rope of onions that hung on a nail, the devil himself might have had part, and of them he kept such strait account, that if I had taken at any time more than my ordinary[8], I should dearly have bought it.[9]

After that I had continued a while with him, I was ready everyhour to fall down dead for hunger. His use was, to dine and sup with as much flesh as mounted to the value of five blanks, whereof I was sure never to taste, unless it were of the broth, which sometimes he would friendly part between us, and so for bread, I would to God I might have had half as much as was sufficient. Upon Saturdays, as the *A blank the twelfth part of an English penny. The custom is there upon Saturday to eat the heads, the feet and the bowels of all beasts with his licence.* custom was in that city, he would send it me for a sheep's head that should cost three maravedies, whereof when it was sodden[10], he would eat both the eyes, the tongue, and the brain, yea, and all the *Two blanks, a maravedi.* flesh on both the cheek bones. Then reaching me the platter, with a few naked bones, would say,

'Take down this to thee, and rejoice, seeing that thou hast the world at will.[11] I am sure the Pope himself hath now no better life than thou hast.'

Then would I answer him, with low voice: 'God send thee always the like.'

---

4   i.e. bread given to the church in honour of the dead.
5   Rowland's translation is free here; the last six words are his additions.
6   i.e. hesitation.
7   Valencia was famous for candied fruits, sweets and jams.
8   i.e. allowance.
9   i.e. paid dear.
10 i.e. cooked by boiling. Since the Middle Ages, there was some abstention from meat on Saturdays as a penance in Spain except in Castile, where the heads, giblets and feet of animals by custom were eaten.
11 An echo of Biblical parody, literally 'Take, eat, rejoice, for yours is the world'.

A cabo de tres semanas que estuve con él, vine a tanta flaqueza que no me podía tener en las piernas de pura hambre. Vime claramente ir a la sepultura, si Dios y mi saber no me remediaran. Para usar de mis mañas no tenía aparejo, por no tener en qué dalle salto; y aunque algo hubiera, no podía[1] cegalle, como hacía al que Dios perdone, si de aquella calabazada feneció, que todavía, aunque astuto, con faltalle aquel preciado sentido no me sentía; mas estotro, ninguno hay que tan aguda vista tuviese como él tenía. Cuando al ofertorio estábamos, ninguna blanca en la concha caía que no era dél registrada: el un ojo tenía en la gente y el otro en mis manos. Bailábanle los ojos en el caxco[2] como si fueran de azogue. Cuantas blancas ofrecían tenía por cuenta; y acabado el ofrecer, luego me quitaba la concheta y la ponía sobre el altar. No era yo señor de asirle una blanca todo el tiempo que con él veví[3] o, por mejor decir, morí. De la taberna nunca le traje una blanca de vino, mas aquel poco que de la ofrenda había metido en su arcaz compasaba de tal forma que le turaba[4] toda la semana, y por ocultar su gran mezquindad decíame:

'Mira, mozo, los sacerdotes han de ser muy templados en su comer y beber y por esto yo no me desmando como otros.'

Mas el lacerado mentía falsamente, porque en cofradías[5] y mortuorios que rezamos, a costa ajena comía como lobo y bebía más que un saludador. Y porque dije de mortuorios, Dios me perdone, que jamás fui enemigo de la naturaleza humana sino entonces, y esto era porque comíamos bien y me hartaban. Deseaba y aun rogaba a Dios que cada día matase el suyo. Y cuando dábamos sacramento a los enfermos, especialmente la extrema unción, como manda el clérigo rezar a los que están allí, yo cierto no era el postrero de la oración, y con todo mi corazón y buena voluntad rogaba al Señor, no que la echase[6] a la parte que más servido fuese, como se suele decir, mas que le llevase de aqueste mundo[7]. Y cuando alguno de éstos

---

1   pudiera.
2   i.e. casco
3   i.e. viví.
4   duraba.
5   confradías.
6   le echase. Burgos seems to refer to Lázaro's prayer, Antwerp, to the dying man.
7   deste mundo.

I had not dwelt with him three weeks, but I was so lean that my legs were scarce able to bear me; the hunger was so great which I sustained, that I never thought to escape death, unless that God's help and mine own industry would find some remedy to save my life. And for to use my accustomed subtlety, there was no wherewithal, seeing that there was nothing there to give assault unto. Yea, although there had been, I might never have been able to deceive him, as I had done the poor blind man, upon whom I pray God take mercy if he be dead with his last blow. For howbeit he was crafty, yet wanting his precious sight, I was sure he could never see what I hourly did. But there was never man that had quicker eyesight than this priest. For at offering time, the silver was not so soon fallen into the basin, but that straight he had it registered, having always one eye to my hand, and another to the people; and his eyes would so roll in his head, as if they had been of quicksilver. As soon as offering was done he would take the basin out of my hands, and lay it upon the altar, so that I was never able to deceive him of one blank. And whiles I continued with him (or to say better), whiles that I consumed myself in this miserable service, he never sent me to the tavern for as much as the value of a blank of wine, but that small quantity which he had offered on the Sunday[12], he kept always in his coffer so sparingly, that it would last him all the week over. And for to hide his covetousness, he would sometimes say unto me,

'My boy, all priests ought to be sober in eating and drinking and therefore I dare not break order[13] as many other do.'

Now you shall see how the miser lied falsely therein, for at burials and dirges[14], where he had meat at other men's charges, and would eat like a wolf, more than four men, and drink as it were a Saluter[15]; and because his office was always to say dirge, at such time (God forgive me) I was *A Saluter is a kind of drunken prophets in Spain which take upon them the healing of mad dogs, etc* always an enemy to human nature[16], and only because that then we should fare well, and have meat at liberty[17], I wished and prayed God that he would every day call up one to heaven. When we went to minister the Sacrament to such as were sick, my master would desire those that were there, to pray for the sick man, surely I was never one of the last that prayed, desiring God with all my heart, not that he would do to the patient according to his will (as others prayed), but that he would dispatch him out of the world; and when any of them escaped death, I was ready (God

---

12   i.e. the wine left over from mass.

13   i.e. indulge myself.

14   i.e. the food and drink that followed burial of a member of a church guild or funeral service.

15   'Saluter' is Rowland's translation of quack. Quacks used spittle for healing and were therefore notorious for thirst.

16   i.e. unlike his fellow human beings, Lazarillo prayed that the sick would die, because then he would eat better.

17   i.e. liberally.

escapaba, ¡Dios me lo perdone!, que mil veces le daba al diablo, y el que se moría otras tantas bendiciones llevaba de mí dichas. Porque en todo el tiempo que allí estuve, que sería[1] cuasi seis meses, solas veinte personas fallecieron, y éstas bien creo que las maté yo o, por mejor decir, murieron a mi recuesta; porque viendo el Señor mi rabiosa y continua muerte, pienso que holgaba de matarlos por darme a mí vida. Mas de lo que al presente padecía, remedio no hallaba, que si el día que enterrábamos yo vivía, los días que no había muerto, por quedar bien vezado de la hartura, tornando a mi cuotidiana hambre, más lo sentía. De manera que en nada hallaba descanso, salvo en la muerte, que yo también para mí como para los otros deseaba algunas veces; mas no la vía, aunque estaba siempre en mí.

Pensé muchas veces irme de aquel mezquino amo, mas por dos cosas lo dejaba: la primera, por no me atrever a mis piernas, por temer de la flaqueza que de pura hambre me venía; y la otra, consideraba y decía:

'Yo he tenido dos amos: el primero traíame muerto de hambre y, dejándole, topé con estotro, que me tiene ya con ella en la sepultura. Pues si deste desisto y doy en otro más bajo, ¿qué será sino fenecer?'

Con esto no me osaba menear, porque tenía por fe que todos los grados había de hallar más ruines; y a abajar otro punto, no sonara Lázaro ni se oyera en el mundo.

Pues, estando en tal aflición, cual plega al Señor librar della a todo fiel cristiano, y sin saber darme consejo, viéndome ir de mal en peor, un día que el cuitado ruin y lacerado de mi amo había ido fuera del lugar, llegóse acaso a mi puerta un calderero, el cual yo creo que fue ángel enviado a mí por la mano de Dios en aquel hábito. Preguntóme si tenía algo que adobar.

'En mí teníades[2] bien que hacer, y no haríades poco si me remediásedes', dije paso, que no me oyó; mas como no era tiempo de gastarlo en decir gracias, alumbrado por el Spíritu[3] Santo, le dije:

'Tío, una llave de este arte he perdido, y temo mi señor me azote. Por vuestra vida, veáis si en ésas que traéis hay alguna[4] que le haga, que yo os lo pagaré.'

---

1   serían.
2   i.e. old Spanish forms for teníais, haríais and remediáseis.
3   espíritu.
4   algunas.

forgive me) to wish him at the devil, and whosoever died *Lazaro had not cared* was sure to have of me many blessings and prayers for his *though the King had died* soul. I dwelt with this master about six months, and in that *that he might have had* time there died only twenty persons, which I certainly slew, *meat to stay his hunger.* or at the least, the earnest request of my prayers was cause of their death; for God the father perceiving the raging hunger which I continually sustained, rejoiced (as I think) to slay them, to save my life thereby, considering that otherwise my disease could not be remedied, for I was never at ease, but when we had burials. The day that there was none, my teeth should have no work; but my heart would faint, because that I had been used sometimes to have my belly filled. At such times I found ease in nothing but in death, which then I wished, as well for myself, as I had done before for the sick men.[18]

I determined oftentimes to depart from that miserable master, yet fearing so to do for two causes, first, because I durst not trust my legs, which by hunger were brought to great weakness, secondly, considering with myself , saying,

'I have had two masters, with the first I died for hunger, whom when I had forsaken I chanced upon this other, which with the very same disease hath almost brought me to my grave.'

Therefore I made account that if I should forsake the second and meet with a third that were worse than these two, then there were no remedy but plain death. Wherefore I never durst depart from him, being assured to find all estates worse and worse, knowing that to descend another degree, *Lazaro* should soon be forgotten, being once rid out of this world.

And being in such affliction (God of his grace deliver *Lazaro was a good* every faithful Christian from the like) not knowing how to *Christian, believing that* counsel myself, my misery daily increasing, upon a day, *all goodness came from* when by chance my wretched master had gone abroad, there *God.* arrived by chance to the door a tinker, which I believe was an angel disguised, sent from God, who demanded for[19] work. I answered softly,

'Thou hast enough to amend in me, and I believe more than thou canst do.'
But as it was no time then to delay the matter (by inspiration[20] of the Holy Ghost), I said unto him,

'Uncle, I have lost the key of this coffer, I fear that my master will beat me, for God's sake look amongst your keys if there be any that will open it, I will consider your pains.'

---

18   Rowland leaves out that Lazarillo did not see death face to face, though it hovered very close.

19   i.e. asked for jobs.

20   Interestingly, the Spanish uses the word 'alumbrado', the same as was used for the pietist religious movement.

Comenzó a probar el angélico calderero una y otra de un gran sartal que dellas traía, y yo ayudalle con mis flacas oraciones. Cuando no me cato, veo en figura de panes, como dicen, la cara de Dios dentro del arcaz; y, abierto, díjele:

'Yo no tengo dineros que os dar por la llave, mas tomad de ahí el pago.'

Él tomó un bodigo de aquellos, el que mejor le pareció, y dándome mi llave se fue muy contento, dejándome más a mí.

Mas no toqué en nada por el presente, porque no fuese la falta sentida, y aun, porque me vi de tanto bien señor, parecióme que la hambre no se me osaba allegar[1]. Vino el mísero de mi amo, y quiso Dios no miró en la oblada que el ángel había llevado.

Y otro día, en saliendo de casa, abro mi paraíso panal, y tomo entre las manos y dientes un bodigo, y en dos credos le hice invisible, no se me olvidando el arca abierta; y comienzo a barrer la casa con mucha alegría, pareciéndome con aquel remedio remediar dende en adelante la triste vida. Y así estuve con ello aquel día y otro gozoso.

Mas no estaba en mi dicha que me durase mucho aquel descanso, porque luego al tercero día me vino la terciana derecha, y fue que veo a deshora al que me mataba de hambre sobre nuestro arcaz volviendo y revolviendo, contando y tornando a contar los panes.

Yo disimulaba, y en mi secreta oración y devociones y plegarias decía: '¡Sant Juan y ciégale!'

Después que estuvo un gran rato echando la cuenta, por días y dedos contando, dijo:

'Si no tuviera a tan buen recado esta arca, yo dijera que me habían tomado della panes; pero de hoy más, sólo por cerrar la puerta a la sospecha, quiero tener buena cuenta con ellos: nueve quedan y un pedazo.'

'¡Nuevas malas te dé Dios!', dije yo entre mí.

---

1   llegar.

The heavenly[21] tinker began to assay[22], now one key, now another, of his great bunch, and I helped with my prayers, so that immediately before I was aware, he opened it; whereof I was so glad, that methought I did see in figure (as they say), the face of God, when I beheld the bread within it.[23]

And when he had done all, I said unto him, 'I have no money, but take this for thy payment.'

So he took one of his fairest loaves, and after he had delivered me the key, he departed right well pleased, and I as well content as he.

At that time I touched nothing[24], partly because I perceived myself to be the lord of such treasure, that by reason of that key hunger durst never again approach me. Incontinently[25] after, who cometh in but my unhappy master, and as God would, he never took heed of the loaf which the heavenly tinker[26] had borrowed.

The next day after, as soon as he went abroad, I began to open my paradise of bread[27], and what between my hands and teeth, with the twinkling of an eye[28] I made a loaf invisible, forgetting in no wise to lock the chest again. Then I began cheerfully to sweep the house, judging by such remedy I might ease my sorrowful life. So I passed that day and the next, with much mirth.

But my contrary Fortune went about to hinder me to enjoy such pleasure long, for the third day just, a tercian ague came upon me, in perceiving him that had slain me with hunger, at an undue hour, over the chest, turning and tossing, accounting and reckoning his bread.

I dissembled the matter, as I had not perceived him, and in my secret prayer and devotion, I prayed Saint John[29] to blind him.

And after that he had been a good while casting his account upon his fingers, he said unto me,

'If it were not that this coffer is so sure, I would say that some of my bread hath been taken away, but from henceforth I will keep good account of it, there is now nine loaves besides a broken piece.'

Then said I with low voice, 'Nine evils[30] God send unto thee.'

---

21   literally angelic, like a good angel disguised.

22   i.e. try, test.

23   The religious parody continues: Lazarillo sees the countenance of God in the loaves of bread. This section is rich in sacramental ironies against the Adoration of the Blessed Sacrament in the Tabernacle or Monstrance.

24   'partly that the loss should not be noticed', left out by Rowland.

25   i.e. straightway, immediately.

26   The Spanish reads 'the angel'.

27   a more precise reading might be 'breadly paradise' on the model of earthly.

28   Literally, the original means 'in the time it takes to recite the Creed twice'. As already noted, Rowland mutes the religious satire in places.

29   i.e the patron saint of servants.

30   More literally, 'evil tidings', 'misfortune'.

Parecióme con lo que dijo pasarme el corazón con saeta de montero, y comenzóme el estómago a escarbar de hambre, viéndose puesto en la dieta pasada. Fue fuera de casa; yo, por consolarme, abro el arca, y como vi el pan, comencélo a adorar, no osando recebillo. Contélos, si a dicha el lacerado se errara, y hallé su cuenta más verdadera que yo quisiera. Lo más que yo pude hacer fue dar en ellos mil besos y, lo más delicado que yo pude, del partido partí un poco al pelo que él estaba; y con aquél pasé aquel día, no tan alegre como el pasado.

Mas como la hambre creciese, mayormente que tenía el estómago hecho a más pan aquellos dos o tres días ya dichos, moría mala muerte; tanto que otra cosa no hacía en viéndome solo sino abrir y cerrar el arca y contemplar en aquella cara de Dios, que ansí[1] dicen los niños. Mas el mesmo[2] Dios, que socorre a los afligidos, viéndome en tal estrecho, trujo[3] a mi memoria un pequeño remedio; que, considerando entre mí, dije:

'Este arquetón es viejo y grande y roto por algunas partes, aunque pequeños agujeros. Puédese pensar que ratones, entrando en él, hacen daño a este pan. Sacarlo entero no es cosa conveniente, porque verá la falta el que en tanta me hace vivir. Esto bien se sufre.'

Y comienzo a desmigajar el pan sobre unos no muy costosos manteles que allí estaban; y tomo uno y dejo otro, de manera que en cada cual de tres o cuatro desmigajé su poco; después como quien toma gragea, lo comí, y algo me consolé.

Mas él, como viniese a comer y abriese el arca, vio el mal pesar, y sin dubda[4] creyó ser ratones los que el daño habían hecho, porque estaba muy al propio[5] contrahecho de como ellos lo suelen hacer. Miró todo el arcaz de un cabo a otro y viole ciertos agujeros por do[6] sospechaba habían entrado. Llamóme, diciendo:

'¡Lázaro! ¡Mira, mira qué persecución ha venido aquesta noche por nuestro pan!'

Yo híceme muy maravillado, preguntándole qué sería.

'¡Qué ha de ser! — dijo él — Ratones, que no dejan cosa a vida.'

Pusímonos a comer, y quiso Dios que aun en esto me fue bien, que me cupo más pan que la laceria que me solía dar, porque rayó[7] con un cuchillo todo lo que pensó ser ratonado, diciendo:

'Cómete eso, que el ratón cosa limpia es.'

---

1   así.
2   mismo.
3   i.e. trajo.
4   duda.
5   proprio.
6   i.e. donde.
7   i.e. ralló, grated.

It seemed unto me with that which he had said, my heart to be pierced through with an arrow[31], and my stomach began to rive for hunger[32], perceiving how I was put to my former diet. He then departed out, and I opened the said coffer to comfort myself a little, and beholding the bread, which I durst not receive, but worshipping it[33], I beheld and counted it over, to see if the wretch had over–reckoned himself; but I found his account more just than I would have wished it by the one half. The most that I could do, was to give it a thousand kisses, and to cut a little delicately of that place where it was cut before; and with that I passed over that day, yet not so merrily as I did the other.

But now because two or three days before I had bread at will, the appetite in my stomach did increase in such sort, that I was almost dead for hunger; wherefore being alone, I did nothing but open and lock again the coffer, beholding always that bread as a God[34]. And God himself which succoureth those that are afflicted, seeing me in such necessity, brought a little remedy to my memory, which was, that I remembered with myself this coffer to be old and broken in many places, and although the holes were little, yet might it be thought that mice had entered therein to damage the bread. And to take out a whole loaf, the wretch would soon espy the fault, yet this may be better borne withal. So then I began to claw the bread with my nails, upon a simple napkin that was there, taking one loaf and leaving another, so that of every third or fourth, I would be sure to take some crumbs, and even as if they were confects[35] I did swallow the same, to comfort my stomach.

When he should come to dinner, opening his chest, and espying incontinently the hurt, he did judge that rats had done that spoil[36], for I had so counterfeited their gnawing, that any man would have thought the same; wherefore he sought all corners of the chest, and at the last he espied certain holes where he suspected they had entered. Whereupon he called me in all haste, saying,

'*Lazaro*, see here what persecution hath been done this night upon our bread.'
I began to marvel, demanding what it should be.

'What should it be,' said he, 'but rats, which leave nothing whole?'[37]
We went then to dinner, and as God would I had better allowance than I was wont, for with his knife he pared away all that he thought the mice had touched, saying,

'Take, eat this, my boy; mice are clean.'

---

31 Literally, a hunting arrow.
32 i.e. split painfully, rumble.
33 The sacramental irony continues: Lazarillo uses the language of the mass, a community act of worship from which he is excluded.
34 Again Rowland mutes the religious parody. The Spanish suggests that Lazarillo contemplated the bread as the countenance of God.
35 As in 'liquorice comfits'; sugar candy.
36 i.e. damage.
37 i.e. leave nothing alone.

Y así aquel día, añadiendo la ración del trabajo de mis manos, o de mis uñas, por mejor decir, acabamos de comer, aunque yo nunca empezaba. Y luego me vino otro sobresalto, que fue verle andar solícito, quitando clavos de las paredes[1] y buscando tablillas, con las cuales clavó y cerró todos los agujeros de la vieja arca.

'¡Oh, Señor mío! — dije yo entonces — ¡a cuánta miseria y fortuna y desastres estamos puestos los nacidos, y cuán poco turan[2] los placeres de esta nuestra trabajosa vida! Heme aquí que pensaba con este pobre y triste remedio remediar y pasar mi laceria, y estaba ya cuanto que alegre y de buena ventura; mas no quiso mi desdicha, despertando a este lacerado de mi amo y poniéndole más diligencia de la que él de suyo se tenía (pues los míseros por la mayor parte nunca de aquella carecen), agora, cerrando los agujeros del arca, cierrase[3] la puerta a mi consuelo y la abriese a mis trabajos.'

Así lamentaba yo, en tanto que mi solícito carpintero con muchos clavos y tablillas dio fin a sus obras, diciendo: 'Agora, donos[4] traidores ratones, conviéneos mudar propósito, que en esta casa mala medra tenéis.'

De que salió de su casa, voy a ver la obra y hallé que no dejó en la triste y vieja arca agujero ni aun por donde le pudiese entrar un moxquito[5]. Abro con mi desaprovechada llave, sin esperanza de sacar provecho, y vi los dos o tres panes comenzados, los que mi amo creyó ser ratonados, y dellos todavía saqué alguna laceria, tocándolos muy ligeramente, a uso de esgremidor[6] diestro. Como la necesidad sea tan gran maestra, viéndome con tanta, siempre, noche y día, estaba pensando la manera que ternía[7] en sustentar el vivir; y pienso, para hallar estos negros remedios, que me era luz la hambre, pues dicen que el ingenio con ella se avisa y al contrario con la hartura, y así era por cierto en mí.

Pues estando una noche desvelado en este pensamiento, pensando como me podría valer y aprovecharme del arcaz, sentí[8] que mi amo dormía, porque lo mostraba con roncar y en unos resoplidos grandes que daba cuando estaba durmiendo. Levantéme muy quedito y, habiendo en el día pensado lo que había de hacer y dejado un cuchillo viejo que por allí andaba en parte do le hallase, voyme al triste arcaz, y por do había mirado tener menos defensa le acometí con el cuchillo, que a manera de barreno dél usé. Y como la antiquísima arca, por ser de tantos años,

---

1   de paredes.
2   i.e. duran.
3   cerrase.
4   i.e. dones
5   i.e. mosquito.
6   i.e. esgrimidor.
7   i.e. tendría.
8   sintí.

I chanced that day to fare better, for he augmented my allowance with that which I had made by the travail of my hands, or to say truth, of my nails. We ended our dinner for all that somewhat too soon, yet there came another plunge[38] upon me, perceiving how the priest was earnest in pulling nails out of the wall, and seeking little boards to stop the holes again. Wherefore I said to myself:

'Lord God, unto how many perils and calamities of Fortune are human creatures subject! How short a time do the pleasures of our troublesome life last! Lo, where I am now, which trusted by this my poor remedy, to ease my misery, being in best hope of good adventure, my evil luck would not consent, but opened the sight of my covetous master's understanding, causing his to have more subtle wit than he had given him by nature, although such wretches are commonly subtle enough.[39]

When he had dummed up[40] the holes, I thought this chest should be shut to my comfort, and opened to my pain, and therefore I never left lamenting, until that the curious carpenter with his company of boards had ended his work of nailing, and when he had done he said:

'Now, ye traitorly mice, you must change purpose, for there is no more profit for you in this house.'

As soon as he went abroad, I went to view his work, and I perceived that he had not left in his old chest one hole unstopped, not so much as a place for a fly to get in. Notwithstanding without hope of gain, I opened the chest with my unprofitable[41] key, and there visited two loaves begun, which he had thought the mice had carved, and from them once again I scraped a little quantity, touching them lightly like a nimble master of defence[42], for necessity at that time my mistress, caused me day and night to imagine how I might live and seek remedy for my sore, whereunto hunger taught me the way, which commonly maketh men have ready wits.

I began then to study about my affairs, seeking means to draw some commodity out of the said covetous[43] coffer. Perceiving one night that my master slept soundly (or at least made me believe so) by his snorting and blowing, I rose to my feet, and as I had taken order with myself the day before what should be done that night, I had left an old knife which was cast about the house, in a place where it might be found at need, and went to that happy[44] coffer; and where it seemed to have least defence, I gave the assault with my rusty knife, which served my turn well for a gimlet. But the chest by reason of good years, being weak, without

---

38   i.e. crisis, difficulty.

39   Rowland catches the parody of Biblical lamentation of the original.

40   i.e. sealed.

41   i.e. of no use, useless.

42   i.e. in the manner of a skilled fencer, swordsman.

43   Not in the Spanish. Rowland means that Lazarillo wished to take advantage of the stingy coffer.

44   Probably an original typographical error. Read 'unhappy.'

la hallase sin fuerza y corazón, antes muy blanda y carcomida, luego se me rindió, y consintió en su costado por mi remedio un buen agujero. Esto hecho, abro muy paso la llagada arca y, al tiento, del pan que hallé partido hice según deyuso está escrito. Y con aquello algún tanto consolado, tornando a cerrar, me volví a mis pajas, en las cuales reposé y dormí un poco, lo cual yo hacía mal, y echábalo al no comer; y ansí[1] sería, porque cierto en aquel tiempo no me debían de quitar el sueño los cuidados del rey de Francia.

Otro día fue por el señor mi amo visto el daño así del pan como del agujero que yo había hecho, y comenzó a dar a los diablos[2] los ratones y decir:

'¿Qué diremos a esto? ¡Nunca haber sentido ratones en esta casa sino agora!'

Y sin dubda[3] debía de decir verdad; porque si casa había de haber en el reino justamente de ellos privilegiada[4], aquélla de razón había de ser, porque no suelen morar donde no hay qué comer. Torna a buscar clavos por la casa y por las paredes y tablillas a atapárselos. Venida la noche y su reposo, luego era yo[5] puesto en pie con mi aparejo, y cuantos él tapaba de día, destapaba yo de noche. En tal manera fue, y tal priesa[6] nos dimos, que sin dubda por esto se debió decir: 'Donde una puerta se cierra, otra se abre.' Finalmente, parecíamos tener a destajo la tela de Penélope, pues cuánto él tejía de día, rompía yo de noche; ca[7] en pocos días y noches pusimos la pobre despensa[8] de tal forma, que quien quisiera propiamente[9] della hablar, más corazas viejas de otro tiempo que no arcaz la llamara, según la clavazón y tachuelas sobre sí tenía.

De que vio no le aprovechar nada su remedio, dijo:

'Este arcaz está tan maltratado y es de madera tan vieja y flaca, que no habrá ratón a quien se defienda; y va ya tal que, si andamos más con él, nos dejará sin guarda; y aun lo peor, que aunque hace poca, todavía hará falta faltando, y me pondrá en costa de tres o cuatro reales. El mejor remedio que hallo, pues el de hasta aquí no aprovecha, armaré por dentro a estos ratones malditos.'

---

1   así.
2   al diablo.
3   duda.
4   previlegiada.
5   yo era.
6   i.e. prisa.
7   i.e. because Antwerp reads 'y'.
8   dispensa.
9   propriamente.

strength, very soft and tender, did straightway render and consent that I should make for my commodity[45] a good hole in the side of it, and that done, opening the wounded chest, and knowing every loaf severally by the touch, I did as I had done before, and by that means being somewhat comforted, having locked the chest again, I returned to my pallet, whereupon I slept little, and (as I think) mine evil supper was cause for that, for otherwise, at that time of the night the King of France[46] his cares could never break me of my sleep.

On the morning the priest my master perceiving the hurt which was done as well to the bread as to the coffer, began to curse the mice, saying:

'What meaneth this? There was never mouse wont to go here before now.'

And certainly his words were true, for if any house in the whole Kingdom might be privileged from mice it might be his, for mice are never wont to dwell where no parings of meat do fall. But now he began again to seek nails about the ways[47], and little boards, to make defence against the traitorous mice. But as soon as night came that he went to his rest, I rose up with my tools, and look[48] what he stopped in the day time, I broke up again in the night. Finally, the one and the other of us took such pain, that this proverb was fulfilled: when one door is shut the other openeth. At the last, we seemed to have *Penelope's*[49] web in hand, whatsoever he wrought in the day, I undid again in the night, in so much that we brought the poor coffer[50] to such estate[51], that whosoever would properly talk of it, might compare it to an old boat or brigantine[52], for that number of old nails that were driven into each side of it.

When he saw his remedy prevailed not, he said:

'This coffer is so old and so weak, that it is no longer able to defend our victuals from vermin; it is now at that point that if I meddle anymore with it, the more it will decay, and so at length be able to do us no service at all, and peradventure evil fortune will cause me to spend two or three shillings to buy another. The best remedy that I can find, seeing this doth not prevail, is to set up a trap within it, to take these cruel[53] rats.'

---

45   i.e. advantage.

46   The reference to the King of France could be proverbial or mean François I, defeated by Charles V at Pavia in 1525 and taken prisoner

47   i.e. wherever he could find them.

48   i.e. Lo! not in the original and possibly a Welsh English expression

49   To defeat her unwelcome suitors, Penelope, wife of Ulysses, undid by night the cloth she wove by day.

50   Spanish reads 'larder'.

51   i.e. state, condition.

52   Rowland embellishes. Strictly, armour or a vessel's armour plating.

53   i.e. merciless, accursed.

Luego buscó prestada una ratonera, y con cortezas de queso que a los vecinos pedía, contino el gato estaba armado dentro del arca, lo cual era para mí singular auxilio; porque puesto caso que yo no había menester muchas salsas para comer, todavía me holgaba con las cortezas del queso que de la ratonera sacaba, y sin esto no perdonaba el ratonar del bodigo.

Como hallase el pan ratonado y el queso comido y no cayese el ratón que lo comía, dábase al diablo, preguntaba a los vecinos qué podría ser comer el queso y sacarlo de la ratonera, y no caer ni quedar dentro el ratón, y hallar caída la trampilla del gato. Acordaron los vecinos no ser el ratón el que este daño hacía, porque no fuera menos de haber caído alguna vez. Díjole un vecino:

'En vuestra casa yo me acuerdo que solía andar una culebra, y ésta debe ser sin dubda[1]. Y lleva razón que como es larga, tiene lugar de tomar el cebo; y aunque la coja la trampilla encima, como no entre toda dentro, tórnase a salir.'

Cuadró a todos lo que aquél dijo, y alteró mucho a mi amo; y dende en adelante no dormía tan a sueño suelto, que cualquier gusano de la madera que de noche sonase, pensaba ser la culebra que le roía el arca. Luego era puesto en pie, y con un garrote que a la cabecera, desde que aquello le dijeron, ponía, daba en la pecadora del arca grandes garrotazos, pensando espantar la culebra. A los vecinos despertaba con el estruendo que hacía y a mí no me dejaba dormir. Íbase a mis pajas y trastornábalas, y a mí con ellas, pensando que se iba para mí y se envolvía en mis pajas o en mi sayo, porque le decían que de noche acaecía a estos animales, buscando calor, irse a las cunas donde están criaturas y aun mordellas y hacerles peligrar. Yo las más veces hacía del dormido, y en las mañanas decíame él:

'Esta noche , mozo, ¿no sentiste nada? Pues tras la culebra anduve, y aun pienso se ha de ir para ti a la cama, que son muy frías y buscan calor.'

'Plega a Dios que no me muerda — decía yo — que harto miedo le tengo.'

Desta manera andaba tan elevado y levantado del sueño, que, mi fe, la culebra (o culebro[2], por mejor decir) no osaba roer de noche ni levantarse al arca; mas de día, mientras estaba en la iglesia o por el lugar, hacía mis saltos: los cuales daños viendo él y el poco remedio que les podía poner, andaba de noche, como digo, hecho trasgo.

---

1   duda.
2   el culebro.

Whereupon he went immediately and borrowed one of his neighbour's, which he had continually bent[54] within the coffer, with a bait of cheese–paring, which was laid only for my comfort and ease; for although I could well have eaten my bread alone, without the help of anything else to cause my appetite, yet the cheese–paring which I would pull out of the trap gave me trim taste with my mouse–eaten bread. But when he should perceive the bread so spoiled with rats, and the cheese eaten, and the rat that did the deed not taken, then would he wish the trap at the devil, demanding of his neighbours what it might be, that the cheese should be eaten, and the rat not taken, yea, and the trap fallen? The neighbours would answer that it was no rat that did that harm, for at one time or other she had been taken[55]. And amongst the rest one said,

Snakes are wont there to resort much to men's houses for food.

'I do remember that a snake was wont to haunt your house, and by all reason it is she that hath done the deed, for she being long, might easily eat the cheese, and although the trap did fall, yet because her body entered not in all, she might well and easily get out and escape.

This neighbour's saying did satisfy the whole company, and especially my master, which from that time forward never slept one night soundly, for when he had heard the least noise amongst the wood, he would think that it were the snake gnawing the coffer, wherefore he would straight be up with a cudgel, which since he entered into such suspicion, was always ready at his bed's head, wherewith he would beat the poor coffer so hard, to fear the snake, that he waked all the neighbours with the noise. And as for me, I never slept, for oftentimes in the night he would turn me and my pallet over and over, thinking that the snake had gotten thither into my bed or into my apparel, for he was informed, that those beasts oftentimes seeking heat, have come into children's cradles, and bitten them to death. I would always make as though I slept: then he would in the morning say unto me:

'*O Lazaro*, hast thou heard no noise this night? I did pursue the snake, and I was afraid he had gotten into thy bed; for they are cold, and therefore seek heat.' Then answered I:

'I pray God she hath not bitten me[56]. I fear snakes as the devil.'

He continued in such fearful fantasy that he never slept, so that I being the snake, durst never approach the coffer, but only in the daytime, whilst he was at church or abroad in the town, then would I make my assault; whereof when we had knowledge, perceiving that he was not able to find any further remedy, would every night (as I have told you) be raging mad.

---

54 He kept the mousetrap set.

55 i.e. would have been caught. In Spanish, a mouse is a small rat, hence Rowland uses 'rat' and 'mouse' interchangeably.

56 i.e. she will not bite me. The commonest Spanish word for snake is feminine. There is clear parody in introducing a snake into a paradise of bread.

Yo hube miedo que con aquellas diligencias no me topase con la llave que debajo de las pajas tenía, y parecióme lo más seguro metella[1] de noche en la boca. Porque ya, desde que viví con el ciego, la tenía tan hecha bolsa, que me acaeció tener en ella doce o quince maravedís, todo en medias blancas, sin que me estorbasen[2] el comer; porque de otra manera no era señor de una blanca que el maldito ciego no cayese con ella, no dejando costura ni remiendo que no me buscaba muy a menudo. Pues ansí[3], como digo, metía cada noche la llave en la boca, y dormía sin recelo que el brujo de mi amo cayese con ella; mas cuando la desdicha ha de venir, por demás es diligencia.

Quisieron mis hados, o por mejor decir mis pecados, que una noche que estaba durmiendo, la llave se me puso en la boca, que abierta debía tener, de tal manera y postura, que el aire y resoplo que yo durmiendo echaba salía por lo hueco de la llave, que de cañuto era, y silbaba, según mi desastre quiso, muy recio, de tal manera que el sobresaltado de mi amo lo oyó y creyó sin duda ser el silbo de la culebra; y cierto lo debía parecer.

Levantóse muy paso con su garrote en la mano, y al tiento y sonido de la culebra se llegó a mí con mucha quietud, por no ser sentido de la culebra; y como cerca se vio, pensó que allí en las pajas do yo estaba echado, al calor mío se había venido. Levantando bien el palo, pensando tenerla debajo y darle tal garrotazo que la matase, con toda su fuerza me descargó[4] en la cabeza un[5] tan gran golpe, que sin ningún sentido y muy mal descalabrado me dejó.

Como sintió que me había dado, según yo debía hacer gran sentimiento[6] con el fiero golpe, contaba él que se había llegado a mí y dándome grandes voces, llamándome, procuró recordarme. Mas como me tocase con las manos, tentó la mucha sangre que se me iba y conoció el daño que me había hecho, y con mucha priesa fue a buscar lumbre. Y llegando con ella, hallóme quejando, todavía con mi llave en la boca, que nunca la desamparé, la mitad fuera, bien de aquella manera que debía estar al tiempo que silbaba con ella.

Espantado el matador de culebras qué podría ser aquella llave, miróla, sacándomela del todo de la boca, y vio lo que era, porque en las guardas[7] nada de la suya diferenciaba. Fue luego a proballa[8], y con ella probó el maleficio. Debió de decir el cruel cazador: 'El ratón y culebra que me daban guerra y me comían mi hacienda he hallado.'

---

1   i.e. meterla.
2   estorbase.
3   así.
4   descarga.
5   not in Antwerp.
6   i.e. groans.
7   i.e. the wards of the key.
8   i.e probarla.

All that I feared then was, that he with his diligence would meet with my privy key which I had hid under the bedstraw. But for more sure, at night time I would always keep it in my mouth, for when that I dwelt with the blind man, I had brought my mouth to such use by conveying money into it, that it served me often for a purse. I can well remember, when sometimes I have had in it fourteen or fifteen deniers[57], and not hindering my eating, otherwise I had never been master of a denier, but that the cursed blind man would have found out, not leaving one seam or a wrinkle of my coat unsought. Therefore as I tell you, I did every night put the key in my mouth for a safeguard, and by that means slept soundly, not fearing that he should find it. Notwithstanding, when that the evil hour could not be escaped, my diligence was all but vain.[58]

It pleased my fatal destiny (or to say truth my sins), that upon a night when I was asleep, the key happened so to turn in my mouth, being wide open , in such sort, that my breath coming forth through the hole in the key, which was hollow, made such loud whistling (as evil fortune would[59]) that my careful[60] master heard it, who thought certainly that it had been the hissing of the snake (as surely it might be like). He rose up very softly holding his cudgel fast, and by the noise of the hissing came by little and little straight to me, without making any noise, to the intent the snake should not hear him. When he was near me, he thought certainly that the snake was there in the straw, wherefore he lifted up his cudgel to kill her, and with all his strength he discharged upon my head such a cruel blow, that he wounded me to death.

Whereupon, he knowing that he had stricken me, belike by the groaning that I made after the receipt of the blow, suspecting what had happened, cried out to awake me, but as soon as he touched me with his hands, he felt abundance of blood issue out of my head. Wherefore considering what hurt he had done me, he went in haste for a candle, and returning with it in his hand, found me groaning and gasping with my key in my mouth, which I never let go, being half out, even as it was when it made such hissing.

Whereat the killer of snakes marvelled, especially when he beheld the key, which he took out of my mouth, and viewing it, he perceived what it was, for in workmanship it differed nothing from his. But for more surety he went straight to prove it, and so then espied the whole deceit. God knoweth then how he bragged, that he had taken the rat and the snake that had made him such war, and that so destroyed his bread.

---

57   The French coin, an eighth of a sou. This may betray Rowland's use of Samgrain's French translation. The Spanish coin was the 'maravedi' (see page 85 for Rowland's own note).

58   Literally the Spanish reads, 'when bad luck must come, precaution is fruitless.'

59   i.e. as my bad luck would have it.

60   i.e. painstaking, wary. The Spanish reads startled, aroused.

De lo que sucedió en aquellos tres días siguientes ninguna fe daré, porque los tuve en el vientre de la ballena; mas de cómo esto que he contado oí, después que en mí torné, decir a mi amo[1], el cual a cuantos allí venían lo contaba por extenso.

A cabo de tres días yo torné en mi sentido y vime echado en mis pajas, la cabeza toda emplastada y llena de aceites y ungüentos y, espantado, dije: '¿Qué es esto?'

Respondióme el cruel sacerdote:

'A fe, que los ratones y culebras que me destruían ya los he cazado.'

Y miré por mí, y vime tan maltratado que luego sospeché mi mal.

A esta hora entró una vieja que ensalmaba[2], y los vecinos, y comiénzanme a quitar[3] trapos de la cabeza y curar el garrotazo. Y como me hallaron vuelto en mi sentido, holgáronse mucho y dijeron:

'Pues ha tornado en su acuerdo, placerá a Dios no será nada.'

Ahí tornaron de nuevo a contar mis cuitas y a reírlas, y yo, pecador, a llorarlas. Con todo esto diéronme de comer, que estaba transido de hambre, y apenas me pudieron remediar[4]. Y ansí, de poco en poco, a los quince días me levanté y estuve sin peligro, mas no sin hambre, y medio sano.

Luego otro día que fui levantado, el señor mi amo me tomó por la mano y sacóme la puerta fuera y, puesto en la calle, díjome:

'Lázaro, de hoy más eres tuyo y no mío. Busca amo y vete con Dios, que yo no quiero en mi compañía tan diligente servidor. No es posible sino que hayas sido mozo de ciego.'

Y santiguándose de mí como si yo estuviera endemoniado, tórnase[5] a meter en casa y cierra su puerta.

---

1   i.e. mas [daré fe] de cómo, después que en mí torné, esto que he contado [lo] oí decir a mi amo, el cual.
2   i.e. she prayed for Lázaro's recovery.
3   a quitar: not in Antwerp.
4   demediar.
5   se torna.

What happened the three days following, I am not able to tell, for I was as it were in a whale's belly[61], but only this that I have told you, which I had heard my master report, after that I was returned to myself, for he declared the whole matter to as many as came in and out.

The third day after, I began to recover, marvelling much, when I perceived myself being in my straw, my head full of plasters, oils, and ointments, and being thereat amazed, I said: 'What meaneth this?'

The[62] priest then answered,

'The meaning of this is, that I have chased away the rat and the snake that have done me such hurt.'

Then calling to mind my affairs, I suspected my hurt, and the cause thereof; then came there in an old woman[63], with certain of the neighbours, to undo the clouts about my head, and to dress my wounds, and being glad to see me recovered, said: 'There is no danger now in him[64], seeing that he hath his senses.'

They began then to recite my afflictions, they laughing and I[65] weeping. After all this, they gave me meat, I being almost dead for hunger. Much ado they had to recover me, but by little and little I waxed strong, and at fifteen days' end, I rose up and was out of danger, yet not without hunger, howbeit half healed.

The next day after that I rose, my master took me by the hand, and brought me out at the door, and leaving me in the street, said unto me:

'*Lazaro*, from this day forth, thou shalt be at thine own liberty, and not under my subjection, the Lord be with thee; go seek thee a master, I have no need of such a diligent servant. It is not possible, but that thou hast been servant to some blind man.'

And therewith blessing himself from me[66], as though I had been possessed with some evil spirit, he getteth him in and locketh fast his door.

---

61   The reference to Jonah pursues the religious parody. See *Jonah*, 1.17 and *Matthew*, 12.40.

62   Rowland again softens the Spanish, which reads 'the cruel priest'.

63   The Spanish explicitly says that the old woman cured with prayers, a fact perhaps that was intended to contrast with the unChristian conduct of the priest.

64   Literally, 'God will be pleased [that] it will be nothing.'

65   ' Sinner that I was', suppressed by Rowland.

66   i.e. crossing himself.

Tratado Tercero

Cómo Lázaro se asentó con un escudero, y de lo que le acaeció con él

Desta manera me fue forzado sacar fuerzas de flaqueza y, poco a poco, con ayuda de las buenas gentes di comigo en esta insigne ciudad de Toledo, adonde con la merced de Dios dende a quince días[1] se me cerró la herida; y mientras estaba malo, siempre me daban alguna limosna, mas después que estuve sano, todos me decían:

'Tú, bellaco y gallofero[2] eres. Busca, busca un amo a quien sirvas.'

'¿Y adónde se hallará ése — decía yo entre mí — si Dios agora de nuevo, como crió el mundo, no le criase?

Andando así discurriendo de puerta en puerta, con harto poco remedio, porque ya la caridad se subió al cielo, topóme Dios con un escudero que iba por la calle con razonable vestido, bien peinado, su paso y compás en orden. Miróme, y yo a él, y díjome:

'Mochacho, ¿buscas amo?'

Yo le dije: 'Sí, señor.'

'Pues vente tras mí — me respondió — que Dios te ha hecho merced en topar comigo. Alguna buena oración rezaste hoy.'

Y seguíle, dando gracias a Dios por lo que le oí, y también que me parecía, según su hábito y continente, ser el que yo había menester.

Era de mañana cuando este mi tercero amo topé, y llevóme tras sí gran parte de la ciudad. Pasábamos[3] por las plazas do se vendía pan y otras provisiones. Yo pensaba y aun deseaba que allí me quería cargar de lo que se vendía, porque ésta era propria hora cuando se suele proveer de lo necesario; mas muy a tendido paso pasaba por estas cosas. 'Por ventura no lo[4] vee aquí a su contento — decía yo — y querrá que lo compremos en otro cabo.'[5]

---

1   i.e. a fortnight later.
2   i.e. idler, originally a poor pilgrim who received alms from a monastery.
3   pasamos.
4   no le.
5   i.e. place, part of town.

Third Treatise

How Lazaro placeth himself to serve a Squire[1], and what happened to him in his service.

By this means I was forced to help myself being weak, and shortly after, I came by help of good people, to this noble city of Toledo, where[2] (I thank God) my wound closed up. As long as I was sick, every man gave me his charity, but after that I was once whole, every man would say, 'Thou vagabond and loiterer, why dost thou not seek a master?' Then I murmuring with myself, would say, 'And where the devil shall I find him, unless God, as he made the world, make me one?' But now I demanding alms from door to door for God's sake, I found little remedy, for charity had then ascended up to heaven .

At the last God caused me to meet with a squire which walked through the street, in very sumptuous[3] apparel, and cleanly, his pace in going well measured after good order[4]. He beheld me and I him, and he said unto me:

'Boy, dost thou want a master?'

I answered: 'I would fain have a good master, sir.'

'Then follow me,' said he: 'God hath sent thee good fortune to meet with me, thou hast prayed well this day.'

I thanked God, for that which I had heard him say, and for that he seemed by his behaviour and countenance to be even he, that I had so much longed for.

I met with this third master betime in the morning, and he led me after him through the most part of the city. We passed through the market–place, where there was sold bread, and other provisions; I looked when he would have laden me there with meat[5]; for it was then that every man provided and *Gentlemen use to buy their meat in the market themselves.* bought things necessary for their dinner. But with comely and large pace went he by, and left that place behind him. Then I said to myself, 'Peradventure he doth not see here that which doth content him, he not will buy in another place.' We so

---

1   Within the tradition of chivalry, a squire was a young man of gentle birth, intending to become a knight, who in preparation, attended upon a knight and carried his shield. In peacetime in sixteenth century Spain, squires might wait upon ladies or have some office in a noble household. They were often proverbial for poverty. In the present context, the Squire perhaps represents the lowest rung of the nobility and a military caste made increasingly redundant by professional armies and the growth of capitalism.

2   ' A fortnight later' (omitted).

3   'Cleanly' would be a better rendering, alone. Rowland has added 'very sumptuous'.

4   The Elizabethan and Jacobean dramatists especially associated Spaniards with a measured gait indicative of pride.

5   i.e. food, necessaries.

Desta manera anduvimos hasta que dio las once. Entonces se entró en la iglesia mayor, y yo tras él, y muy devotamente le vi oír misa y los otros oficios divinos, hasta que todo fue acabado y la gente ida. Entonces salimos de la iglesia.

A buen paso[1] tendido comenzamos a ir por una calle abajo. Yo iba el más alegre del mundo en ver que no nos habíamos ocupado en buscar de comer. Bien consideré que debía ser hombre, mi nuevo amo, que se proveía en junto, y que ya la comida estaría a punto y tal como yo la deseaba y aun la había menester.

En este tiempo dio el reloj la una después de mediodía, y llegamos a una casa ante la cual mi amo se paró, y yo con él; y derribando el cabo de la capa sobre el lado izquierdo, sacó una llave de la manga y abrió su puerta y entramos en casa; la cual tenía la entrada obscura y lóbrega de tal manera que parece[2] que ponía temor a los que en ella entraban, aunque dentro della estaba un patio pequeño y razonables cámaras.

Desque fuimos entrados, quita de sobre sí su capa y, preguntando si tenía las manos limpias, la sacudimos y doblamos, y muy limpiamente soplando un poyo que allí estaba, la puso en él. Y hecho esto, sentóse cabo della, preguntándome muy por extenso de dónde era y cómo había venido a aquella ciudad; y yo le di más larga cuenta que quisiera, porque me parecía más conveniente hora de mandar poner la mesa y escudillar la olla que de lo que me pedía. Con todo eso, yo le satisfice de mi persona lo mejor que mentir supe, diciendo mis bienes y callando lo demás, porque me parecía no ser para en cámara.

Esto hecho, estuvo ansí[3] un poco, y yo luego vi mala señal, por ser ya casi las dos y no le ver más aliento de comer que a un muerto. Después desto, consideraba aquel tener cerrada la puerta con llave ni sentir arriba ni abajo pasos de viva persona por la casa. Todo lo que yo [4]había visto eran paredes, sin ver en ella silleta, ni tajo[5], ni banco, ni mesa, ni aun tal arcaz como el de marras[6]: finalmente, ella parecía casa encantada.

---

1   y a buen paso.

2   parecía.

3   así.

4   yo: not in Antwerp.

5   i.e. a chopping block.

6   i.e. of former days.

walked long that the clock struck eleven, then went he to the *There is not such* chief church, and I after him, where I saw him most *provision of meat in Spain* devoutly hear service[6]. When all was ended, and the people *as there is in. England* departed, he came out of the church and marched leisurely down a street: and as for me, I went joyfully, the best content in the world, perceiving *He went so late to the* how that we did not stay to seek our dinner, imagining that *church to tarry that his* this my new master had been some great personage, and that *dinner might be made* he had his house provided before hand, that we should find *ready.* dinner ready, yea, such as I desired, and as I had need of.[7]

At this time the clock struck one after noon, when we arrived at a house before which my master had stayed[8], I with him; then he throwing his cloak over his left shoulder very civilly[9], drew out a key out of his sleeve to open his door.

We then entered in, the entrance whereof was so dark and unhandsome[10], that it might fear any man living to enter in, howbeit, there was within it a pretty little court and reasonable chambers; and when we were within, he putteth off his cloak, and demanding me whether my hands were clean, we shook it, and then doubled it handsomely[11], and after he had blown cleanly the dust away from an old bench[12] that was there, he laid it up.

That being done, he sat him down, demanding of me at large what countryman I was, and how I came to the city. I gave him a larger account than I was willing; for I thought it a more convenient time to command me to lay the cloth and take out pottage, than to make such inquiries. Yet for all that, bringing forth the best lies I could frame for myself, I made him account what I was, reckoning all the goodness that was in my personage, leaving apart all that which I thought was not to be rehearsed in that place. When I had declared all he stayed awhile, and by that time I did see an evil sign; for it was almost two o'clock, and yet he was no readier to dine than he that had been dead. I marvelled moreover, when I perceived that he had locked his door with his key, and that I could not hear any living creature stir, neither above, not beneath; all that ever I *As the Priest had.* did see was the naked walls, not so much as a chair or stool[13], not a table, nor yet a coffer, as the other man had. Finally you would have said, it had been a house, not inhabited.[14]

---

6   The Spanish more explicitly says that he heard mass and other divine services.
7   Again the theme of hunger.
8   i.e. stopped, halted.
9   Again, Rowland's addition.
10   i.e. dismal, gloomy. Indeed, the Spanish word 'lóbrega' is a key word in the Third Treatise and has associations with death.
11   Rowland's additions, both.
12   Literally, a stone seat against a wall
13   Or chopping block for meat (omitted).
14   Literally, 'bewitched'.

Estando así, díjome: 'Tú, mozo, ¿has comido?'

'No, señor — dije yo — que aún no eran dadas las ocho cuando con vuestra merced encontré.'

'Pues, aunque de mañana, yo había almorzado, y cuando ansí[1] como algo, hágote saber que hasta la noche me estoy ansí[2]. Por eso, pásate como pudieres, que despúes cenaremos.'

Vuestra merced crea, cuando esto le oí, que estuve en poco de caer de mi estado, no tanto de hambre como por conocer de todo en todo la fortuna serme adversa. Allí se me representaron de nuevo mis fatigas, y torné a llorar mis trabajos; allí se me vino a la memoria la consideración que hacía cuando me pensaba ir del clérigo, diciendo que aunque aquél era desventurado y mísero, por ventura toparía con otro peor: finalmente, allí lloré mi trabajosa vida pasada y mi cercana muerte venidera. Y con todo, disimulando lo mejor que pude[3]:

'Señor, mozo soy que no me fatigo mucho por comer, bendito Dios. Deso me podré yo alabar entre todos mis iguales por de mejor garganta,y ansí[4] fui yo loado della fasta[5] hoy día de los amos que yo he tenido.'

'Virtud es ésa — dijo él — y por eso te querré yo más; porque el hartar es de los puercos y el comer regladamente es de los hombres de bien.'

'¡Bien te he entendido! — dije yo entre mí — '¡maldita tanta medicina y bondad como aquestos mis amos que yo hallo hallan en la hambre!'

Púseme a un cabo del portal y saqué unos pedazos de pan del seno, que me habían quedado de los de por Dios[6].

El, que vio esto, díjome:

'Ven acá, mozo. ¿Qué comes?'

Yo lleguéme a él y mostréle el pan. Tomóme él un pedazo, de tres que eran el mejor y más grande, y díjome:

'Por mi vida, que parece éste buen pan.'

'¡Y cómo! ¿Agora — dije yo — señor, es bueno?'

'Sí, a fe — dijo él — ¿Adónde lo hubiste? ¿Si es amasado de manos limpias?'

---

1   así.
2   así.
3   Antwerp adds: le dije.
4   así.
5   hasta.
6   i.e. those that I had begged.

A while after he had demanded me whether I had dined, I answered, saying:

'No, sir, for it was not eight o'clock when I met with your mastership this morning.'

'Then,' said he, 'as early as it was, I had broken my fast, and whensoever I break my fast in the morning, I never eat again until it be night, therefore pass thou over the time as well as thou canst, and we will make amends at supper.'[15]

Your worship may think that when I heard these words I was ready to fall down dead, not so much for hunger, as for plainly perceiving, that then fortune was altogether mine enemy. Then began my sorrows to appear unto me again, and I to lament my misfortune; then came there to my mind, the consideration that I made when I was about to depart from the priest, weighing with myself, that although he was most wretched and miserable, yet peradventure I might meet with a worse; finally, I lamented and wept my trouble-some life that was past, and my death that did approach. And yet for all this I disembled the matter as well as I could, and said unto him:

Poor Lazaro did bear his master's dinner and his own in his bosom for fear of losing it.

'Sir, I thank God, I am a boy that doth not greatly care for eating and drinking, for I may well compare with any of my age for soberness and measure in eating, and so I have been always esteemed of[16] as many masters as I have served.'

He then answered, saying:

'It is a virtue to live soberly, therefore I commend thee much. Hogs fill themselves, and wise men eat discreetly[17] what is only sufficient for them.'

'I now understand you well, sir,' said I to myself, 'evil luck light upon such virtue and goodness as these my masters do find in hunger.'

Immediately after all this[18], I conveyed myself behind the door, where I drew certain pieces of bread out of my bosom, which were left of that I had received for God's sake[19] two days before.

But he perceiving me, said,

'Come hither, boy, what dost thou eat?'

I came unto him, and did shew the bread, whereof he took a piece, which of two[20] or three was the best and the biggest, saying,

'By my soul, methinks this bread is good and savorous[20].'

'Yea marry, sir, at this time especially,' said I.

'It is so indeed,' said he, 'but where hadst thou it? Was it moulded with clean hands?'

---

15   Elizabethan and Jacobean dramatists also seized upon the material destitution of Spaniards.

16   i.e. by.

17   i.e. temperately, moderately.

18   Rowland's addition.

19   i.e. from begging.

20   Addition of Rowland.

'No sé yo eso — le dije — mas a mí no me pone asco el sabor dello.'

'Así plega a Dios', dijo el pobre de mi amo.

Y llevándolo a la boca, comenzó a dar en él tan fieros bocados como yo en lo otro.

'Sabrosísimo pan está — dijo — por Dios.'

Y como le sentí de qué pie coxqueaba[1], dime priesa, porque le vi en disposición, si acababa antes que yo, se comediría a ayudarme a lo que me quedase; y con esto acabamos casi a una. Y mi amo[2] comenzó a sacudir con las manos unas pocas de migajas, y bien menudas, que en los pechos se le habían quedado, y entró en una camareta que allí estaba, y sacó un jarro desbocado y no muy nuevo, y desque hubo bebido convidóme con él. Yo, por hacer del continente, dije:

'Señor, no bebo vino.'

'Agua es — me respondió, — Bien puedes beber.'

Entonces tomé el jarro y bebí, no mucho, porque de sed no era mi congoja. Ansí[3] estuvimos hasta la noche, hablando en cosas que me preguntaba, a las cuales yo le respondí lo mejor que supe. En este tiempo metióme en la cámara donde estaba el jarro de que bebimos, y díjome:

'Mozo, párate allí y verás cómo hacemos esta cama, para que la sepas hacer de aquí adelante.'

Púseme de un cabo y él del otro y hecimos la negra cama, en la cual no había mucho que hacer, porque ella tenía sobre unos bancos un cañizo, sobre el cual estaba tendida la ropa que, por no estar muy continuada a lavarse, no parecía colchón, aunque servía dél, con harta menos lana que era menester. Aquél tendimos, haciendo cuenta de ablandalle, lo cual era imposible, porque de lo duro mal se puede hacer blando. El diablo del enjalma[4] maldita la cosa tenía dentro de sí, que puesto sobre el cañizo todas las cañas se señalaban y parecían a lo proprio entrecuesto de flaquísimo puerco; y sobre aquel hambriento colchón un alfamar[5] del mesmo [6]jaez, del cual el color yo no pude alcanzar.

Hecha la cama y la noche venida, díjome:

---

1   i.e. cojeaba literally 'on which foot he limped', 'what his weakness was'.
2   mi amo: not in Antwerp.
3   así.
4   i.e. mattress.
5   i.e. blanket or coverlet.
6   mismo.

'That I know not,' said I, 'howbeit I find it good.'

'I pray God it be clean,' said the poor gentleman, and with that putting his hand to his mouth, devoured quickly all that I had given him; and somewhat before we had ended, he said, 'By God, this bread hath a good taste, how savorous it is.'

And as for me, when I perceived upon which foot he halted[21], I made haste to eat, perceiving him to be so disposed, that if he had made an end before me, I thought he would gently have offered to help me; therefore we ended both at one time in good order.

He began with his hand to brush away a few crumbs, which had fallen upon his breast, and after that entered into a chamber that was there, and thence brought forth an old pot broken mouthed, and drank well and then he offered me the pot.

But I to seem sober and modest, said:

'Sir, I drink no wine.'

'It is water,' said he, 'thou mayest well drink of it.'

Then I took the pot, but I drank not much, for it was not thirst, but hunger troubled me.

In Spain many drink nothing but water and some that may have wine, but this squire drank it for want of better.

We passed the time so until it was night, reasoning of sundry matters which he demanded of me, whereunto I answered as well as I could. Then we entered into the chamber from whence he had brought forth his drinking pot, he saying:

'Boy, go to the other side, and mark how we make this bed, that thou mayest know how to make it from henceforth.'

I went to the one side and he to the other, and made the poor bed, which was an easy matter to do, for it was thus as I will tell you. A sheep's hurdle laid overthwart two trestles, a silly rotten hard mattress[22], and upon that his bedclothes, which by reason of seldom washing could not be discerned in colour from the mattress, the which had not half so much wool as need required. We turned it to make it soft, but that was impossible to do, for very hard it is for a man to make a hard thing soft, and the devil a thing was within the cruel mattress at all, for when it was spread upon the hurdle of big sticks, every stick appeared through, even as like as could be to the ribs of a carrion lean hog. We spread upon the hungry miserable mattress a coverlet suitable to the rest of the stuff, what stuff[23] it was of, I cannot well devise[24].

Before that we had made the bed it was night, and he said:

---

21   i.e. what his weakness was.

22   Addition of Rowland; 'silly' means 'homely' or 'frail'.

23   'Colour' in the Spanish.

24   i.e. guess.

'Lázaro, ya es tarde, y de aquí a la plaza hay gran trecho. También en esta ciudad andan muchos ladrones que siendo de noche capean[1]. Pasemos como podamos y mañana, venido el día, Dios hará merced; porque yo, por estar solo, no estoy proveído, antes he comido estos días por allá fuera, mas agora hacerlo hemos de otra manera.'

'Señor, de mí — dije yo — ninguna pena tenga vuestra merced, que sé pasar una noche y aun[2] más, si es menester, sin comer.'

'Vivirás más y más sano — me respondió — porque, como decíamos hoy, no hay tal cosa en el mundo para vivir mucho que comer poco.'

'Si por esa vía es — dije entre mí — nunca yo moriré, que siempre he guardado esa regla por fuerza, y aun espero en mi desdicha tenella toda mi vida.'

Y acostóse en la cama, poniendo por cabecera las calzas y el jubón, y mandóme echar a sus pies, lo cual yo hice; mas ¡maldito el sueño que yo dormí! Porque las cañas y mis salidos huesos en toda la noche dejaron de rifar y encenderse, que con mis trabajos, males y hambre, pienso que en mi cuerpo no había libra de carne; y también, como aquel día no había comido casi nada, rabiaba de hambre, la cual con el sueño no tenía amistad. Maldíjeme mil veces — ¡Dios me lo perdone! — y a mi ruin fortuna, allí lo más de la noche, y (lo peor) no osándome revolver por no despertalle, pedí a Dios muchas veces la muerte.

La mañana venida, levantámonos, y comienza a limpiar y sacudir sus calzas y jubón y[3] sayo y capa,y yo que le servía de pelillo[4], y vístese[5] muy a su placer de espacio. Echéle aguamanos, peinóse y puso[6] su espada en el talabarte y, al tiempo que la ponías díjome:

'¡Oh, si supieses, mozo, qué pieza es ésta! No hay marco de oro en el mundo por que yo la diese. Mas ansí[7], ninguna de cuantas Antonio hizo, no acertó a ponelle los aceros tan prestos[8] como ésta los tiene.'

Y sacóla de la vaina y tentóla con los dedos, diciendo:

'¿Vesla aquí? Yo me obligo con ella cercenar un copo de lana.'

Y yo dije entre mí:

'Y yo con mis dientes, aunque no son de acero, un pan de cuatro libras.'

---

1   i.e. steal.
2   y más: not in Antwerp.
3   y: not in Antwerp.
4   i.e. attending to him in small matters.
5   vísteseme.
6   púsose.
7   así.
8   i.e. ready for action, sharp.

'*Lazaro*, it is now late, and from hence to the market–place where provision of meat is sold, it is a long way, and besides that ruffians and thieves do meet men every night to spoil[25] them of their cloaks and caps in the dark, therefore let us pass over this night as well as we may, tomorrow God will provide better for us. I am not provided of meat because I have been hitherto alone without a servant, and I have always taken my meals in the City, but from henceforth we will keep a new order.'

The streets are narrow and dark, few lanterns are hung out.

'Sir,' said I, 'take no care for me, I can pass over one night, and more if need be without meat.[26]'

'And that will be cause that thou shalt live longer,' said he, 'for as wise men affirm, there is nothing that can make a man live longer than to eat a little.'

'If that be true,' said I to myself, 'I shall never die, for I have always been constrained to keep that rule, and I think I am fortuned to observe it as long as I live.'

After all this he went to bed, making his hose and his doublet his bolster, and causing me to lie at his feet, where I never slept a wink, for the hard hurdle never left galling my naked bones, which by hunger and sorrow together had not left on them, nor yet on all my body besides, an ounce of flesh; and as I chanced to eat nothing

Hunger is always an enemy to sleep.

that day, my brain was so light, that I could never take rest. Wherefore (God forgive me) I cursed myself and my fortune a thousand times, and that which was worse than all this, I never durst change sides for fear of waking him; wherefore I desired death.[27]

The next morning when he rose, he began to shake and to make clean his hose, his doublet, and his cloak, I was his brush[28], so he arrayed himself at leisure. I gave him then water for his hands, and when he had occupied[29] his comb, he taketh his sword and kisseth the pommel[30], and as he was putting it to his girdle, said unto me:

'My boy, if thou knewest what a blade this is, thou wouldest marvel, there is no gold that can buy it of me, for of as many as *Antonio*[31] made, he could never give such temper to any as he gave this.'

Then drawing it out of the scabbard he tested the edge with his fingers, saying,

'Seest thou it? I dare undertake to cut asunder with it a whole fleece of wool.'

I answered him softly to myself, saying: 'And I with my teeth though they be not of such hard metal, a loaf of bread weighing four pound.'

---

25   i.e. steal, rob.

26   i.e food.

27   Literally, 'I asked God for death'

28   i.e. served as a humble assistant.

29   i.e. used.

30   These actions are additions of Rowland.

31   A famous sword–maker of Toledo in the fifteenth century.

Tornóla a meter y ciñósela y un sartal de cuentas gruesas del talabarte, y con un paso sosegado y el cuerpo derecho, haciendo con él y con la cabeza muy gentiles meneos, echando el cabo de la capa sobre el hombro y a veces so[1] el brazo, y poniendo la mano derecha en el costado, salió por la puerta, diciendo:

'Lázaro, mira por la casa en tanto que voy a oír misa, y haz la cama, y ve por la vasija de agua al río, que aquí bajo está, y cierra la puerta con llave, no nos hurten algo, y ponla aquí al quicio[2], porque si yo viniere en tanto pueda entrar.'

Y súbese por la calle arriba con tan gentil semblante y continente, que quien no le conociera pensara ser muy cercano pariente al conde de Arcos, o a lo menos camarero que le daba de vestir.

'¡Bendito seáis vos, Señor — quedé yo diciendo — que dais la enfermedad y ponéis el remedio! ¿Quién encontrara a aquel mi señor que no piense, según el contento de sí lleva, haber anoche bien cenado y dormido en buena cama, y aunque agora es de mañana, no le cuenten por muy[3] bien almorzado? ¡Grandes secretos son, Señor, los que vos hacéis y las gentes ignoran! ¿A quién no engañara aquella buena disposición y razonable capa y sayo, y quién pensara que aquel gentil hombre se pasó ayer todo el día sin comer, con aquel mendrugo de pan que su criado Lázaro trujo un día y una noche en el arca de su seno, do no se le podía pegar mucha limpieza, y hoy, lavándose las manos y cara, a falta de paño de manos, se hacía servir de la halda[4] del sayo? Nadie por cierto lo sospechara. ¡Oh señor, y cuántos de

---

1   i.e. under.
2   i.e. the crack between the door and the jamb.
3   muy: not in Antwerp.
4   i.e. falda.

Then up went the sword again, hanging it at his girdle[32], and after all this he marched out into the street, with a leisurely well–measured pace, holding his body straight, making therewith and with his head a very good countenance[33], casting the end of his cloak sometimes upon his shoulder, and otherwhiles under his arm, with his right hand always on his side, and as he was going forth, said,

'*Lazaro*, look well about the house, while I do go and hear service, make the bed, and then fetch some water here at the river beneath[34], lock the door lest anybody rob us, and lay the key underneath the threshold, that I may come in.'

He went up the street with such comely gesture and countenance, that he that had not known him, would have judged him to have been near kinsman unto the high Constable[35] of Spain, or at the least his chief Chamberlain. I remained then alone, saying to myself,

'Blessed art thou O God which sendest the sickness and givest the remedy[36]. Who would think that should meet my lord and master, with such gesture and countenance, but that he had supped well yesternight, yea, and that he had slept in a good bed? And although it be now early, who would think but that he had broken his fast well? Great are thy secret doings, O Lord, and all people are ignorant of them[37]; might not his good disposition, his reasonable cloak and coat deceive any man? Who would distrust[38] that such a noble gentleman had eaten nothing at all yesterday, but one piece of bread which his servant *Lazaro* had kept in the chest of his bosom a day and a night, so that it could not be (to say the truth) very clean? Who would suspect that he had dried this morning his face and his hands upon the skirts of his coat for want of a towel? I am certain no man would judge[39] it in him. O Lord, how many

---

32 Again Rowland mutes the religious satire; the Spanish reads that additionally the squire hung a string of large rosary beads from his sword belt.

33 Perhaps better rendered as 'graceful movements'.

34 The river Tagus flows around the foot of the eminence on which Toledo stands.

35 The Spanish reads Conde de Arcos (Arcos had become a dukedom in 1493), or Conde Alarcos, a character in a famous ballad, which again may be a mistake for Conde Claros, another ballad–character. The Constable of Castile represented the Spanish Crown at the peace ceremonies in London, August 1604. In the ballad, the Count says, 'Rouse yourself my chamberlain, Help me dress and put on my boots.'

36 Compare Deuteronomy 32.39; 'I kill and I make alive, I wound, and I heal'; and Job 5, 17–18: 'happy is the man whom God correcteth …For he maketh sore, and bindeth up: he woundeth, and his hands make whole.'

37 Compare Job 5.9: '[God] which doeth great things and unsearchable; marvellous things without number;' Deuteronomy 29.29: 'The secret things which belong unto the Lord our God'; and Romans 11.33: 'God! how unsearchable are his judgements, and his ways past finding out!' These Biblical echoes convey the inscrutable God of the Old Testament.

38 i.e. think, suspect.

39 i.e. suspect it.

aquéstos debéis vos tener por el mundo derramados, que padecen por la negra que llaman honra lo que por vos no sufrirían!'

Ansí[1] estaba yo a la puerta, mirando y considerando estas cosas y otras muchas[2], hasta que el señor mi amo traspuso la larga y angosta calle, y como lo vi trasponer[3], tornéme a entrar en casa, y en un credo la anduve toda, alto y bajo, sin hacer represa ni hallar en qué. Hago la negra dura cama y tomo el jarro y doy conmigo en el río, donde en una huerta vi a mi amo en gran recuesta con dos rebozadas mujeres, al parecer de las que en aquel lugar no hacen falta, antes muchas tienen por estilo de irse a las mañanicas del verano a refrescar y almorzar sin llevar qué por aquellas frescas riberas, con confianza que no ha de faltar quién se lo dé, según las tienen puestas en esta costumbre aquellos hidalgos del lugar.

Y como digo, él estaba entre ellas hecho un Macías, diciéndoles más dulzuras que Ovidio escribió. Pero como sintieron dél que estaba bien enternecido, no se les hizo de vergüenza pedirle de almorzar con el acostumbrado pago. Él, sintiéndose tan

---

1   así.
2   y otras muchas: not in Antwerp.
3   y como lo vi trasponer: not in Antwerp.

are there in the world, that are in such bravery as this my master is in, which do suffer more for a little vain glory's sake, than they would do for the love of thee[40].'

I stood in the door so long remembering[41] all those things, that[42] my master passed through a long and narrow street; then I went in, and within a minute of an hour[43], I visited the whole house above and beneath, without staying, or finding whereat to stay. When I had made the unlucky bed[44], I took my pot and went straight to the river, and being ready to take up my water, I might perceive[45] my master in a garden over the water, in great talk with two comely[46] women, which by their countenance seemed to be some of them, whereof in *Toledo* a number are rifely[47] found; and many of them take a use[48] of going abroad early in the morning in summer time, to take the air in those gardens, and to break their fast without provision of their own under trees and shadows, near that pleasant river, trusting[49] to find out some that would bestow charges upon them,[50] especially such as they had accustomed thereto, such lusty young gentlemen of the city as delighted in such pastime.

He was (as I mean to tell you) between these women devising and counterfeiting all kinds of bravery,[51] reciting more pleasant and sweet words than ever *Ovid*[52] wrote. But when they perceived that their beauty had vanquished him clean, and that he was left without shame, they demanded of him their breakfast, and he therefore to have the accustomed payment[53]. Whereupon he being as cold in the

---

40   An alternative rendering of the Spanish might be 'which endure for that accursed thing they call honour, what they would not suffer for thee.' Clearly one of the objects of attack is the code of honour of the knightly caste.

41   i.e. reflecting upon.

42   i.e. until.

43   The Spanish reads: 'in the time it takes to recite the creed', another instance of Rowland's softening the religious parody.

44   i.e. unfortunate. The Spanish original reads 'black and hard'.

45   The Spanish reads 'saw'.

46   More literally 'earnestly courting two women muffled up in shawls.'

47   i.e. there is no shortage of such women.

48   i.e. have the custom.

49   i.e. confident.

50   Rowland seems embarrassed and makes heavy weather of an explicit Spanish original. The women are prostitutes who provide sex in return for the wherewithall to buy food and break their fast. Their clients are not 'lusty young gentlemen' but 'gentlemen of the place', i.e. of Toledo, and the practice is an established arrangement.

51   In the Spanish original, the squire is compared to the fourteenth–century Galician troubadour and model of faithful lovers, Macias, who died at the hands of a jealous husband. Rowland possibly did not expect English readers to know the reference.

52   The classical Latin poet Ovid wrote *The Art of Loving* and *Remedies for Love*.

53   More literally, 'when they saw that he was moved to pity (and sexually aroused) they were brazen enough to ask him for their breakfast in return for the usual payment.'

frío de bolsa cuanto estaba[1] caliente del estómago, tomóle tal calofrío[2] que le robó la color del gesto, y comenzó a turbarse en la plática y a poner excusas no válidas. Ellas, que debían ser bien instituídas, como le sintieron la enfermedad, dejáronle para el que era.

Yo, que estaba comiendo ciertos tronchos de berzas, con los cuales[3] me desayuné, con mucha diligencia, como mozo nuevo, sin ser visto de mi amo, torné a casa, de la cual pensé barrer alguna parte, que era bien[4] menester, mas no hallé con qué. Púseme a pensar que haría, y parecióme esperar a mi amo hasta que el día demediase y si viniese y por ventura trajese algo que comiésemos; mas en vano fue mi experiencia.

Desque vi ser las dos y no venía y la hambre me aquejaba, cierro mi puerta y pongo la llave do mandó, y tórnome a mi menester. Con baja y enferma voz e inclinadas mis manos en los senos, puesto Dios ante mis ojos y la lengua en su nombre, comienzo a pedir pan por las puertas y casas más grandes que me parecía. Mas como yo este oficio le hobiese[5] mamado en la leche, quiero decir que con el gran maestro el ciego lo aprendí, tan suficiente discípulo salí que, aunque en este pueblo no había caridad ni el año fuese muy abundante, tan buena maña me di que, antes que el reloj diese las cuatro, ya yo tenía otras tantas libras de pan ensiladas en el cuerpo y más de otras dos en las mangas y senos. Volvíme a la posada y al pasar por la tripería pedí a una de aquellas mujeres, y diome un pedazo de uña de vaca con otras pocas de tripas cocidas.

Cuando llegué a casa, ya el bueno de mi amo estaba en ella, doblada su capa y puesta en el poyo, y él paseándose por el patio. Como entro[6], vínose para mí. Pensé que me quería reñir la tardanza, mas mejor lo hizo Dios. Preguntóme do[7] venía. Yo le dije:

'Señor, hasta que dio las dos estuve aquí, y de que vi que V.M. no venía, fuime

---

1   estaba: not in Antwerp.
2   i.e. escalofrío.
3   las cuales.
4   bien era.
5   hubiese.
6   entré.
7   i.e. de dónde, whence

purse as he was hot in stomach, fell in such a trance, that he lost all the colour in his face; his tongue not able to talk, was fain to allege vain excuses. But they which in their science were well instructed[54], when they perceived his infirmity[55], they gave him over for such a one as he was indeed.

All this while I was breaking my fast with stalks of colworts[56], and when I had done, like a diligent servant, not seen of my master, returned home, meaning to sweep some part of the house that had most need; but I could not find wherewithall to do the deed. Wherefore not knowing what to do, I began to muse wherein I should occupy myself; and after study[57], I determined to tarry until noon, that[58] my master came, for peradventure he would bring something with him for us to eat.

Wherefore I tarried his coming, yet all for nothing, for it was now two o'clock, and he not yet come. But because hunger oppressed me sore, I came out and locked the door, laying the key where he had commanded. With a low and sorrowful voice, my hands thrust into my bosom, I began to return to my former practice, in so much, that having God before mine eyes and my tongue, in his name, I fell to beg bread from door to door, and from house to house, where I thought best to speed[59]. Having learned this trade in my sucking years, I mean with the blind master, I became such a scholar, that although in that city there was small charity, nor the year was not abundant[60]; yet notwithstanding I had put my affairs in such good order, that before the clock struck four, I had laid a pound of bread in my belly, and twice as much in my bosom and sleeves. I returned then homeward, and in my way went through the streets where they sold tripe, where I demanded[61] a woman that was there her charity, she gave me a piece of a neat's[62] foot, and a few sodden[63] tripes.

When I came home, my courteous master was within, having folded his cloak and laid up, walking up and down the court[64]; and as soon as he did see me, he came towards me, wherefore I feared he would have beaten me, because I had tarried so long, but it was not God's will. The first thing he demanded me, was, where I had been. I answered,

'Sir, I was here until it was two o'clock, and when I perceived that your mastership came not, I went forth into the city, to recommend myself to good

---

54   i.e. they must have been very experienced.
55   i.e. weakness of pocket.
56   i.e. cabbages.
57   i.e. thought.
58   i.e. in case.
59   i.e. prosper, be successful.
60   i.e. a year of poor harvest.
61   i.e. begged.
62   i.e. cow's.
63   i.e. boiled.
64   i.e. the inner patio.

por esa ciudad a encomendarme a las buenas gentes, y hanme dado esto que veis.'

Mostréle el pan y las tripas que en un cabo de la halda traía, a lo cual él mostró buen semblante y dijo:

'Pues esperado te he a comer, y de que vi que no veniste, comí. Mas tú haces como hombre de bien en eso, que más vale pedillo por Dios que no hurtallo[1], y ansí[2] Él me ayude como ello me parece bien. Y solamente te encomiendo que no sepan que vives conmigo, por lo que toca a mi honra, aunque bien creo que será secreto, según lo poco que en este pueblo soy conocido. ¡Nunca a él yo hubiera de venir!'

'De eso pierda, señor, cuidado — le dije yo — que maldito aquél que ninguno tiene de pedirme esa cuenta ni yo de dalla.'

'Agora pues, come, pecador. Que, si a Dios place, presto nos veremos sin necesidad; aunque te digo que después que en esta casa entré, nunca bien me ha ido. Debe ser de mal suelo[3], que hay casas desdichadas y de mal pie[4], que a los que viven en ella pegan la desdicha. Ésta debe de ser sin dubda[5] de ellas; mas yo te prometo, acabado el mes, no quede en ella aunque me la den por mía.'

Sentéme al cabo del poyo y, porque no me tuviese por glotón, callé la merienda; y comienzo a cenar y morder en mis tripas y pan, y disimuladamente miraba al desventurado señor mío, que no partía sus ojos de mis faldas, que aquella sazón servían de plato. Tanta lástima haya Dios de mí como yo había dél, porque sentí lo que sentía, y muchas veces había por ello pasado y pasaba cada día. Pensaba si sería bien comedirme a convidalle; mas por me haber dicho que había comido, temíame no aceptaría el convite. Finalmente, yo deseaba aquel[6] pecador ayudase a su trabajo[7] del mío, y se desayunase como el día antes hizo, pues había mejor aparejo, por ser mejor la vianda y menos mi hambre.

Quiso Dios cumplir mi deseo, y aun pienso que el suyo; porque, como comencé a comer y[8] él se andaba paseando, llegóse a mí y díjome:

---

1   hurtalle i.e. hurtarle.
2   así.
3   i.e. unlucky.
4   i.e. ill-omened.
5   duda.
6   de quel i.e. de que el.
7   there is a pun: trabajo can mean both 'travail' and 'work'.
8   y: not in Antwerp.

people, which have given me thus much for God's sake,' and so shewed him the tripes which I kept in the skirt of my coat.

Whereat he made no angry countenance, but said:

'I have tarried for thee to dinner, and because I could not see thee come, I dined alone. As for thee, thou hast done like an honest boy, for it is better to beg than to steal; as God help me I am of that opinion. One thing only I will desire thee to do, that thou wilt not let them know that thou dost dwell with me nor that I am thy master. For that toucheth mine honour, and I do not doubt but that will be kept secret, for very few do know me in this city; I would to God I had never come to it.'

'Of that matter, sir, take you no care,' said I, 'for no man will ask me that question, I need not therefore make[65] such account to any of them.'

'But why dost thou not fall now to thy victuals, poor soul; if it be God's will we shall soon be out of this misery. Thou shalt understand, that since I came in hither[66], I had never good hour, this house is surely built in an unhappy[67] place, and certainly some houses are so unlucky, that look[68] whosoever doth dwell within them, he shall be sure to have evil fortune. But I promise thee, that as soon as the month is ended, I will not dwell here (no, though they would give it me rent free).'

I sat down then, and because he should not think me a covetous[69] glutton, I drew out my victuals, and there began to sup honestly, biting my tripes with my bread handsomely, beholding dissemblingly my miserable master which[70] had his eye always upon my skirt[71], being at that time my only platter. God take such compassion on me, as I did then upon him, for I had oftentimes endured, yea, and daily felt that sorrow, which I knew tormented him; wherefore I imagined with myself, how I might well invite him; but because he told me that he had dined, I was afraid lest he would refuse the banquet. Finally, I wished that the poor man would have eased his pain, by help of mine[72] and that he would have eaten with me for company, as he had done the day before, especially, because that then I had better victuals, and more store, and moreover that then my hunger was less.

It pleased God to accomplish my desire and his together, for when as I had begun my meat[73], as he walked he came near to me, saying:

---

65   i.e. give.
66   i.e. live in this house.
67   i.e. unlucky.
68   i.e. lo: – the expletive perhaps betrays Rowland's Welsh English.
69   Rowland's addition; 'selfish'.
70   i.e. who.
71   i.e. skirts of his coat or possibly shirt.
72   Rowland's attempt to translate a pun in the Spanish: 'should relieve his suffering by what I had earned by my work'.
73   i.e. food.

'Dígote, Lázaro, que tienes en comer la mejor gracia que en mi vida vi a hombre, y que nadie te lo verá[1] hacer que no le pongas gana aunque no la tenga.'

'La muy buena que tú tienes — dije yo entre mí — te hace parecer la mía hermosa.'

Con todo, parecióme ayudarle, pues se ayudaba y me abría camino para ello, y díjele:

'Señor, el buen aparejo hace buen artífice. Este pan está sabrosísimo y esta uña de vaca tan bien cocida y sazonada, que no habrá a quien no convide con su sabor.'

'¿Uña de vaca es?'

'Sí, señor.'

'Dígote que es el mejor bocado del mundo, y que no hay faisán que ansí[2] me sepa.'

'Pues pruebe, señor, y verá qué tal está.'

Póngole en las uñas la otra y tres o cuatro raciones de pan de lo más blanco y asentóseme[3] al lado, y comienza a comer como aquel que lo había gana, royendo cada huesecillo de aquéllos mejor que un galgo suyo lo hiciera.

'Con almodrote[4] — decía — es éste singular manjar.'

'Con mejor salsa lo comes tú', respondí yo paso.

'Por Dios, que me ha sabido como si hoy no hobiera[5] comido bocado.'

'¡Ansí[6] me vengan los buenos años como es ello!' dije yo entre mí.

Pidióme el jarro del agua y díselo como lo había traído. Es señal que, pues no le faltaba[7] el agua, que no le había a mi amo sobrado la comida. Bebimos, y muy contentos nos fuimos a dormir como la noche pasada.

Y por evitar prolijidad, desta manera estuvimos ocho o diez días, yéndose el pecador en la mañana con aquel contento y paso contado a papar aire por las calles, teniendo en el pobre Lázaro una cabeza de lobo[8]. Contemplaba yo muchas veces mi desastre, que escapando de los amos ruines que había tenido y buscando mejoría, viniese a topar con quien no solo no me mantuviese, mas a quien yo había de mantener.

---

1   te lo vee.
2   así.
3   y asentóseme: not in Antwerp.
4   i.e. a sauce or gravy made with olive oil, garlic, cheese and other ingredients.
5   como si no hubiera hoy comido.
6   así.
7   i.e. the water was not amiss.
8   i.e. a front or cat's paw.

'*Lazaro*, I promise thee thou hast the best grace[74] in eating that ever I did see any man have, for there is no man that seeth thee eat, but by seeing thee feed, shall have appetite, although they be not a hungered.'

Then would I say to myself; 'The hunger which thou sustainest, causeth thee to think mine own beautiful.'

Then I trusted I might help him, seeing that he had so helped himself, and had opened me the way thereto; wherefore I said unto him:

'Sir, the good tools make the workman good; this bread hath good taste, and this neat's foot is so well sodden, and so cleanly dressed, that it is able with the savour of it only, to entice any man to eat of it.'

'What is it, a neat's foot?'

'Yea, sir.'

'Now I promise thee it is the best morsel in the world, there is no pheasant that I would like so well.'

'I pray you, sir, prove of it better and see how you like it.'

At home in his own country he did eat nothing else.

I delivered then unto his nails the neat's foot, with two or three pieces of the whitest bread that I had, whereupon he sitteth down by me, and there began to eat like one that had great need, gnawing every one of those little bones, better than any greyhound could have done for life, saying:

'With sauce this is a singular good meat.'

And I to myself said: 'The sauce that thou eatest withal is better .'

'By God, I have eaten it with as good a stomach, as if I had eaten nothing all this day before.'

Then I with a low voice said: 'God send me to live long, as sure as that is true.' And having ended his victuals, he commanded me to reach him the pot of water, which I gave his even as full as I had brought it from the river, and it was a sign that since he wanted no water, that the residue of his dinner was but small[75]. We drank both, and went to bed, as the night before, at that time well satisfied.

He had fasted until then.

And now for to avoid long talk, we continued after this sort eight or nine days; and the poor gentleman went every day to brave it out in the street, to content himself with his accustomed stately pace, and always I poor Lazaro was fain to be his purveyor[76]. I oftentimes considered my disgraces[77], that escaping from evil, and seeking better, I happened to meet now with him, who not only did not maintain me, but whom I was fain to maintain, or else he to die.

---

74   i.e. pleasing manners.

75   i.e. since the squire had not drunk any of the water, he had eaten nothing else that day.

76   The Spanish literally describes Lazarillo as the Squire's 'wolf's head', i.e. cat's paw, doing someone's dirty work.

77   i.e. misfortunes.

Con todo, le quería bien, con ver que no tenía ni podía más, y antes le había lastima que enemistad; y muchas veces, por llevar a la posada con que él lo pasase, yo lo pasaba mal. Porque una mañana, levantándose el triste en camisa, subió a lo alto de la casa a hacer sus menesteres, y en tanto yo, por salir de sospecha, desenvolvíle el jubón y las calzas que a la cabecera dejó, y hallé una bolsilla de terciopelo raso hecho[1] cien dobleces y sin maldita la blanca ni señal que la hobiese[2] tenido mucho tiempo.

'Éste — decía yo — es pobre y nadie da lo que no tiene. Mas el avariento ciego y el malaventurado mezquino clérigo que, con dárselo Dios a ambos[3], al uno de mano besada y al otro de lengua suelta[4], me mataban de hambre, aquéllos es justo desamar y aquéste[5] de haber mancilla.'[6]

Dios es testigo que hoy día, cuando topo con alguno de su hábito, con aquel paso y pompa, le he lástima, con pensar si padece lo que aquél le vi sufrir; al cual con toda su pobreza holgaría de servir más que a los otros por lo que he dicho. Sólo tenía dél un poco de descontento: que quisiera yo que no tuviera tanta presunción, mas que abajara un poco su fantasía con lo mucho que subía su necesidad. Mas, según me parece, es regla ya entre ellos usada y guardada; aunque no haya cornado de trueco[7], ha de andar el birrete en su lugar. El Señor lo remedie, que ya con este mal han de morir.

Pues, estando yo en tal estado, pasando la vida que digo, quiso mi mala fortuna, que de perseguirme no era satisfecha, que en aquella trabajada y vergonzosa vivienda no durase. Y fue: como el año en esta tierra fuese estéril de pan, acordaron el Ayuntamiento que todos los pobres estranjeros se fuesen de la ciudad, con pregón

---

1   hecha.
2   hubiese.
3   i.e. although God gave to them both.
4   i.e. ready tongue.
5   aquéste es.
6   i.e. to have pity on.
7   i.e. tuppence to their name.

Yet for all that, I loved him well, perceiving that he was able to do no more; yea, and I did pity him, for oftentimes with carrying him home wherewith to pass the day, I felt grief myself. One morning, the poor gentleman rose up in his shirt, and went up to the top of the house to ease himself, and in the mean season[78] to be out of the suspicion that I was in[79], I unfolded his doublet and his hose, which were his bolster, and there found a little purse of velvet, which had a hundred wrinkles in it, but the devil a penny, nor yet any sign that there had been any there long time before. Then did I say to myself:

'This man is poor, no man can give that which he hath not; but my covetous blind man, and my wretched priest, unto whom God hath given so much goods, that one got with smooth[80] hand, and other gained with his loose[81] tongue, and yet they famished me continually; there was good reason why I should hate such people, so there is cause why this man's case should be lamented.[82]'

God knoweth that when I met with any of his estate[83], being of like gravity, pace, and countenance, how I pitied them, thinking that they did endure that which I did see him daily suffer, whom I had rather serve for all his poverty, than any of the others for the causes above named. I did like him well, but only that methought[84] he was too presumptuous[85], where I often wished that seeing he so plainly perceived his own poverty, he would something have hid[86] his fantastical pride. But as I think, it is a common usual rule amongst such as he, which though they have not a cross[87] in the world, nor a denier, the cap must needs stand in his[88] old place; but if God of his mercy do not order[89] the matter, all such are like to die of that vile disease.

As I continued in such estate, sustaining[90] the life that I have told you, my evil fortune which never ceased to pursue me, would not yet suffer me to continue in that troublesome and shameful kind of life. For the matter happened thus: the Lords of the Council[91] made proclamation with sound of trumpet, because that that year there

---

78   i.e. mean time.
79   i.e. to make sure he was as poor as I suspected.
80   Literally the Spanish original reads 'kissed' i.e. his parishioners kissed his hand on making him gifts.
81   i.e. ready, glib.
82   i.e. should have my pity.
83   i.e. social rank.
84   It seemed to me.
85   i.e. proud.
86   i.e. reduced.
87   i.e. a coin embossed with a cross. The Spanish means 'without a penny's worth of change.'
88   i.e. its.
89   i.e. reform.
90   i.e. in such a condition, suffering ….
91   i.e. the city Council of Toledo.

que el que de allí adelante topasen fuese punido con azotes. Y así, ejecutando la ley, desde a cuatro días que el pregón se dio, vi llevar una procesión de pobres azotando por las Cuatro Calles, lo cual me puso tan gran espanto, que nunca osé desmandarme a demandar.[1]

Aquí viera, quien vello pudiera, la abstinencia de mi casa y la tristeza y silencio de los moradores[2], tanto que nos acaeció estar dos o tres días sin comer bocado, ni hablaba[3] palabra. A mí diéronme la vida unas mujercillas hilanderas de algodón, que hacían bonetes y vivían par[4] de nosotros, con las cuales yo tuve vecindad y conocimiento; que de la laceria que les traían[5] me daban alguna cosilla, con la cual muy pasado me pasaba.[6]

Y no tenía tanta lástima de mí como del lastimado de mi amo, que en ocho días maldito el bocado que comió. A lo menos, en casa bien lo[7] estuvimos sin comer. No sé yo cómo o dónde andaba y qué comía. ¡Y velle venir a mediodía la calle abajo con estirado cuerpo, más largo que galgo de buena casta! Y por lo que toca[8] a su negra que dicen honra, tomaba una paja de las que aun asaz no había en casa, y salía a la puerta escarbando los dientes[9] que nada entre sí tenían, quejándose todavía de aquel mal solar, diciendo:

'Malo está de ver, que la desdicha de esta vivienda lo hace. Como ves, es lóbrega, triste, obscura. Mientras aquí estuviéremos, hemos de padecer. Ya deseo que[10] se acabe este mes por salir della.'

Pues, estando en esta afligida y hambrienta persecución un día, no sé por cual dicha o ventura, en el pobre poder de mi amo entró un real, con el cual él[11] vino a

---

1   i.e. be so rash as to beg.
2   moradores della.
3   hablar.
4   i.e. next door.
5   i.e. of the pittance they earned.
6   i.e. I suffered but got along.
7   los i.e. the eight days.
8   tocaba.
9   dientes: not in Antwerp.
10   que: not in Antwerp.
11   él: not in Antwerp.

was scarcity of corn, all poor people being strangers, should forsake the City, upon pain that he which from thenceforth should be taken[92], should be punished with stripes. And so executing the law, within three days after the proclamation, I saw a whole procession of poor folk whipped through the four principal streets[93], which sight did so fear[94] me, that never after I durst venture to beg.

Then might you have seen a strange diet we kept at home, and the great silence that was there, so that we were constrained to fast two or three days together, without eating any morsel, or speaking a word; and as for me, the best shift I made, was amongst certain poor women, which were spinners and cap knitters, which saved my life, by reason of the acquaintance I had with them, being our near neighbours.

For of that meat they had, I should have a little, wherewith I did not so lament mine own case as I did my poor master's, which in eight days did not eat one morsel, at the least, we were so long at home without meat, but indeed I know not whether[95] he went, nor what he did eat abroad. Yet notwithstanding, for all this, you should see him come some times up the street, with a body as large as any greyhounds of good race[96]: and for to maintain his poor honour, he was wont to take a straw in his hand, whereof *Small need to pick his* also there was want in our house, and standing without the *teeth for any meat he had* door, would therewith pick those[97] which had little need of *eaten.* picking, for anything that had stuck in them with eating. Lamenting still the unluckiness of that house, he would say,

'It grieveth me, to see how all our sorrow cometh of this house, thou seest how uncomfortable and dark it is, and as long as we dwell here, we are like to be thus tormented, therefore I would to God the month were ended, that we might depart out of it.[98]'

As we continued in this afflicted and famishing *Six pence English. Belike* persecution, one day a real[99] entered into the power of my *some gamesters had given* master, I know not by what good luck and adventure, *him and it was full time.*

---

92   i.e. caught.

93   Rowland has misunderstood. The Spanish original refers to the square of the Four Ways, between the Cathedral and old market.

94   i.e. frighten.

95   i.e. whither.

96   i.e. breed.

97   i.e. teeth.

98   Possibly more Biblical parody, for example of *Ecclasiastes* 7.2: it is better to go to the house of mourning, than to go to the house of feasting: for that is the end of all men.

99   A 'real' was a coin worth about ten and a half pence sterling. The word is still used for the name of currency of present day Saudi Arabia and Brazil.

casa tan ufano como si tuviera el tesoro de Venecia; y con gesto muy alegre y risueño me lo dio, diciendo:

'Toma, Lázaro, que Dios ya va abriendo su mano. Ve a la plaza y merca[1] pan y vino y carne: ¡quebremos el ojo al diablo! Y más, te hago saber, porque te huelgues, que he alquilado otra casa, y en ésta desastrada no hemos de estar más de en cumpliendo el mes. ¡Maldita sea ella y el que en ella puso la primera teja, que con mal en ella entré! Por Nuestro Señor, cuanto ha que en ella vivo, gota de vino ni bocado de carne no he comido, ni he habido descanso ninguno; mas ¡tal vista tiene y tal obscuridad y tristeza! Ve y ven presto, y comamos hoy como condes.'

Tomo mi real y jarro y a los pies dándoles priesa, comienzo a subir mi calle encaminando mis pasos para la plaza muy contento y alegre. Mas ¿qué me aprovecha si está constituído en mi triste fortuna que ningún gozo me venga sin zozobra? Y ansí[2] fue éste; porque yendo la calle arriba, echando mi cuenta en lo que le emplearía que fuese mejor y más provechosamente gastado, dando infinitas gracias a Dios que a mi amo había hecho con dinero[3], a deshora me vino al encuentro un muerto, que por la calle abajo muchos clérigos y gente en unas andas traían. Arriméme a la pared por darles lugar, y desque el cuerpo pasó, venían[4] luego a par del lecho una que debía ser mujer del difunto, cargada de luto, y con ella otras muchas mujeres; la cual iba llorando a grandes voces y diciendo:

'Marido y señor mío, ¿adónde os me llevan? ¡A la casa triste y desdichada, a la casa lóbrega y obscura, a la casa donde nunca comen ni beben!'

Yo que aquello oí, juntóseme el cielo con la tierra[5], y dije:

'Oh desdichado de mi! Para mi casa llevan este muerto.'

Dejo el camino que llevaba y hendí por medio de la gente, y vuelvo por la calle abajo a todo el más correr que pude para mi casa, y entrando en ella cierro a grande priesa, invocando el auxilio y favor de mi amo, abrazándome dél, que me venga ayudar y a defender la entrada. El cual, algo alterado, pensando que fuese otra cosa, me dijo:

'¿Qué es eso, mozo? ¿Qué voces das? ¿Qué has? ¿Por qué cierras la puerta con tal furia?'

'¡Oh señor — dije yo — acuda aquí, que nos traen acá un muerto.'

---

1   i.e. buy.
2   así.
3   i.e. had brought into money.
4   venía.
5   i.e. the Heavens fell about me.

wherewith he came home so blowing, as if he had brought with him the whole treasure of Venice[100], and so with a merry and lively countenance he giveth it to me, saying:

'Take here, *Lazaro*, now God beginneth to open his hand, and to smile upon us, go quickly to the market–place and buy bread, wine, and flesh, that we may break the devil's envious eye[101]; and furthermore, because thou shalt have good cause to rejoice, thou shalt understand, that I have hired another house, therefore, the month once ended, we will no longer abide in this miserable unlucky house, cursed be it, and he that laid the first tile on it, for in evil time did I come in. By our Lord, all the time that I have been here I never drank a drop of wine, nor a morsel of flesh entered into my belly, nor yet have I had any rest in it, such is the sorrow and misery that belongeth to it, go thy ways and make speed, and let us dine this day like Earls.'

Then I took my real and my pot, and with all haste I began to go up the street, towards the market–place, with joy and mirth. But what profiteth all this, now that I am born under such a planet that I can never enjoy any pleasure long, without hindrance? It appeareth so now, for as I went on my way, making my account[102] how I should bestow my money upon that which should be most profitable and best, giving infinite thanks to God (that he had given my master that money), upon a sudden I might see right before me a dead corpse come down the street, accompanied with many priests and other people. I leaned to the wall to give them place, and as the corpse went by, I might see a woman which belike was the dead man's wife, following the bier, all in mourning weed, accompanied with other women, and she weeping and lamenting, said:

'O my husband and my lord, alas, whither do they carry you? to the uncomfortable and sad house where they never eat nor drink?'

When I heard her speak these words, methought heaven and earth had met, and I said: 'O unfortunate wretch that I am, they carry this dead corpse to our house.'

Wherefore I forsook my way, and brake in between[103] the people, and running down the street as fast as ever I could, I got into the house, and when I entered therein, I locked the door with all haste, calling out to my master for help, and embracing him, I desired his aid to keep them out.
Whereof he was somewhat amazed, thinking it had been some other matter, and said,

'What is the matter, boy? What aileth thee to cry out so? Why dost thou lock the door with such fury?'

'O, sir,' then I answered, 'I pray you help me, for they bring us in here a dead corpse.'

---

100   This was proverbial.
101   A traditional call to celebration.
102   i.e. calculating.
103   i.e. broke through the crowd of mourners.

'¿Cómo así?' respondió él.

'Aquí arriba lo encontré, y venía diciendo su mujer: "Marido y señor mío, ¿adónde os llevan? ¡A la casa lóbrega y obscura, a la casa triste y desdichada, a la casa donde nunca comen ni beben!" Acá, señor, nos le traen.'

Y ciertamente, cuando mi amo esto oyó, aunque no tenía por qué estar muy risueño, rio tanto que muy gran rato estuvo sin poder hablar. En este tiempo tenía ya yo echada la[1] aldaba a la puerta y puesto el hombro en ella por más defensa. Pasó la gente con su muerto, y yo todavía me recelaba que nos le habían de meter en casa; y desque fue ya más harto de reír que de comer, el bueno de mi amo díjome:

'Verdad es, Lázaro; según la viuda lo va diciendo, tú tuviste razón de pensar lo que pensaste. Mas, pues Dios lo ha hecho mejor y pasan adelante, abre, abre, y ve por de comer.'

'Déjalos, señor, acaben de pasar la calle — dije yo.

Al fin vino mi amo a la puerta de la calle, y ábrela esforzándome, que bien era menester, según el miedo y alteración, y me torno a encaminar. Mas aunque comimos bien aquel día, maldito el gusto yo tomaba en ello, ni en aquellos tres días torné en mi color; y mi amo muy risueño todas las veces que se le acordaba aquella mi consideración.

De esta manera estuve con mi tercero y pobre amo, que fue este escudero, algunos días, y en todos deseando saber la intención de su venida y estada en esta tierra; porque desde el primer día que con él asenté, le conocí ser estranjero, por el poco conocimiento y trato que con los naturales della tenía. Al fin se cumplió mi deseo y supe lo que deseaba; porque un día que habíamos comido razonablemente y estaba algo contento, contóme su hacienda[2] y díjome ser de Castilla la Vieja, y que había dejado su tierra no más de por no quitar el bonete a un caballero su vecino.

---

1   el.
2   i.e. his affairs.

'How so?' said he.

'I met the corpse above in the street, and his wife followed him, saying, 'O my husband and my Lord, whither do they carry you? To the uncomfortable and sad house, to the house where they never eat nor drink?' Therefore without doubt, sir, they do bring him in here to you.'

Now truly when my master heard this, although he had no great cause to be joyful, he laughed so earnestly, that he stood a good while and could not speak. In this mean season[104], I had barred the door, and for more surety, had laid my shoulders fast against it. The people passed by with their corpse, and yet still I was afraid, and durst not remove[105], lest they would bring him in; and when my master had satisfied himself with laughing, though not with meat, he said unto me:

'Truly, *Lazaro*, thou hast said the truth, and according to the widow's crying words, thou hadst good reason to suspect that which thou hast said; but now, seeing that God hath dealt better with us than so, and that they are past us, open the door, and go to buy us some meat.'

'Sir,' then said I, 'let them first be all past.'

In the end, my master came and opened the door against my will, and it was as much as he could do, I held it so hard, being in great fear. Then he caused me to return to my voyage[106], and although we dined well that day, notwithstanding, I found no taste at all in my meat, nor within three days after I never recovered my own colour, and as often as the rememberance of these vain things came to my master's mind, he was never able to stay himself from laughing.

After such sort[107] I continued a time with this my third poor master, which was a Squire, seeking continually occasion [108] to know his estate[109], and for what cause he had come to dwell in this city, for I perceived that he was a stranger long before, by reason that he had so little acquaintance with those of the city. Finally, my wish was accomplished, and I understood that which I coveted to know; for upon a day, after that we had dined reasonably well, he being at that time indifferently well satisfied, declared unto me his affairs, in so much that he certified me, that he was born in *Castilla* the old[110], and how that he had[111] forsaken his country for nothing in the world, but because he would not abase himself so much as put off his cap to a gentleman his neighbour.

---

104 i.e. meanwhile.

105 i.e. feared to budge.

106 i.e. journey.

107 i.e. in this manner.

108 i.e. opportunity.

109 i.e. circumstances, background.

110 Modern Spain still distinguishes Old and New Castile. The former lies to the north, borders the Cantabrian Mountains and includes the major centres of Salamanca and Valladolid.

111 i.e. would have.

'Señor — dije yo — si él era lo que decís y tenía más que vos, ¿no errabádes[1] en no[2] quitárselo primero, pues decís que él también os lo quitaba?'

'Sí es, y sí tiene, y también me lo quitaba él a mí; mas, de cuantas veces yo se le quitaba primero, no fuera malo comedirse[3] él alguna y ganarme por la mano.'

'Paréceme, señor — le dije yo — que en eso no mirara, mayormente con mis mayores que yo y que tienen más.'

'Eres mochacho[4] — me respondió — y no sientes las cosas de la honra, en que el día de hoy está todo el caudal de los hombres de bien. Pues te hago[5] saber que yo soy, como vees[6], un escudero; mas ¡vótote a Dios!, si al conde topo en la calle y no me quita muy bien quitado del todo el bonete, que otra vez que venga, me sepa yo entrar en una casa, fingiendo yo en ella algún negocio, o atravesar otra calle, si la hay, antes que llegue a mí, por no quitárselo. Que un hidalgo no debe a otro que a Dios y al rey nada, ni es justo, siendo hombre de bien, se descuide un punto de tener en mucho su persona. Acuérdome que un día deshonré[7] en mi tierra a un oficial[8], y quise ponerle[9] las manos, porque cada vez que le topaba me decía: "Mantenga Dios a vuestra merced." "Vos, don villano ruin — le dije yo — ¿por qué no sois bien criado? ¿Manténgaos Dios, me habéis de decir, como si fuese quienquiera?"

De allí adelante, de aquí acullá, me quitaba el bonete y hablaba como debía.'

'¿Y no es buena manera de saludar un hombre a otro — dije yo — decirle que le mantenga Dios?'

'¡Mira mucho de enhoramala![10] — dijo él — A los hombres de poca arte dicen eso, mas a los más altos, como yo, no les han de hablar menos de: "Beso las manos

---

1   i.e. errabais.
2   no: not in Antwerp.
3   i.e. be civil and obliging.
4   muchacho.
5   hágote.
6   ves.
7   i.e. took to task.
8   i.e. journeyman.
9   poner en él.
10   i.e. Damn you!

And having heard all his discourse, I said unto him:

'Sir, if he were such a one as you say, and besides that, if he were richer than you, it had been but your duty to put off your cap first to him, for I believe he would have done the like to you.'

'Indeed he is a gentleman, and richer than I, and he would always put off his cap to the uttermost, when I did put off mine, but seeing that oftentimes mine was first off, reason would have required, that his should once have been first, and so have won of me by quick hand, the courtesy.'

'As for me,' said I, 'I would never have regard to that.'

'Thou art a child,' said he, 'and therefore thou knowest not what doth belong to honour, which at this day is the only refuge of such as be honest[112]. Therefore thou shalt understand, that I am as thou seest a poor esquire, and I make a vow to God, that if I should meet in the midst of the street an Earl, that would not put his cap altogether off, as well as I do mine, the next time I see him come, I will enter into some house, as if I had some business there, or else cross over into another street, if there be any between me and him, so that I shall not need to put off my cap to him; for a gentleman is bound to none but to God and the Prince[113], and therefore it is reason[114] that an honest man shall be curious to esteem[115] his own person. I do remember that upon a day, I dishonoured[116], and had almost beaten a craftsman where I was born, because that when so ever he met me, he would say, *Mantenga Dios a vuestra merced*, which is to say, 'Sir, God maintain your worship.' I took him once with the deed, and said:

'How now, sir clown, what mean you by this, who hath so instructed you, doth it become you to say unto me, God maintain you, even as I were one of the common sort?'

From thenceforth he would put off his cap to me afar off, and salute me as he ought.'[117]

'Why, sir,' said I, 'was not that kind of salutation[118] good enough for any man, is it not sufficient for a man to say, 'God maintain your mastership'?'

He answered angrily:

'Thou must know in an evil hour[119], that that kind of salutation is used to a mean man; but no man ought to salute one of my estate[120] after such a sort, but

---

112 The Spanish is perhaps bettered rendered 'is nowadays the entire wealth of honest men'
113 i.e. King.
114 i.e. right.
115 i.e. keen to value himself.
116 i.e. insulted, abused.
117 The craftsmen used the greeting appropriate to the lower classes. The style of greeting used at Court was 'I kiss your worship's hands.'
118 i.e. greeting.
119 i.e. damn you!
120 i.e. status, social standing.

de vuestra merced", o por lo menos: "Bésoos [1], señor, las manos", si el que me habla
es caballero. Y ansí[2], de aquél de mi tierra que me atestaba de mantenimiento, nunca
más le quise sufrir, ni sufriría ni sufriré a hombre del mundo, del rey abajo, que
"Manténgaos Dios", me diga.'

    'Pecador de mí — dije yo — por eso tiene tan poco cuidado de mantenerte, pues
no sufres que nadie se lo ruegue.'

    'Mayormente — dijo — que no soy tan pobre que no tengo en mi tierra un solar
de casas, que a estar ellas en pie y bien labradas, diez y seis leguas de donde nací, en
aquella costanilla[3] de Valladolid, valdrían más de docientas[4] veces mil maravedís,
según se podrían hacer grandes y buenas; y tengo un palomar que, a no estar
derribado como está, daría cada año más de docientos palominos; y otras cosas que
me callo, que dejé por lo que tocaba a mi honra. Y vine a esta ciudad, pensando que
hallaría un buen asiento, mas no me ha sucedido como pensé. Canónigos y señores
de la iglesia, muchos hallo, mas es gente tan limitada que no los sacaran[5] de su paso
todo el mundo. Caballeros de media talla, también me ruegan; mas servir con[6] éstos
es gran trabajo, porque de hombre os habéis de convertir en malilla[7] y si no. "Andá
con Dios" os dicen. Y las más veces son los pagamentos a largos plazos, y las más y
las más ciertas, comido por servido[8]. Ya cuando quieren reformar conciencia y
satisfaceros vuestros sudores, sois librados[9] en la recámara, en un sudado jubón o
raída capa o sayo. Ya cuando asienta un[10] hombre con un señor de título, todavía

---

1   besos.
2   así.
3   i.e. steep street, then the best part of Valladolid.
4   docientos.
5   sacara i.e. would not make them change their step or ways.
6   servir a.
7   There is reference here to the card game hombre (or 'ombre'); 'malilla' is 'joker', the
       force of the metaphor is that the squire must contend with a social world of biting
       tongues, risking spite and quarrelling.
8   i.e. you serve only for your keep.
9   Librado i.e. paid in old clothes from the wardrobe.
10   un: not in Antwerp.

always he ought to say, *Beso las manos de vuestra merced*, which is as much to say, as I kiss your worship's hands, or at the least *Bésoos, señor, las manos*, I do kiss your hands, if so be that he that saluteth me be a knight or a gentleman; so from that day forward I could never abide to hear talk of maintenance, nor suffer any man, unless it were the King[121], to say unto me, 'sir, God maintain you'.'

'Alas, wretch that I am (said I to myself), that is the cause, that He [122] hath so little care to maintain thee, for thou canst abide no man to wish it thee.'
Furthermore he said:

'I am not so poor, but that I have in my country ground, where foundation of houses is well and surely laid, which if they were built up as *Two and thirty maravedis* they ought, sumptuous and great, and by exchange placed in *is six pence English.* *Valladolid*, sixteen miles on this side the place where I was born, they would be worth no less than a thousand *maravedis*[123]. And I have a dovehouse, which if it were built up as it is now fallen, it would yield me yearly above two hundred pigeons; beside other things which I will not now speak of, all which things I forsook for matters which touched mine honour, and came to this city, meaning to serve one of the chief nobles, but it happened otherwise with me. I find indeed many Doctors and Prebends[124] belonging to the Church, but they keep such modest orders[125], that all the world is not able to bring them out of their pace[126]; many gentlemen which are of the basest sort[127], covet to have me, but to serve such men is great travail, for from a man, you must become a cloak–bag[128], or else they will straight bid you farewell. And most commonly, their wages is paid with long terms[129], sometime your meat and drink only for your painful service. And when they mean to reform their conscience[130], and to consider the servant's pain, there shall be delivered out of the wardrobe, some cut doublet, or some threadbare cloak, or coat; but when a man serveth a Nobleman of the Order[131], he shall better

---

121   More literally, 'from the King down'.
122   i.e. God.
123   Rowland's marginal gloss suggests that Lazarillo's Squire has very little grasp of real money value.
124   A prebend is a portion of the revenues of a cathedral or collegiate church granted to a canon or member of the chapter as a stipend. Rowland means 'Prebendaries'.
125   i.e. they are so stingy.
126   i.e. make them change their ways.
127   Strictly the Spanish original means 'of middle rank'.
128   i.e. a man for all purposes. [Literally, 'the joker in the pack'.]
129   i.e. greatly in arrears.
130   i.e. they have pangs of conscience.
131   i.e. with title.

pasa su laceria. ¿Pues por ventura no hay en mí habilidad para servir y contentar a éstos?

Por Dios, si con él topase, muy gran su privado[1] pienso que fuese y que mil servicios le hiciese, porque yo sabría mentille tan bién como otro, y agradalle a las mil maravillas: reílle hía[2] mucho sus donaires y costumbres, aunque no fuesen las mejores del mundo; nunca decirle[3] cosa con que le pesase, aunque mucho le cumpliese; ser muy diligente en su persona en dicho y hecho; no me matar por no hacer bien las cosas que él no había de ver, y ponerme a reñir, donde lo[4] oyese, con la gente de servicio, porque pareciese tener gran cuidado de lo que a él tocaba; si riñese[5] con algún[6] su criado, dar unos puntillos[7] agudos para le encender la ira y que pareciesen en favor del culpado; decirle bien de lo que bien le estuviese y, por el contrario, ser malicioso, mofador, malsinar[8] a los de casa y a los de fuera; pesquisar y procurar de saber vidas ajenas para contárselas; y otras muchas galas de esta calidad que hoy día se usan en palacio. Y a los señores dél parecen bien, y no quieren ver en sus casas hombres virtuosos, antes los aborrecen y tienen en poco y llaman necios y que no son personas de negocios ni con quien el señor se puede descuidar. Y con éstos los astutos usan, como digo, el día de hoy, de lo que yo usaría. Mas no quiere mi ventura que le halle.'

---

1   i.e. favourite.
2   i.e. le reiría.
3   decille.
4   donde él lo.
5   reñiese.
6   alguno.
7   i.e. sly remarks.
8   i.e. slander.

pass over his misery[132]. But peradventure there is not in me ability to serve and to content such men.'

'By God, if I had met with one of them, I think certainly, I should quickly have been chief of his counsel[133], for I would have done him a thousand kind of services. I could have dissembled as well as any other, yea, and pleased him a thousandfold, that it would have been marvellous. I would have smiled merrily at his doings[134], although they had not been the best in the world, I would never have recited that which should have displeased him, no although[135] it had been much for his profit, most diligent about[136] his person in word and deed, never vexing myself about the well doing of things that should never come to his sight, but sometimes[137] have chid such as served, where he might hear me, that I might seem to be careful about that which touched him: and whensoever he should happen to fall out with any of his men, then would I put forth two or three smooth words[138] to set him forward, which should seem to be in the favour of the offender, affirming always that which I thought he liked of; and on the contrary side, [139]a malicious mocker of the ignorant and rude sort. Furthermore, I would always demand and procure[140], how to know the lives of strangers, to account them unto him, with other such tricks of like quality which at this day are used in great palaces and courts, and which please the chief dwellers herein, which cannot abide to see in their houses virtuous men, but do abhor, and esteem them as nought, despising and calling them fools, and ignorant in the traffic of weighty affairs so that the Lord[141] cannot safely trust to their simple doings in weighty matters. Therefore nowadays, those that are subtle and crafty, get into favour, and use such means as I would have used, if fortune would have suffered me to have found out such a noble Lord.'

---

132 To preserve the sense of the Spanish, a negative should be inserted i.e. he shall no better pass over his misery, still suffer the same degree of misery.

133 i.e. favourite, someone indispensable.

134 i.e. witticisms and habits.

135 i.e. not even if.

136 i.e. I should be most attentive to.

137 i.e. I should have.

138 The Spanish original suggests that a clearer rendering would be 'utter sly and provocative remarks that would make the employer angrier whilst seeming to mitigate the servant's offence.'

139 i.e. I should be... Rowland here suppresses an original passage which literally reads: 'I should speak well to him of whatever mattered to him, and, on the contrary, be evil–tongued, mocking and spiteful about people within his palace or from outside.' Presumably Rowland found the original too severe, or possibly he disagreed with the portrayal of service in a great house. His translation is, after all, dedicated to Sir Thomas Gresham.

140 i.e. inquire into and get information about the lives of other people, to pass on to him.

141 i.e. nobleman.

Desta manera lamentaba también su adversa fortuna mi amo, dándome relación de su persona valerosa.

Pues, estando en esto, entró por la puerta un hombre y una vieja. El hombre le pide el alquiler de la casa y la vieja el de la cama. Hacen cuenta, y de dos en dos[1] meses le alcanzaron lo que él en un año no alcanzara: pienso que fueron doce o trece reales. Y él les dio muy buena respuesta: que saldría a la plaza a trocar una pieza de a dos[2], y que a la tarde volviesen. Mas su salida fue sin vuelta. Por manera que a la tarde ellos volvieron, mas fue tarde. Yo les dije que aún no era venido. Venida la noche, y él no, yo hube miedo de quedar en casa solo, y fuime a las vecinas y contéles el caso, y allí dormí. Venida la mañana, los acreedores vuelven y preguntan por el vecino, mas a estotra[3] puerta. Las mujeres le[4] responden: 'Veis aquí su mozo y la llave de la puerta.'

Ellos me preguntaron por él y díjele que no sabía adónde estaba y que tampoco había vuelto a casa desde que[5] salió a trocar la pieza, y que pensaba que de mí y de ellos se había ido con el trueco. De que esto me oyeron, van por un alguacil y un escribano. Y helos do vuelven luego con ellos[6], y toman la llave, y llámanme, y llaman testigos, y abren la puerta, y entran a embargar la hacienda de mi amo hasta ser pagados de su deuda. Anduvieron toda la casa y halláronla desembarazada, como he contado, y dícenme:

'¿Qué es de la hacienda de tu amo, sus arcas y paños de pared y alhajas de casa[7]?'

'No sé yo eso', le respondí.

'Sin duda — dicen ellos — esta noche lo deben de haber alzado y llevado a alguna parte. Señor alguacil, prended a este mozo, que él sabe dónde está'

En esto vino el alguacil, y echóme mano por el collar del jubón diciendo:

---

1   en dos: not in Antwerp.
2   i.e. a doubloon.
3   i.e. esta otra
4   les
5   desque
6   i.e. they come back with them at once.
7   i.e hangings and furniture.

After this sort my master lamented his evil fortune, making relation[142] unto me, what a valiant person he was.

And being in such talk, there cometh in to us, a man, and an old woman, the man demanded the rent of the house, and the woman the hire of the bed, and there made straightways accounts[143], so that he for two months was indebted more than he was able to pay in a whole year. I think his debts came to twelve or thirteen reals of plate[144]; he gave them gentle[145] answers, that he would go to the market–place to change a double piece of gold[146], desiring them to come again in the evening, but his departure was without return. When evening came, they returned, but it was too late, wherefore I told them that he was[147] not yet come. The night being come and he not, I was afraid to lie alone in the house, therefore I went to my neighbour's, and there declared unto them the whole matter, and there lay all night. The next day in the morning, the creditors came and inquired for my master, but at the other door, unto whom the woman answered:

'There is his servant, with the key of the door.'

They demanded me for him[148], I answered that I knew not where he was, for he was not come home since he went abroad to change his gold, and that therefore I thought that he was gone both from them and me with the exchange.

When they heard me say so, they go straight and seek a Sergeant and a Scrivener[149], and as soon as they had brought them thither, without delay they took the key and opened the door in the presence of witnesses, and entered in to sequester on [150]my master's goods that the debt might be paid them; but when they had sought the house all over, they found it as empty as I have told you, wherefore they demanded of me where my master's goods were conveyed, his chests, his tapestry, and his household stuff.

I answered, saying: 'I know nothing that he hath, sir.'

'Without doubt they have been taken away this night,' say they, 'and carried to some other place; therefore, master Sergeant, take hold on this boy, for he knoweth all.'

Then the officer approacheth unto me and taking fast hold on the collar of my coat, said:

---

142   i.e. giving me a lengthy account of.
143   i.e. presented their bills.
144   See (99) above. 'Plate' means silver.
145   i.e. polite.
146   i.e. the doubloon, beloved of pirates, sometimes called 'pieces of eight'. At the time Rowland wrote, a doubloon might have been worth roughly between 20 and 40 'reals'.
147   i.e. had.
148   i.e. asked me his whereabouts.
149   i.e. a constable and notary.
150   i.e. attach, confiscate.

'Mochacho, tú eres preso si no descubres los bienes deste tu amo.'

Yo, como en otra tal[1] no me hubiese visto, porque asido del collar, sí, había sido muchas e infinitas veces, mas era mansamente dél trabado[2], para que mostrase el camino al que no vía, yo hube mucho miedo, y llorando prometíle de decir lo que me preguntaban.

'Bien está — dicen ellos — pues di todo[3] lo que sabes, y no hayas temor.'

Sentóse el escribano en un poyo para escrebir el inventario, preguntándome qué tenía.

'Señores — dije yo — lo que este mi amo tiene, según él me dijo, es un muy buen solar de casas y un palomar derribado.'

'Bien está — dicen ellos —. 'Por poco que eso valga, hay para nos entregar de la deuda. ¿Y a qué parte de la ciudad tiene eso?', me preguntaron.

'En su tierra', les respondí.

'Por Dios, que está bueno el negocio — dijeron ellos — ¿Y adónde es su tierra?.

'De Castilla la Vieja me dijo él que era', le[4] dije yo.

Riéronse mucho el alguacil y el escribano, diciendo:

'Bastante relación es ésta para cobrar vuestra deuda, aunque mejor fuese.'

Las vecinas, que estaban presentes, dijeron:

'Señores, éste es un niño inocente, y ha pocos días que está con ese escudero, y no sabe dél más que vuestras mercedes, sino, cuanto el pecadorcico se llega aquí a nuestra casa, y le damos de comer lo que podemos por amor de Dios, y a las noches se iba a dormir con él.'

Vista mi inocencia, dejáronme, dándome por libre.

Y el alguacil y el escribano piden al hombre y a la mujer sus derechos[5], sobre lo cual tuvieron gran contienda y ruido, porque ellos alegaron no ser obligados a pagar, pues no había de qué ni se hacía el embargo. Los otros decían que habían dejado de ir a otro negocio que les importaba más por venir a aquél. Finalmente, después de dadas muchas voces, al cabo carga un porquerón[6] con el viejo alfamar de la vieja,

---

1   i.e. in such a fix.
2   i.e. seized.
3   todo: not in Antwerp.
4   les.
5   i.e. fees.
6   i.e. a constable.

'Thou art prisoner, unless thou tell where thy master his goods are become[151].'

But as never no man had taken hold on me in that place before saving only my blind master, who never laid hand on me so rudely, but gently, that I might lead him that could not see, I was afraid, and crying[152] mercy, I promised to tell all that they demanded.

'Go to then,' say they, 'say on God's name what thou knowest and be not afraid.'

The Scrivener sitteth down in haste, to write the Inventory, demanding what goods he had. I then began to declare what I knew, saying:

'Sir, the goods that he hath, or at least that which he told me he had, was a piece of ground, where foundation of houses is laid, and moreover a dove house, which is fallen[153].'

'Well said,' say they, 'my boy, though that be little worth, it is sufficient to pay us. In what place of the city[154] standeth it?' say they.

I answered, 'Marry, it standeth a good way hence in his own country.'

'The matter is then in a fair case[155],' say they, 'but where is his country?'

'He told me that he was born in *Castilla* the old.'

The Sergeant, and the Scrivener, laughing a pace[156], said: 'This confession is sufficient for you to recover the debt (though it were greater).'

The neighbours[157] that were there present, said: 'This child is an innocent, and he hath not dwelt long with the Squire, therefore he knoweth no more of him than you do, he hath oftentimes come to us, and we have given him such meat as we had, for God's sake, and at nights gone in to lie with his master.'

When they perceived my innocency, they did set me at liberty.

The Sergeant and the Scrivener did demand of the man and the woman their fee, whereupon there rose great contention, and they alleged that they were not bound to pay, seeing that there was no execution made, especially, seeing there was no wherewithal. The officers alleged, for that coming thither, they had left undone matters of much greater importance. Finally, after many angry words, a poor carrier[158] was laden with the old mattress, which was the woman's, scant half a load

---

151 i.e. where your master's possessions are located, hidden.
152 i.e. begging, an addition of Rowland.
153 i.e. a dovecot that has tumbled down.
154 i.e. Toledo.
155 i.e. the creditors' demands may be met, satisfied.
156 i.e. heartily.
157 In the Spanish, these are female.
158 Strictly the Spanish word means a petty officer of justice or constable. Rowland's contemporary translation is a warning that modern dictionaries may miss a nuance of that time. The Spanish word derives from the name of someone who keeps pigs. Perhaps then, a sort of filthy bailiff.

aunque[1] no iba muy cargado. Allá van todos cinco dando voces. No sé en qué paró. Creo yo que el pecador alfamar pagara por todos, y bien se empleaba, pues el tiempo que había de reposar y descansar de los trabajos pesados, se andaba alquilando.

Así, como he contado, me dejó mi pobre tercero amo, do[2] acabé de conocer mi ruin dicha, pues, señalándose todo lo que podría contra mí, hacía mis negocios tan al revés, que los amos, que suelen ser dejados de los mozos, en mí no fuese ansí[3], mas que mi amo me dejase y huyese de mí.

Tratado Cuarto
Cómo Lázaro se asentó con un fraile de la Merced, y de lo que le acaeció con él

Hube de buscar el cuarto, y éste fue un fraile de la Merced, que las mujercillas que digo me encaminaron, al cual ellas le llamaban pariente: gran enemigo del coro y de comer en el convento, perdido por andar fuera, amicísimo de negocios seglares y visitar[4], tanto que pienso que rompía él más zapatos que todo el convento. Éste me dio los primeros zapatos que rompí en mi vida, mas no me duraron ocho días, ni yo pude con su trote durar más. Y por esto y por otras cosillas que no digo, salí dél.

Tratado Quinto
Cómo Lázaro se asentó con un buldero, y de las cosas que con él pasó

En el quinto por mi ventura di, que fue un buldero, el más desenvuelto y desvergonzado y el mayor echador dellas que jamás yo vi ni ver espero ni pienso

---

1   y aunque.
2   i.e. de donde, whence.
3   así.
4   visitas.

to the bearer; then went they all five out together chiding. What became of them after, I know not, I believe the poor mattress paid for all.[159]

And thus, as I tell you, I lost my third master when as I fully perceived evil fortune wrought altogether against me, insomuch that my affairs went so backward, that whereas masters are wont to be forsaken of their servants, it was not so with me, but my master was fain to forsake me, yea, and run away in haste.

Fourth Treatise

How Lazaro placeth himself to dwell with a Friar of the Abbey of Grace.

I was then constrained to seek the fourth master, which was a Friar of the Abbey of Grace[1], unto whom the poor women[2] which I have told you of, preferred me. They called him cousin. This man was an enemy to the Choir, not liking well of his meals in the convent, a man lost[3] for going abroad, desirous to see worldly affairs and [4]visitations, wherefore I think that he alone did tear[5] more shoes than all the rest of his brethren. It was he that gave me the first shoes that ever I wore in all my life, which lasted me but eight days, for he never left trotting abroad. Wherefore for this, and for other small matters[6], which at this time I will not speak of, I was fain to forsake him.

Fifth Treatise

How Lazaro placeth himself with a Pardoner, and what things happened to him in his service.

I met by evil chance with the fifth master, which was an utterer of Pardons, the deceitfullest merchant and most shameless, that ever I did see, or any man else. For

---

159 For clarity of narrative, Rowland cuts, not translating twenty Spanish words. These could be rendered 'and the mattress was well used, since the time it would [otherwise] have had to take a breather and rest from its past travails, was now earning rent.'

1 Strictly, of the Order of Mercy, a royal and military order, founded in the twelfth century with the primary mission of ransoming captives. In the sixteenth century it became known for its worldly ambitions, especially in America.

2 See Third Treatise ,note 157.

3 i.e. both 'passionately fond of' and 'damned'.

4 i.e. 'make'.

5 i.e. wear out.

6 Much ink has been spilt on guessing what these matters were, and general agreement that they were of a sexual nature.

que[1] nadie vio; porque tenía y buscaba modos y maneras y muy sotiles invenciones.

En entrando en los lugares do habían de presentar la bula, primero presentaba a los clérigos o curas algunas cosillas, no tampoco de mucho valor ni substancia: una lechuga murciana, si era por el tiempo, un par de limas o naranjas, un melocotón, un par de duraznos, cada sendas peras verdiñales. Ansí[2] procuraba tenerlos propicios porque favoreciesen su negocio y llamasen sus feligreses a tomar la bula.

Ofreciéndosele a él las gracias, informábase de la suficiencia dellos. Si decían que entendían, no hablaba palabra en latín por no dar tropezón; mas aprovechábase de un gentil y bien cortado romance[3] y desenvoltísima lengua. Y si sabía que los dichos clérigos eran de los reverendos, digo que más con dineros que con letras y con reverendas[4] se ordenan, hacíase entre ellos un Santo Tomás[5] y hablaba dos horas en latín: a lo menos, que lo parecía aunque no lo era.

Cuando por bien no le tomaban las bulas, buscaba cómo por mal se las tomasen, y para aquello hacía molestias al pueblo e otras veces con mañosos artificios. Y

1　　que: not in Antwerp.
2　　así.
3　　i.e. Castilian, Spanish.
4　　i.e. letters authorising a priest to be ordained in another diocese. The use of 'reverend' twice contains an obvious sarcasm.
5　　i.e. Saint Thomas Aquinas.

to dispatch away his pardons, he had fine means and traffic, and daily imagined[1] therefore most subtle inventions.

As soon as he arrived to such towns, where he should utter his pardons, he would first present some gift of small value or substance to the priests and curates of that place: sometimes a cabbage lettuce[2], a couple of lemons or oranges; otherwhiles an apricot, or else a couple of peaches, or at the least, to every one a fair pear; and by that means he went about to make them his friends, that they might favour his affairs, and cause their parishioners to receive the pardons.

Yea, and that they should thank him, he would always be informed before he came, which were learned, and which not. When he came to those which he understood were learned, he would be sure never to speak a word of Latin, for fear of stumbling; but used in such places, a gentle kind of *Castilian Spanish*[3], his tongue always at liberty[4]; and contrariwise, whensoever he was informed of the reverend *Domines*[5] (I mean such as are made priests, more for money than for learning and good behaviour) to hear him speak among such men, you would say it were St. Thomas[6]. For he would then, two hours together talk Latin, at least which seemed to be, though it was not.

When that they received not his pardons friendly, he sought means to make them to take them perforce; so that oftentimes, he therefore molested the parishioners, otherwhiles causing them to receive them by subtle inventions[7]. And

---

1   i.e. devised. This was a Pardoner of the Holy Crusade, who sold indulgence granting full remission of their sins to those who contributed in this manner towards the campaigns against the infidels in North Africa and other places; the sale of these printed sheets, with blank spaces for the name of the buyer and the amount paid, brought considerable profits to the state. Serious abuses were denounced in the Cortes (or Parliament) on numerous occasions, and in 1524, Charles V issued a decree to prevent pardoners from forcing their indulgences upon the people.

2   Strictly a lettuce from Murcia.

3   i.e. He used an elegant form of the vernacular. The Spanish employs a metaphor from tailoring.

4   i.e. fluent, relaxed.

5   There is a play on words in the Spanish. We should understand: 'when, on the contrary, he learned that the priest were of the reverend sort who are ordained more through money than education and episcopal conferment ...' In Scotland, a well educated teacher is still known as a 'dominie'. Letters from a bishop authorising the ordination or appointment of a priest began with the words, 'Reverend in Christ the Father...' Rowland repeats the sarcasm of the Spanish.

6   i.e. Thomas Aquinas 1225–74, Dominican friar and Christian apologist, here used as an instance of a supreme Christian scholar.

7   i.e. cunning tricks or ruses.

porque todos los que le veía hacer sería largo de contar, diré uno muy sotil y donoso, con el cual probaré bien su suficiencia.

En un lugar de la Sagra de Toledo había predicado dos o tres días, haciendo sus acostumbradas diligencias, y no le habían tomado bula, ni a mi ver tenían intención de se la tomar. Estaba dado al diablo con aquello[1] y, pensando qué hacer, se acordó de convidar al pueblo, para otro día de mañana despedir la bula.

Y esa noche, después de cenar, pusiéronse a jugar la colación[2] él y el alguacil, y sobre el juego vinieron a reñir y a haber malas palabras. Él llamó al alguacil ladrón, y el otro a él falsario. Sobre esto, el señor comisario mi señor tomó un lanzón que en el portal do jugaban estaba. El alguacil puso mano a su espada, que en la cinta tenía. Al ruido y voces que todos dimos, acuden los huéspedes y vecinos y métense en medio, y ellos muy enojados procurándose desembarazar de los que en medio estaban, para se matar. Mas como la gente al gran ruido cargase y la casa estuviese llena della, viendo que no podían afrentarse con las armas, decíanse palabras injuriosas, entre las cuales el alguacil dijo a mi amo que era falsario y las bulas que predicaba que[3] eran falsas.

Finalmente, que los del pueblo, viendo que no bastaban a[4] ponellos en paz, acordaron de llevar el[5] alguacil de la posada a otra parte. Y así quedó mi amo muy enojado; y después que los huéspedes y vecinos le hubieron rogado que perdiese el enojo y se fuese a dormir, se fue. Y[6] así nos echamos todos.

La mañana venida, mi amo se fue a la iglesia y mandó tañer a misa y al sermón para despedir la bula. Y el pueblo se juntó, el cual andaba murmurando de las bulas, diciendo como eran falsas y que el mesmo[7] alguacil riñendo lo había descubierto; de

---

1   i.e. he was furious about it.
2   i.e. a sort of sweet night cap.
3   que: not in Antwerp.
4   a: not in Antwerp.
5   al.
6   se fue. Y: not in Antwerp.
7   mismo.

now, seeing that it were too long to account all such parts[8] as I did see him use, I will recite one, whereby he showed right well how sufficient[9] he was.

He had preached two or three days, in a village, within the diocese of the Archbishop of *Toledo*[10], without omitting any part of his accustomed diligence, and the people had not taken one pardon, not no man (as far as I could perceive) was minded to receive any; wherefore he was in great rage. And as he imagined[11] what he had best do, determined[12] to invite and bid all the people to come thither the next day, so to dispatch his pardons.

And that night after supper, he and his sergeant went to play for their breakfast[13], and as they played, they fell at such debate[14], that the one gave evil words to the other. Insomuch, that at the last he said to his sergeant, that he was a thief, and the sergeant answered, saying that he was a falsifier, wherefore the commissary[15] my master laid hand upon a short pike that stood behind the door where they

Pardoners have always with them a sergeant to take up gages in such houses as refuse to pay for their pardons at the time appointed.

played, and the sergeant, on the other side, put his hand to his sword which hung by his side, so that with the great noise that we made, our host and our neighbours came in, and went between them.

Then they being sore angry, sought all means to come together, that the one might kill the other; but the house was so full of people, that they could by no means come near to one another, wherefore they never left giving one another injurious words, in so much that the sergeant said to my master, that he was a falsifier, and that the pardons which he preached of daily, were most false.

To be brief, when the people perceived that they could by no means pacify them, they determined to carry the sergeant away to another lodging, and master remained still there in great rage. Whereupon our host, with his neighbours, desired him heartily that he would forget his anger, and go to bed; and so then we went all to sleep.

As soon as day appeared in the morning, my master went to the church and caused them there to ring[16] to Mass, and to sermon, that he might dispatch his pardons; then the people assembled together, murmuring amongst themselves at the pardons, saying that they were false and nothing worth, seeing that the sergeant

---

8   i.e. tricks.
9   i.e. skilled.
10   In fact in Sacra, an area north east of Toledo.
11   i.e. thought up.
12   i.e. decided.
13   Probably a misunderstanding. Read 'play for their nightcap', by custom largely sweets. They probably played at dice.
14   i.e. a heated row.
15   i.e. in the sense that he held a commission to sell indulgences.
16   i.e. ring the bell summoning the people to mass and to hear his sermon.

manera que tras[1] que tenían mala gana de tomalla, con aquello de todo la aborrecieron.

El señor comisario se subió al púlpito y comienza su sermón, y a animar la gente a que no quedasen sin tanto bien e indulgencia como la santa bula traía. Estando en lo mejor del sermón, entra por la puerta de la iglesia el alguacil y, desque hizo oración, levantóse y con voz alta y pausada cuerdamente[2] comenzó a decir:

'Buenos hombres, oídme una palabra, que después oiréis a quien quisiéredes. Yo vine aquí con este echacuervo que os predica, el cual me engañó y dijo que le favoreciese en este negocio y que partiríamos la ganancia. Y agora, visto el daño que haría a mi conciencia y a vuestras haciendas, arrepentido de lo hecho, os declaro claramente que las bulas que predica son falsas, y que no le creáis ni las toméis, y que yo *directe* ni *indirecte* no soy parte en ellas, y que desde agora dejo la vara[3] y doy con ella en el suelo; y si algún tiempo éste fuere castigado por la falsedad, que vosotros me seáis testigos como yo no soy con él ni le doy a ello ayuda, antes os desengaño y declaro su maldad.'

Y acabó su razonamiento. Algunos hombres honrados que allí estaban se quisieron levantar y echar el[4] alguacil fuera de la iglesia, por evitar escándalo. Mas mi amo les fue a la mano[5] y mandó a todos que so pena de excomunión no le estorbasen, mas que le dejasen decir todo lo que quisiese. Y ansí[6], él también tuvo silencio, mientras el alguacil dijo todo lo que he dicho.

Como calló, mi amo le preguntó, si quería decir más, que lo dijese. El alguacil dijo:

'Harto hay más[7] que decir de vos y de vuestra falsedad, mas por agora basta.'

El señor comisario se hincó de rodillas en el púlpito y, puestas las manos[8] y mirando al cielo, dijo ansí[9]:

'Señor Dios, a quien ninguna cosa es escondida, antes todas manifiestas, y a quien nada es imposible, antes todo posible, tú sabes la verdad y cuán injustamente

---

1   atrás.
2   i.e. calmly.
3   i.e. rod of office.
4   al.
5   i.e. stopped them.
6   así.
7   más hay.
8   i.e. hands joined in prayers.
9   así.

himself had affirmed the same. So that before that time, they having small mind to receive any, they then utterly abhorred them[17].

Master commissary mounteth up into the pulpit, and beginneth his sermon, encouraging the people not to forsake such great goodness and indulgence, as the holy pardon contained; and being in the midst of the sermon, the sergeant cometh in at the church door, and when that he had ended his prayers, he rose up suddenly, and with a loud voice discreetly said:

All sergeants in Spain do bear a white rod in their hands, higher than themselves by half a foot, as big as a man's finger.

'Ye honest and godly people, give ear that I may tell you a word or two, and then hear whom ye will. I am come hither in the company of this crow keeper[18] which now preacheth, who hath deceived me, promising, that if I would help him in his affairs, I should have half the gains. But now perceiving the damage that my conscience should receive, and besides that, the loss of your goods, I do earnestly repent that which I have done, and I will tell you plainly, that the pardons which he hath brought, are false; therefore ye ought not to believe him, nor yet take any one of them. As for me, I will neither be partaker with him[19], one way or other, therefore from this time forward, I do forsake the rod of them[20], which I now cast to the ground; for if hereafter he be punished for his falsehood, you may be witness with me that I am no doer with him herein, nor yet help him, but do rather betray unto you his craft and falsehood.'

And when he had said all, certain men of honour which were there, would needs have cast him out of the church, to avoid slander; but my master did forbid them so to do, commanding them all upon pain of excommunication, to suffer him to say all that ever he could, and he himself kept silence whiles that the sergeant declared all that which I have rehearsed. And as soon as he held his tongue, my master demanding him whether he would say any more, the sergeant answered:

They were no Lords, every man is of honour there.

'There may be much more said of thee, and of thy falsehood, but at this time this is sufficient.'

Then my master commissary falling down upon his knees in the pulpit, holding up his hands, his eyes looking up to heaven, said these words:

'O Lord God, from whom nothing is hid, unto whom all things are manifest, and unto whom nothing is impossible, who can do all things, thou knowest the truth,

---

17   i.e. Consequently whereas previously they had been little inclined to buy any, now, they utterly rejected them.

18   Thus Rowland attempts to render a piece of abusive slang, often applied to pardoners in Spain, and meaning 'swindler', 'charlatan'.

19   More accurately, 'I have nothing to do with them (i.e. the false pardons) openly or in secret'.

20   Such a rod or staff was the emblem of office for various judicial positions. The Spanish terminology parodies legal formulae.

yo soy afrentado. En lo que a mí toca, yo lo¹ perdono porque tú, Señor, me perdones. No mires a aquél que no sabe lo que hace ni dice; mas la injuria a ti hecha, te suplico, y por justicia te pido, no disimules; porque alguno que está aquí, que por ventura pensó tomar aquesta santa bula, dando crédito a las falsas palabras de aquel hombre, lo dejará de hacer. Y pues es tanto perjuicio del prójimo, te suplico yo, Señor, no lo disimules, mas luego muestra aquí milagro, y sea desta manera: que si es verdad lo que aquél dice y que traigo maldad y falsedad, este púlpito se hunda conmigo y² meta siete estados³ debajo de tierra, do él ni yo jamás parezcamos. Y si es verdad lo que yo digo y aquél, persuadido del demonio, por quitar y privar a los que están presentes de tan gran bien, dice maldad, también sea castigado y de todos conocida su malicia.'

Apenas había acabado su oración el devoto señor mío, cuando el negro alguacil cae de su estado y da tan gran golpe en el suelo que la iglesia toda hizo resonar, y comenzó a bramar y a echar espumajos por la boca y torcella, y hacer visajes con el gesto, dando de pie y de mano, revolviéndose por aquel suelo a una parte y a otra. El estruendo y voces de la gente era tan grande, que no se oían unos a otros. Algunos estaban espantados y temerosos. Unos decían:

'El señor le socorra y valga.'

Otros: 'Bien se le emplea⁴, pues levantaba tan falso testimonio.'

Finalmente, algunos que allí estaban, y a mi parecer no sin harto temor, se llegaron y le trabaron de los brazos, con los cuales daba fuertes puñadas a los que cerca dél estaban. Otros le tiraban por las piernas y tuvieron reciamente, porque no había mula falsa en el mundo que tan recias coces tirase. Y así le tuvieron un gran rato, porque más de quince hombres estaban sobre él, y a todos daba las manos llenas, y si se descuidaban, en los hocicos⁵.

A todo esto, el señor mi amo estaba en el púlpito de rodillas, las manos y los ojos puestos en el cielo, transportado en la divina esencia, que⁶ el planto y ruido y voces que en la iglesia había no eran parte para⁷ apartalle de su divina contemplación.

---

1   le.
2   i.e. se meta.
3   i.e. feet.
4   i.e. it serves him right.
5   i.e. kept them busy, and if they did not watch out, punched them on the nose.
6   i.e. de modo que
7   i.e. were not distraction enough to.

and how unjustly I am accused and slandered. As for me (O Lord) I forgive him, that thou mayest forgive me. Have no regard to him that knoweth not what he doth nor sayeth: notwithstanding, O Lord, I do beseech thee, and through justice I demand of thee, that thou wilt not dissemble[21] this injury which is done unto thee. Peradventure, some that are here present, were minded to take this divine pardon, which[22] now will not, giving place and credit to the wicked man's words. And because this matter is so hurtful to Christian neighbours, I beseech thee once again, good Lord, that thou wilt not dissemble it, but immediately, that it may please thee to show here a miracle, and that it may be thus; if it be true that this man saith, that is, that the pardons which I have here are false, that this pulpit may then sink with me, as far as the depth of seven men under the ground, that neither it nor I may never be seen again[23]. And on the other side, if that be true which they say, that he being persuaded by the devil, hath said these words falsely and untruly, only to deprive the people of such goodness, that then it may also please thee to punish him, that his malicious perversity may be known to all men.'[24]

My devout master had scant ended his prayers, but that the poor sergeant fell in a trance, giving himself such a blow against the ground, that all the church sounded of it, stretching out his body with great abundance of foam at his mouth, making strange visages, and striking the ground both with hand and foot, tumbling up and down from one side to another, insomuch that the noise which the people made, was so great, that one could not hear another. Some were amazed and sore afraid, saying, 'God be his help,' and other said, 'He hath that which he hath deserved, seeing that he durst affirm such falsehood.'

Finally some of those that were there, which to my judgement were not without great fear, came near to hold fast his hands, wherewith he struck all such as came near him. Others held him fast by the feet, for there was never false mule in the world that ever kicked so fast; and so they held him a good while. There were above fifteen men upon him, and he gave them all their hands full[25]; so that if they had forgotten their business, he would have given some of them overthwart[26] the teeth.

All this while my master was in the pulpit upon his knees, holding his hands together still, his eyes bent towards heaven, transported into such divine essence, that all the noise and rumour[27] which was in the church, was not sufficient to bring him out of his divine contemplation.

---

21   i.e. pretend not to know, disregard.

22   i.e. who (as so often in Tudor English).

23   Double negatives were once standard in English as they continue to be in Spanish.

24   This staged miracle to confound unbelievers perhaps echoes Moses' invocation in Numbers 16.30. An identical story will be found in Masuccio da Salerno.

25   i.e. he kept them busy.

26   Or, as the Spanish puts it, 'bashed them on the snout'.

27   i.e. uproar.

Aquellos buenos hombres llegaron a él, y dando voces le despertaron y le suplicaron quisiese socorrer a aquel pobre que estaba muriendo, y que no mirase a las cosas pasadas ni a sus dichos malos, pues ya dellos tenía el pago; mas si en algo podría[1] aprovechar para librarle del peligro y pasión que padecía, por amor de Dios lo hiciese, pues ellos veían clara la culpa del culpado y la verdad y bondad suya, pues a su petición y venganza el Señor no alargó el castigo.

El señor comisario, como quien despierta de un dulce sueño, los miró y miró al delincuente y a todos los que alderredor[2] estaban, y muy pausadamente les dijo:

'Buenos hombres, vosotros nunca habíades de rogar por un hombre en quien Dios tan señaladamente se ha señalado; mas pues él nos manda que no volvamos mal por mal y perdonemos las injurias, con confianza podremos suplicarle que cumpla lo que nos manda, y Su Majestad perdone a éste que le ofendió poniendo en su santa fe obstáculo. Vamos todos a suplicalle.'

Y así bajó del púlpito y encomendó a que[3] muy devotamente suplicasen a Nuestro Señor tuviese por bien de perdonar a aquel pecador, y volverle en su salud y sano juicio, y lanzar dél el demonio, si Su Majestad había permitido que por su gran pecado en él entrase. Todos se hincaron de rodillas, y delante del altar con los clérigos comenzaban a cantar con voz baja una letanía. Y viniendo él con la cruz y agua bendita, después de haber sobre él cantado, el señor mi amo, puestas las manos al cielo y los ojos que casi nada se le parecía sino un poco de blanco, comienza una oración no menos larga que devota, con la cual hizo llorar a toda la gente como suelen hazer en los sermones de Pasión de predicador y auditorio devoto, suplicando a Nuestro Señor, pues no quería la muerte del pecador, sino su vida y

---

1	podía.
2	alrededor.
3	aquí.

Certain honest[28] men that were there, came unto him, and awaked him by force of crying[29], desiring that it might please him to succour[30] the poor man which was a–dying, and that he should not regard that which had passed, nor yet his evil words, seeing that now he had received punishment therefore, but that if he could help him in anyway how to escape that peril and danger that he was in, that he would so do for God's sake; and as for them, they plainly perceived that he was in the fault, and so likewise that they knew his truth and goodness, seeing that at his petition, the Lord straightways for revengement, sent him punishment.

Then my master the commissary, like one that had awaked out of a gracious[31] sleep, beholdeth them, and also the patient[32], with all those that were about him, and said:

'Ye honest men, ye ought not to pray for one, on whom God hath so manifestly showed his power; but seeing that he hath commanded that we shall not render evil for evil, but rather that we shall pardon all injuries, to be able to make supplication unto him, that we may fulfil that which he commanded us[33]. And now that his Majesty[34] (being by him offended) may forgive him, so to show miracle of true faith, let us go altogether with humble heart, and pray to him.'

Wherefore he came down out of the pulpit, commanding such as were there present, most devoutly to pray to our Lord, that it might please him, through his grace, to pardon this sinner, and to restore him to his health and bodily senses again; and moreover, if his divine Majesty had permitted any evil spirit to enter into him for his offences, that it might please him likewise, to drive it out again. Incontinently[35] they fell all upon their knees, before the altar, and with the priests they began to sing with low voice, the [36]litany. And the commissary my master, having sung over him, came with the cross and holy water, holding up his hands, and his eyes bent towards heaven, that one might see nothing of them but a little white, began his prayer no less devout than long, wherewith he made those that were there present to weep, as they were wont to do at the sermons of the Passion, and he as a devout preacher, desired almighty God (seeing that he desireth not the death of

---

28   i.e. good, honourable.

29   i.e. shouting.

30   i.e. help, assist.

31   In the Spanish, 'sweet'.

32   Rowland's choice of word is puzzling. The Spanish reads 'delinquent', a word first recorded in English in 1484.

33   The Spanish reads 'we may, confidently beseech [God] to do what He commands us (i.e. forgive).

34   i.e. God, though the text could imply Charles V. Rowland's translation is loose here; a more literal translation is 'that his Majesty forgive this man who offended Him by obstructing his Holy faith.'

35   i.e. forthwith, immediately.

36   The text should read 'a litany'.

arrepentimiento, que aquel encaminado por el demonio y persuadido de la muerte y pecado, le quisiese perdonar y dar vida y salud, para que se arrepintiese y confesase sus pecados.

Y esto hecho, mandó traer la bula y púsosela en la cabeza; y luego el pecador del alguacil comenzó poco a poco a estar mejor y tornar en sí. Y desque fue bien vuelto en su acuerdo, echóse a los pies del señor comisario y demandóle perdón, y confesó[1] haber dicho aquello por la boca y mandamiento del demonio, lo uno por hacer a él daño y vengarse del enojo, lo otro y más principal, porque el demonio recibía mucha pena del bien que allí se hiciera en tomar la bula.

El señor mi amo le perdonó, y fueron hechas las amistades entre ellos; y a tomar la bula hubo tanta priesa, que casi ánima viviente en el lugar no quedó sin ella: marido y mujer, e hijos e hijas, mozos y mozas.

Divulgóse la nueva de lo acaecido por los lugares comarcanos, y cuando a ellos llegábamos, no era menester sermón ni ir a la iglesia, que a la posada la venían a tomar como si fueran peras que se dieran de balde. De manera que en diez o doce lugares de aquellos alderredores[2] donde fuimos, echó el señor mi amo otras tantas mil bulas sin predicar sermón.

Cuando él hizo[3] el ensayo[4], confieso mi pecado que también fui dello espantado y creí que ansí[5] era, como otros muchos; mas con ver después la risa y burla que mi amo y el alguacil llevaban y hacían del negocio, conocí cómo había sido industriado[6] por el industrioso e inventivo de mi amo. Y aunque mochacho, cayóme mucho en gracia, y dije entre mí:

1   demandándole perdón confesó.
2   alrededores.
3   se hizo.
4   i.e. trick.
5   así.
6   i.e. rigged.

a sinner, but rather that he shall repent and live[37]) to pardon, forgive and restore to life, that poor sinner which was led by the devil, overcome with death and sin, that he might repent and confess his sins.

When he had so done, he sent for one of the pardons, and laid it upon his head, whereupon immediately the poor sergeant began to amend and by little and little to return to himself. And as soon as he had recovered his senses, he kneeleth down at master commissary's feet, and there demanded pardon, confessing how that he had said and done all those things by the mouth and instruction of the devil, as well to give him grief, and to be revenged of him[38], as also because the devil was sorry to see the goodness which people received by taking the holy pardons.

My master did then forgive him, and friendship was made between them. Then was there such great haste to take the pardons, that almost no creature living in that town, but took one, the husband, and the wife, sons and daughters, menservants and maidservants, there was none but would have one.

This news was spread abroad through all the towns there about, so that when we arrived thither it was not needful to preach, nor yet to go to the church to dispatch the pardons; for the people came so fast to our lodging for them, as if they had been pears that had been given them for nothing; insomuch that my master dispatched and uttered away ten or twelve thousand pardons in ten or twelve little villages thereabouts, without preaching one sermon.

And as for my part, I will confess my ignorance[39]; for when this their invention was tried[40], I was in a great marvel to see such a strange case[41], and I thought the matter had been so indeed, as many other did. Yet notwithstanding, when I perceived once[42] the jesting and scoffing that my master and the sergeant would make at the matter by the way, I understood plainly, that all that counterfeit show was invented[43] by my master's subtle industrious[44] art. And although I was of tender years, yet I took great pleasure to consider their doings, and would say to myself:

---

37   Again, Biblical allusion: 'As I live, saith the Lord God, I have no pleasure in the death of the wicked; but that the wicked turn from his way and live', Ezekiel 33.11.; and, 'The Lord.... is long suffering to usward, not willing that any should perish, but that all should come to repentance', 2 Peter 3.9. Of particular importance for understanding the book is the fact that the Pardoner echoes the terminology of the Inquisition when it decided to spare a life.

38   i.e. for the quarrel of the previous evening.

39   i.e. I was taken in too.

40   i.e. when their deception took place.

41   i.e. I was both astonished and frightened, as were others, by what I took to be miraculous.

42   i.e. as soon as I noticed.

43   i.e. rigged.

44   i.e. knavish.

'¡Cuántas destas deben[1] hacer estos burladores entre la inocente gente!'

Finalmente, estuve con este mi quinto amo cerca de cuatro meses, en los cuales pasé también hartas fatigas.

Tratado Sexto
Cómo Lázaro se asentó con un capellán, y lo que con él pasó

Después desto, asenté con un maestro de pintar panderos para molelle los colores, y también sufrí mil males.

Siendo ya en este tiempo buen mozuelo, entrando un día en la iglesia mayor, un capellán della me recibió por suyo, y púsome en poder un asno[2] y cuatro cántaros y un azote, y comencé a echar agua[3] por la cibdad[4]. Éste fue el primer escalón que yo subí para venir a alcanzar buena vida, porque mi boca era medida[5]. Daba cada día a mi amo treinta maravedís ganados, y los sábados ganaba para mí, y todo lo demás, entre semana, de treinta maravedís.

---

1   deben de.
2   buen asno.
3   i.e. sell water.
4   ciudad.
5   i.e. my wants were satisfied.

'How many are there such as these that deceive the simple people.'[45]

To conclude, I continued with this fifth master near four months, during which time I suffered much sorrow.[46] [47]

Sixth Treatise

How Lazaro dwelleth with a Chaplain, and what happened to him in his service

Afterward I entered into the service of a painter of drums, unto whom I tempered[1] colours, with whom I suffered a thousand evils, and as I was then of good bigness[2], entering one day into the great Church[3], one of the chaplains received me for his own, and gave me in government[4] an ass, with four great tankards[5], and a whip, to sell water up and down the city, and this was the first stair[6] I climbed up, to come to attain unto good life; for my mouth had then the measure[7]. I delivered up daily to my master in gain thirty *maravedis* and on every Saturday I laboured for myself, and all the week also whatever I could earn over thirty *maravedis* a day, was mine own[8].

They do carry water up and down the city to sell upon asses, with four and sometimes six tankards, for they have no water but from the river.

---

45 i.e. How many deceptions or tricks like these must such swindlers pull off amongst unsuspecting folk!

46 i.e. pain or grief. The Spanish suggests pangs of conscience.

47 The Spanish source of Rowland's translation is the edition published in Burgos. The Alcalá edition has additional material which Jones publishes in his Appendices 2 and 3 and the Penguin translation (*Two Spanish Picaresque Novels*, Alpert (trans.), 1977 on pages 72–77. It is important to note that the Spanish expurgated version of *Lazarillo de Tormes* of 1573 omitted with other anti–clerical comments the story of the Pardoner and the brief account of the Friar of the Order of Mercy.

1 The Spanish reads 'in order to grind his colours for him.'

2 i.e. an adolescent.

3 i.e. the Cathedral of Toledo.

4 i.e. placed under my control, gave me to take care of.

5 i.e. not the modern beer mug but the original bucket like object made of wooden staves and hooped, used for carrying water.

6 i.e. step.

7 i.e. my needs were satisfied.

8 There is no space to summarise the discussion that this passage has generated amongst scholars. Amongst the points at issue are whether there is proverbial mockery of Toledans for relying on outsiders to carry their water and whether the Saturday financial

Fueme tan bien en el oficio que al cabo de cuatro años que lo usé, con poner en la ganancia buen recaudo, ahorré para me vestir muy honradamente de la ropa vieja, de la cual compré un jubón de fustán viejo y un sayo raído de manga tranzada[1] y puerta, y una capa que había sido frisada[2], y una espada de las viejas primeras de Cuéllar.

Desque me vi en hábito de hombre de bien, dije a mi amo se tomase su asno, que no quería más seguir aquel oficio.

Tratado Séptimo

Cómo Lázaro se asentó con un alguacil, y de lo que le acaeció con él

Despedido del capellán, asenté por hombre de justicia con un alguacil, mas muy poco viví con él, por parecerme oficio peligroso; mayormente, que una noche nos corrieron[3] a mí y a mi amo a pedradas y a palos unos retraídos[4], y a mi amo, que

---

1   i.e. braided.
2   i.e. fringed.
3   i.e. chased.
4   i.e. fugitives from justice who have taken sactuary in a church.

This office was so good, that at four years' end I had spared with my wages and my gains, so much, as I bought me apparel honestly[9], with old stuff, whereof I bought an old black fustian[10] doublet, and a coat threadbare with gathered sleeves and whole before[11], and a cloak that had been of felpado[12] and a sword of the old making, one of the first of *Cuellar*[13].

And perceiving myself in apparel like an honest man[14], I desired my master to take his ass again and that I would no more follow that office.

Seventh Treatise

How Lazaro dwelleth with a Sergeant[1], and what happened to him in his service.

After that I had taken my leave of the chaplain I did place myself with a sergeant, to be a member of Justice[2]. But I dwelled few days with him, for in short time I perceived that it was a dangerous office, especially when that one night certain transgressors which retired into a church[3], chased my master and me marvellously[4] with stones and staves; and at that present time my master[5] (whom I tarried for) was evil handled[6], but

A man may escape in Spain the hands of the officers of justice if they can flee into some church, so it be not theft, treason or religion.

---

arrangement implies that the Chaplain was of Jewish descent, a forced convert still culturally a Jew. A severe statute of Toledo Cathedral of 1547 had the purpose of excluding so called New Christians from ecclesiastical office, on the grounds that their blood was not clean.

9   'Honest' commonly meant 'honourable' at that time, as the Spanish confirms. For reasons of honour, Lazarillo buys old clothes and a second hand sword, presumably in imitation of his third master, the Squire.

10 Fustian was a sort of twilled cotton.

11 A possible translation is 'a worn coat with braided sleeves and open collar'.

12 Crofts' proposed correction (meaning plush) for a different Spanish word in the original, usually translated as 'fringed', further testimony to the volume of translation from Spanish into English, and of Spanish words entering English at that time.

13 Cuéllar is in the province of Segovia and was one of the oldest sword making towns in Spain.

14 The Spanish implies respectability, upon gaining which, Lazarillo abandons that particular profitable employment; 'office' of course here means 'job'.

1   This is Rowland's preferred translation of the Spanish 'alguacil', which means little more than a petty constable.

2   i.e. law–enforcement

3   i.e. fugitives from justice who have taken refuge or sanctuary in a church.

4   Rowland's addition to suggest a great level of violence.

5   i.e. my then master.

esperó, trataron mal, mas a mí no me alcanzaron. Con esto renegué del trato.

Y pensando en qué modo de vivir haría mi asiento[1] por tener descanso y ganar algo para la vejez, quiso Dios alumbrarme y ponerme en camino y manera provechosa; y con favor que tuve de amigos y señores, todos mis trabajos y fatigas hasta entonces pasados fueron pagados con alcanzar lo que procuré, que fue un oficio real, viendo que no hay nadie que medre sino los que le tienen; en el cual el día de hoy vivo[2] y resido a servicio de Dios y de vuestra merced.

Y es que tengo cargo de pregonar los vinos que en esta ciudad se venden, y en almonedas[3] y cosas perdidas, acompañar los que padecen persecuciones por justicia y declarar a voces sus delitos: pregonero, hablando en buen romance[4].

Hame sucedido tan bien, yo[5] le he usado tan fácilmente, que casi todas las cosas al oficio tocantes pasan por mi mano: tanto que en toda la ciudad el que ha de echar vino a vender o algo, si Lázaro de Tormes no entiende en ello, hacen cuenta de no sacar provecho.

En este tiempo, viendo mi habilidad y buen vivir, teniendo noticia de mi persona el señor arcipreste de Sant Salvador[6], mi señor, y servidor y amigo de vuestra

---

1   i.e. I would settle down.
2   yo vivo.
3   i.e. auctions.
4   i.e without beating about the bush.
5   y yo.
6   i.e. a Parish in Toledo.

they could never overtake me; yet for all that I did forswear[7] the office.

And as I imagined what kind of life I had best lead, that I might provide something against mine old age, God by his grace lightened[8] my mind to find out the profitable way. So that through the favour which I had of my friends and masters, all the sorrows, which before that time I had sustained, were recompensed with an office royal[9], which I obtained; the which I pretended[10], because that at this day there is no account but of them that have wherewithal[11]. So that at this present, I live in mine office[12], and exercise it to God's service and yours.

Sir, it is so that I have the charge to cry the wines that are sold in this city, and to make inquirance, with open cry, for things that have been lost, and when any suffer persecution by justice, I do accompany them, declaring with loud voice their offence.

I am (in plain language) a common crier[13]. Sir, matters have so well gone forward with me, and I have used myself so well[14], that in manner all things belonging to the office, pass through my hands. Insomuch, that look[15] whosoever within this city doth broach wine, or sell any things and that *Lazarillo de Tormes* be not present, they make account never to get gain.[16]

The criers in Spain do sell all kind of stuff, and when any is whipped through the city, goeth before him, declaring with loud voice what he hath done.

In this meantime, master Archdeacon of *Saint Salvador*[17], your friend and servant at commandment[18], having knowledge of my person and ability, especially

---

6   i.e. received a drubbing. Rowland mis-translated: it was the Sergeant who tarried.

7   i.e. renounce whatever oath he had given on taking up the job.

8   Rowland's excellent translation of the Spanish verb 'alumbrar', associated with pietistic or proto – Protestant tendencies. See notes First Treatise (41) and Second Treatise (20).

9   i.e. a Crown or civil service job.

10   i.e. claimed, asked for.

11   i.e. nobody prospers but those who have such a job.

12   i.e. continue in this job.

13   A town crier was amongst the lowest of Spanish city officials. Lazarillo advertises wines, thereby fulfilling the Blind Beggar's prophecy, (see First Treatise, (54)), lost goods and the misdeeds of those publicly punished. The expression 'persecution by justice' is not a malapropism for the Spanish is ambiguous, also meaning 'persecution for the sake of justice', and echoes what happened to Lazarillo's father at the beginning of the first Treatise.

14   For 'myself' read 'it' (Rowland misread the Spanish) i.e. 'I have carried out the job so well....'

15   Again a Welshism.

16   i.e. if Lazarillo does not receive his cut, then they make no profit either.

17   One of many churches in Toledo. It is surely no accident that it is called Saint Saviour's.

18   It is important to note that the person to whom Lazarillo is giving his account is very possibly senior in the Church hierarchy.

merced, porque le pregonaba sus vinos, procuró casarme con una criada suya; y visto por mí que de tal persona no podía venir sino bien y favor, acordé de lo hacer.

Y así me casé con ella, y hasta agora no estoy arrepentido; porque allende de ser buena hija y diligente, servicial, tengo en mi señor acipreste[1] todo favor y ayuda. Y siempre en el año le da en veces al pie de[2] una carga de trigo, por las pascuas su carne, y cuando[3] el par de los bodigos, las calzas viejas que deja; e hízonos alquilar una casilla par de la suya. Los domingos y fiestas casi todas las comíamos en su casa.

Mas malas lenguas, que nunca faltaron ni faltarán[4], no nos dejan vivir, diciendo no sé qué, y sí sé qué, de que[5] veen a mi mujer irle a hacer la cama y guisalle de comer. Y mejor les ayude Dios que ellos dicen la verdad[6]; porque, allende de no ser ella mujer que se pague destas burlas, mi señor me ha prometido lo que pienso cumplirá. Que él me habló un día muy largo delante della, y me dijo:

'Lázaro de Tormes, quien ha de mirar a dichos de malas lenguas, nunca medrará. Digo esto porque no me maravillaría alguno, viendo entrar en mi casa a tu mujer y salir della.... Ella entra muy a tu honra y suya, y esto te lo prometo. Por tanto, no mires a lo que pueden decir, sino a lo que te toca, digo a tu provecho.'

'Señor — le dije — yo determiné de arrimarme a los buenos. Verdad es que algunos de mis amigos me han dicho algo deso, y aun, por más de tres veces me han

---

1   arcipreste.
2   i.e. adding up to, about.
3   i.e. sometimes.
4   ni faltarán: not in Antwerp.
5   y si sé, que.
6   i.e. may God help them better than they speak the truth.

since I had cried his wine, went about to[19] marry me with his maid. And after that I had considered, that having to do with such a man as master Archdeacon was, I could not receive but honesty and goodness, I determined to do it, so that I took her to wife. Whereof hitherto I do not repent; for besides that she is honest, and a diligent wench, I find great favour and help at master Archdeacon's hand, for every year from one time to another, he giveth her as good as a load of wheat, and against Christmas or Easter, some good morsel of flesh[20], a couple or two[21] of loaves, and such old hose[22] as he leaveth; and he caused us to hire a little house near his dwelling; on every Sunday and holiday we dined (most commonly) in his own house.

But evil tongues which never cease, would not suffer us to live in peace, they would say this and that, and that they did see my wife go and make his bed, and dress his meat[23]. But God help them better than they say truth[24]. For besides that she is a woman that doth not delight in such game[25], master Archdeacon hath promised me that which I trust he will fulfil. For upon a time in her presence, he said at large [26]unto me:

'*Lazarillo de Tormes*, he that will have regard to evil tongues, shall never get profit. I say thus much unto thee, I can never marvel, though some men murmur to see thy wife come in and out of my house, which doing, I promise thee, shall not otherwise redound but to thy great honesty[27] and hers. Therefore let people have their words, have thou only regard to that which shall be for thy profit.'
I answered his, saying:

'Sir, I have determined to join myself with those that are good[28], but truth it is, that certain of my friends have warned me of this, yea and moreover, they have

---

19   Rowland ably renders the ambiguity of the Spanish: the Archdeacon both arranged the marriage and achieved the necessary pretence of social decency and comformity. Rowland preferred to render the Spanish Archpriest as Archdeacon. The subtitle to this Treatise is a decoy: Lazarillo abandoned law enforcement at the end of the first paragraph. Similarly marriage is a decoy. The Archdeacon was Lazarillo's last master.

20   i.e. meat.

21   'or two' is redundant. A redundancy like this and occasional Welsh English expressions may indicate that Rowland dictated his translation to an amanuensis.

22   Not the modern stockings but the earlier garment which covered the body to the waist, breeches.

23   i.e. prepare his food.

24   Rowland perfectly catches the ambiguity of the Spanish. At this point the Alcalá version inserts material, Jones appendix 5 and Penguin Classics, page 78.

25   i.e. shows little sexual appetite.

26   i.e. at length.

27   i.e. honour, as the Spanish confirms.

28   The Spanish repeats the proverb used of Lazarillo's mother, see first Treatise, (3); cross referencing that gives the work cohesion.

certificado que, antes que comigo casase, había parido tres veces, hablando con reverencia de V. M., porque está ella delante.'

Entonces mi mujer echó juramentos sobre sí, que yo pensé la casa se hundiera con nosotros, y después tomóse a llorar y a echar[1] maldiciones sobre quien conmigo la había casado, en tal manera que quisiera ser muerto antes que se me hobiera[2] soltado aquella palabra de la boca. Mas yo de un cabo y mi señor de otro, tanto le dijimos y otorgamos[3] que cesó su llanto, con juramento que le hice de nunca más en mi vida mentalle nada de aquello, y que yo holgaba y había por bien de que ella entrase y saliese, de noche y de día, pues estaba bien seguro de su bondad. Y así quedamos todos tres bien conformes. Hasta el día de hoy, nunca nadie nos oyó sobre el caso; antes, cuando alguno siento que quiere decir algo della, le atajo y le digo:

'Mirá: si sois[4] amigo, no me digáis cosa con que me pese, que no tengo por mi amigo al que me hace pesar; mayormente si me quieren meter mal con mi mujer, que es la cosa del mundo que yo más quiero, y la amo más que a mí. Y me hace Dios con ella mil mercedes y más bien que yo merezco; que yo juraré sobre la hostia consagrada que es tan buena mujer como vive dentro de las puertas de Toledo.[5] Quien otra cosa me dijere, yo me mataré con él[6].'

Desta manera no me dicen nada, y yo tengo paz en mi casa.

Esto fue el mesmo año que nuestro victorioso Emperador en esta insigne ciudad de Toledo entró y tuvo en ella cortes, y se hicieron grandes regocijos[7], como vuestra

---

1   mil [maldiciones].
2   hubiera.
3   i.e. promise.
4   mi amigo.
5   Y.
6   i.e. I'll fight him.
7   y fiestas.

twice or thrice certified me with oaths, that before she was married to me she had two or three children, be it spoken under your mastership's correction, seeing that she is present.'

My wife then began to give such oaths, that I thought the house would have sunk with us all, and then began to weep, cursing the time that ever she married me[29], insomuch that I wished myself dead when that I let scape that word out of my mouth[30]. But I on the one side, and my master on another, said so much, that she left weeping; and I did swear unto her, that as long as I lived, I would never again use the like talk; and how that I rejoiced and was well content, that she should come in and out both day and night, seeing that her honesty and faithfulness was so well known. So then we remained all three with one accord until this day, and never no man heard us since reason of the matter[31]. And from that time forward, whensoever I could happen to hear any man talk of this[32], I would straight break off his matter, and say unto him:

'Look if thou be my friend, speak nothing that shall grieve me, for I do not take him for my friend that causeth me to sorrow, especially that goeth about to sow discord between me and my wife, which[33] I love better than anything in this world, considering how that by her means, God hath done more for me, than I have deserved, and I dare swear by the holy sacrament, that she is as honest a woman as any that dwelleth within the four gates of *Toledo*[34], and he that saith contrary, I will bestow my life upon him[35].'

So from thence forward, they never durst move any such matter unto me[36], and I had peace always in my house.

This was the same year that our victorious Emperor entered into this noble city[37] of *Toledo*, where his Cortes[38] were held with great feasts and triumphs, as

---

29   More literally, 'cursing the man who had married her to me'.
30   i.e. I should rather have died than have uttered that earlier remark.
31   That matter (Spanish 'el caso') is, of course, the matter if the last paragraph of the Prologue (19) which Lazarillo has been commanded to set down in full.
32   The Spanish reads 'of her' i.e. Lazarillo's wife.
33   i.e. whom.
34   There is, of course, a clear hint of the moral standards in Toledo.
35   i.e. I shall fight him to the death.
36   i.e. Nobody says anything to me about our 'ménage à trois'.
37   The formula of Toledo's nobility of the first paragraph of the Third Treatise is here repeated.
38   This could refer to the Cortes or Parliament of 1525, shortly after the defeat of the French at Pavia, or the more stormy session of 1538, when nobles refused to pay subsidies, but which was followed by public celebrations. The Emperor is, of course, Charles V. If Lazarillo's father had died in 1510, the first date may seem more acceptable. No other internal evidence more precisely to date the novel is available.

merced habrá oído. Pues en este tiempo estaba en mi prosperidad y en la cumbre de toda buena fortuna.

~FIN~

your mastership hath heard. Finally, it was then that I was in my prosperity, and in my chiefest time of good adventure[39].

[End Note: Rowland also followed Saugrain's 1561 French translation in adding as a tailpiece the first chapter of the spurious sequel of the novel, printed at Antwerp in 1555. Our present text cuts out this chapter of Rowland since it is redundant to the 1554 Burgos, Alcalá and Antwerp editions.]

To the Reader

Though truth do purchase hate,
and glosing[1] bear the bell[2];
Yet is the man to be beliked,
that truest tale doth tell,
Without respect of place,
of country, or of kind;
For so the law of writing doth
each honest writer bind;
Then Lazaro deserves
no blame, but praise to gain,
That plainly pens the Spaniards' pranks
and how they live in Spain.
He set them out to show
for all the world to see,
That Spain, when all is done, is Spain,
and what those gallants be.
The writer means but well,
and he that took the pain

---

39 A more literal rendering of the Spanish would be 'I was then in my prosperity and at the height of good fortune.' Again the ending catches the last paragraph of the Prologue, referring to the rotation of the wheel of Fortune and the efforts of self made men to achieve prosperity and a safe haven after tempestuous seas.

1 i.e. fawning, flattering.

2 i.e. be triumphant. A bell was a sort of trademark of the printer of *Lazarillo de Tormes*, Abel Jeffs. See the illustration facing the dedication.

To turn it to our mother tongue,
the reader's thanks would gain
For all his former toil
in penning of the book.
The suit[3] is small, allow him that,
that hapst hereon to look.
Though small the volume be,
the value may be great.
Wherefore to yield him thy good will
let this my muse entreat:
Let Rouland have reward
for this his taken pain;
And so thou, reader, mayest perhaps
the like hereafter gain.

---

3   i.e. a petition or request for praise.